*A Dream
of Light
& Shadow*

EDITED BY MARJORIE AGOSÍN

A Dream
of Light
& Shadow

PORTRAITS OF
LATIN AMERICAN
WOMEN WRITERS

UNIVERSITY OF NEW MEXICO PRESS
Albuquerque

Library of Congress Cataloging-in-Publication Data

A dream of light and shadows : portraits of Latin American
women writers / edited by Marjorie Agosín. — 1st ed. p.   cm.
Includes bibliographical references.
ISBN 0-8263-1633-6
1. Women authors, Latin American—Biography. 2. Latin
American literature—Women authors—History and criticism.
3. Women and literature—Latin America. I. Agosín, Marjorie.
PQ7081.3.D74   1995   860.9'9287'098—dc20   94-48679 CIP

© 1995 by the University of New Mexico Press.
All rights reserved.
First edition

Many of the essays were translated
from the Spanish by
Nancy Abraham Hall.

designed by linda mae tratechaud

CONTENTS

INTRODUCTION

From a Room of One's Own to the Garden

MARJORIE AGOSÍN
TRANSLATED BY NANCY ABRAHAM HALL

⟜ A DREAM OF LIGHT AND SHADOW: *Portraits of Latin American Women Writers* is a unique collection of essays about the most outstanding female figures in Latin American culture. Like all anthologies, this one is arbitrary, the product of my own readings, and to a certain extent, my personal selection and vision. By design I have included many prominent voices, as well as some that have yet to receive the recognition they deserve. Rather than simply selecting authors by country and placing them in chronological order, I have focused on women who have forged a destiny and contributed a sense of vision to the cultural landscape of Latin America.

Each woman profiled in this book is vitally aware of the artistry, obsessions, and voices through which she creates her own sense of identity and reaches out to other women. None ever acts as a guardian or promoter of male culture. By bringing these authors together in a single collection, I hope to shed light on a shared tradition, and to show how each woman's individual vision responds to a feminine form of expression, a certain way of looking at writing and at the society in which she chooses to live.

A common thread unites these writers. Each creates her own culture in keeping with a distinctly feminine sensibility. From Sofía Ospina's recipes and books about Antioquian culture to Violeta Parra's autobiography in verse, each writer constructs a creative space in defiance of the limits imposed by society and is able to find freedom through creative imagination. Thus, in order to escape the confines of home and country, Delmira Agustini forges a dual identity for herself, breaking all of society's rules and setting herself free through her erotic poetry. Alejandra Pizarnik also chooses the violence of desire, as well as the liberating power of surrealism, in a stunning journey across the hallucinatory space of poetic language and imaginative discourse.

It would appear that several creative women from the Southern Cone, and more specifically from the River Plate area—women such as Agustini, Pizarnik, and Di Giorgio—resort to a series of "personae," or creative masks, that allow them to invent alternate ways of being and to pursue their true vocation, the search for creative possibilities. We read, for example, in Teresa Porzcekanski's article about Marosa Di Giorgio, of the poet's haunting appearance on a Montevideo stage, and of her secret place of honor, the garden of the imagination. Porzcekanski points out the essential elements—the garden, Di Giorgio's personality, and the kitchen, that feminine realm of magical altars and potions—that fuse to form the essence of Marosa's poetic stage: "[The] altar appeared made of nothing but Bromelias, kitchens, beds. The country brides carried [snails] in baskets . . . stiff as rocks, as eggs, their white shells and bulging rose-colored eyes."

Despite the deep prejudices all the women in this anthology faced during their lifetimes, each was able to overcome obstacles and claim a legitimate place as a writer on the cultural stage. The prejudice was notorious in the case of Gabriela Mistral, who received recognition in her homeland only after she was awarded the

Nobel Prize; in the case of Victoria Ocampo, arrested by the Perón government; and in the case of Marta Traba, who for ideological reasons was threatened with deportation from Colombia in the mid-sixties. Nevertheless, these women forged identities as artists, and always maintained strong connections with other women throughout Latin America and, in the cases of Agustini, Storni, Ocampo, and Mistral, Europe. Above all, they created a network of solidarity and shared reading with other women. This is a point I wish to emphasize: All the articles in this anthology suggest the very real possibility of a culture of sisterhood. That is, they allude to a powerful affirmation regarding feminine essence and its representatives, despite the fact that the term *feminine* is not precisely defined in the texts, nor is feminist ideology debated as a movement.

It is important to recall that all the writers whose portraits make up this collection were vitally concerned with the problems faced by women, and the conditions that affected their collective destiny. Children and mothers form the central texts of all these women's lives, and of many of their writings. There can be no doubt, for example, that Gabriela Mistral's deep concern for women and their struggles was central to her work as both a diplomat and a writer. She published an anthology dedicated to the women of America, wrote poems about motherhood, and was committed to all the issues touching the lives of women and children. According to Elizabeth Horan, Mistral's commitment to women could seem to be at odds with her behavior. After all, the poet was known to drink whiskey, smoke cigarettes, and wear men's clothing. Yet behind that mask of toughness was a tender woman who each year adopted a boy or girl, and always sent clothing to the children of her native Elqui Valley.

The dual mask worn by Gabriela Mistral also figures prominently in the lives of other, more mainstream women writers, such as Victoria Ocampo, Sofía Ospina, and Elena Poniatowska. Public women who have achieved success as editors, journalists, diplomats, or educators, they nevertheless identify with and work on behalf of those who have been relegated to the back rooms, the women who are voiceless, absent. The image of Gabriela Mistral has been appropriated by a nation, but beyond patriotic symbolism we find a complex woman, a world traveler who was also a rural schoolteacher, a woman who held high government posts yet always chose to champion justice and to place women and children center stage. Horan makes a very important point when she states:

> In contrast to taking the life and work of Gabriela Mistral as a pretext for positing various clichés about what is feminine, it is useful to observe Mistral's verse as manifesting a transgressive consciousness. Recent feminist interpretation explores in Mistral's work the possibility of multiple, coexisting identities in women.

Horan's statement provides the true guideline by which the authors in this anthology should be viewed. They are diplomats, like Carmen Naranjo and Gabriela Mistral, but at the same time they are woman submerged in the private details of personal stories, their own and those of others. The fact that these women have participated in very essential and singular ways in the history of their respective countries, and in the intellectual history of Latin America, implies their strong attraction to a profound national and cultural consciousness.

Elizabeth Horan suggests that we would do well to remember Mistral as a woman who discussed the tragic sense of life with Miguel de Unamuno but also prescribed herbal remedies. This image could be extended as well to Elena Poniatowska, who sits facing her father, the sole descendant of the Polish monarch, yet also speaks with Jesusa Palancares, Kay García, seamstresses, earthquake victims, and the masked students of Tlatelolco.

It seems clear that the writers treated in this anthology do not perceive great differences between official worlds and private ones, between what is publishable and how people live. Indeed, they are united by their production of texts, which cast a very deep and rarely fragmented net. This is also the spirit of this anthology, which seeks to capture the passion, freedom, serenity, and rituals of the lives of these extraordinary women.

Each chapter is written by a distinguished critic, and, free of required formulas or strict methodologies, each reflects the personality of the woman in question. As a schoolgirl and on stage, Marosa Di Giorgio always wears a flower in her hair, leading one to believe that she allows her imagination to dictate her life. Delmira Agustini is an obedient woman who, at night, produces torrents of erotic verses that in content and skill go well beyond what could be expected of a seventeen-year-old girl. Carmen Naranjo is an unusual diplomat, who champions reform and social justice over political convenience. Rigoberta Menchú defends the poor, the downtrodden. Her commitment to the struggle for human rights is total. She learns that indigenous women are exploited by mestizos not only in cities but in rural areas as well. Menchú learns Spanish, the language of her oppressors, and then uses it to tell her story.

From Ospina's cookbooks to Clementina Suárez's poems, which recover and discuss female sexuality, each of these women is committed to the struggle for justice, social reform, and recovery. One need only examine the life of Violeta Parra, for example, a woman born into poverty. Her love songs and political anthems are tapestries of words demanding social justice and revindication, pleas for a more just and noble society. The same is true of Naranjo, Mistral, and Storni, who, in their political work and newspaper columns, struggle to recreate a world in which women will find legitimacy and fairness. Even those women who might appear to be obsessed with questions of aesthetics, such as Pizarnik or Lispector, are trailblazers in search of new ways of viewing, of being, of approaching the world. In her final book, *A Hora da Estrêla* for example, Clarice Lispector turned her attention to the stories of the dispossessed and created the character of Macabea, a poor, indigent adolescent from northern Brazil, who searches for a more meaningful and significant existence.

Perhaps some will find the lives of these women excessively glorious or melodramatic. I urge the reader to keep in mind that each of these outstanding women managed to eschew an eclipsed, socially prescribed destiny and to forge a better, far more interesting life and way of being. Of course it is extraordinary that a rural schoolteacher from the Elqui Valley of northern Chile should win the Nobel Prize for literature or that another woman, a Quiché Indian, be named Nobel Peace laureate (1994). Nevertheless, they stand before us, not as loyal guardians of the culture of men, museum tour guides, or proofreaders for books written by men, but as novelists, poets, journalists, directors of museums, folklorists, activists, and politicians. Each made her mark and led a life that, outwardly as well as inwardly, was challenging and full of adventure.

This book explores what is meant and implied when women forge lives of their own and establish their own identities as women. My intention is not to anthologize the great contributions of women to Latin American culture, but rather to present a series of portraits that reflect upon the forms that emerge from the imaginations of creative women. To quote the insightful worlds of Patricia Mayer Spocks on the literary sensibilities of women, "Imagination is the internal sensing of reality, but it is also the capacity to create a substitute reality. Imagination has been for women a seed of grace and often the theme and impetus of their writing."

Woven into all of the chapters are allusions to the feminine sensibility of specific women who, at a given time and place in history, were able to forge distinct ways of being. Each chapter also addresses the complex relationship that has always existed between women, power, and culture. The grand dame of Argentinian literature, Victoria Ocampo, the rural schoolteacher Gabriela Mistral, the peasant Violeta Parra, the Native American Rigoberta Menchú, and the aristocrat Elena Poniatowska, all emerge as able transmitters of an essential tradition based on sorority, social recovery, and a feminine culture of one's own, a culture that includes the preparation of meals, the raising of children, and political activism in solidarity with other women, as rendered so effectively, for example, in the novels about the Mothers of the Plaza de Mayo written by Marta Traba.

It is fitting to recall the words Clarice Lispector wrote and ordered engraved on her tombstone in the Jewish cemetery of Rio de Janeiro: "To stretch out my hand to someone is all I expected from happiness." Each of these women has extended a hand by writing texts of love and pain, and they have done it openly, generously, never begrudgingly, with the hands of extraordinary yet ordinary human beings. This is the spirit of this anthology, which does not establish chronologies or delineate historical periods but celebrates writing in which language is the true homeland without borders.

If Virginia Woolf proposed a room of one's own, a space in which to be free, to dream, a seat of honor from which to exercise the privilege of unrestricted time, one must ask at what hour of the day or night, when and how did creative women use this space? What did those who had such a room do in it? A room of her own, in the history of women's literature and art, is a metaphor for creative space. For some, it was the kitchen, the site of meetings and silenced dialogues, a space for recipes and magic potions as well as perpetual confinement. For others, it was the convents, where, in silence, women heard one another's confessions as an alternative form of intimacy, and their stories were gathered, like so many beads on a string, to create a body of writing set apart from the official reach of the church.

This reflection on a room of one's own questions the absence of historical information about women in relation to their artistic production. For example, we might wonder what was contained in the writings Jane Austen kept hidden under the blotter, and what led George Sand, when she became a writer, to chose her pseudonym and dress like a man. Why is so little known about how these writers created and lived, from colonial times until now? Why have so many stories and cases been ignored, excluded?

Have Latin American women had rooms of their own? How have they validated their lives and work in a predominantly male and authoritarian society? Despite an abundance of translations, and the importance bestowed during the last few decades on women's creativity, we know very little about the cultural, ideological, and political contributions of Latin American women. Their history, still untold and almost unknown, has yet to be written. In literary as well as art criticism, studies continue to focus almost exclusively on those exceptional and anomalous women who were extraordinarily productive. But it is essential to consider the work of those who are missing from the official histories, women whose writings do not appear in newspapers and journals of mass circulation, and whose work does not hang in museums. These individuals constitute the great invisible majority of Latin American women artists and writers. They reside outside official circles and create art within a space of alternative associations, on the margins, for outsiders.

The canonical and classic example of a women who has attained "official" status or recognition is, of course, Sor Juana Inés de la Cruz, the outstanding figure of Mexico's baroque period. In the various genres of the colonial era, it is her name that appears, and yet the work of many of her contemporaries from other regions of Latin America, such as Sor Catalina de Erauso and Sor Francisca Josefa del Castillo, has not been well studied. There is still much to elucidate about why certain women are chosen from each period of history, while the rest pass into anonymity, creating an endless number of gaps in the cultural fabric of Latin America.

It is necessary to start with a serious, critical consideration of the cultural traditions of those women who are not in the literary and art history books, nor in the accepted codes of that "Official History" that recovers only certain texts, certain voices, bestowing value on them in an exclusivistic and arbitrary series of judgments. I believe that critical thought about women's creative work is the true revolution within what can be termed new cultural history, which aims to allow those who have been excluded to finally participate in the yet undefined and unfinished cultural landscape.

The case of Sor Juana suggests that throughout the cultural history of Latin America, outstanding figures have been observed almost in isolation by interlocutors who see them as individual players enacting a cultural tradition on an empty stage. Once again, the presence of certain extraordinary women is considered an anomaly, a mutation within the production of the age in which they live. Those who have lived and worked outside of schools, convents, or universities are excluded. The objective of this collection is to place women writers within a wide cultural context, to install them within a dimension of "their own."

Historically, during the age of convents, it would seem that the "leading" figures chosen to represent the female imagination fit certain molds. A key example is Sor Juana, the nun who defied the orders of her confessor. In the nineteenth century, all attention turns to the dominant presence of Gertrudis Gómez de Avellaneda, author of the first antislavery novel, *Sab*. In the twentieth century, certain women writers from the aristocracy, such as María Luisa Bombal of Chile, Victoria Ocampo of Argentina, and the poets Alfonsina Storni and Gabriela Mistral, become the reiterated figures of the social and creative history of Latin American women.

Obviously, the literary traditions of women have been canonized from the point of view of those in power. One wonders whether the women writers of Latin America have ever identified with their precursors, considered them models, or whether the leading figures have indeed made a series of isolated appearances on the stage of culture. The question is tied to theories of reception that seek to uncover a historic connection, a cultural and communal heritage among writers of different eras who use different modes of expression. We know that letters exchanged between certain twentieth-century figures—Alfonsina Storni, Gabriela Mistral, and Victoria Ocampo—have shed light on shared aspects of their work. But the incipient and central question of this anthology is whether these creative women from a wide variety of Latin American countries share a cultural tradition.

How could a new cultural panorama, one which unites Latin American women through their lives as well as their writing, be proposed? Can unity be found not through male parameters that define literary success but through the lens and perspective of gender? Can we examine how, and through whose eyes, the literary space of women is and has been inscribed?

In this anthology I include women viewed by other women, and incorporate popular and domestic art as well as art of the wealthy classes. Unknown poets appear alongside Nobel Prize winners in a single space governed by the principle of inclusion, not exceptionality, in what could be termed a body of literary work by women.

The purpose of this book is to rethink the cultural tradition of Latin American women and to approach imaginative and creative women as a group, to figure out what has constituted their genius, how it has been viewed, and the contributions these women have made to culture. What made them excel, break away, be included or not in the canon? Do they comprise a canon of their own? A culture of solidarity? A creative alternative? An aesthetic?

In search of new perspectives, this anthology focuses on the connections between women's cultural production and biography. The link between the artist's work and her life is central. The leading female figures of twentieth-century Latin American literature— Gabriela Mistral, Delmira Agustini—always appear wed to their private lives, but there has rarely been a thorough analysis of how those private worlds are revealed in the work. The artist's relationships with her contemporaries have generated interest not for what they can show us about the work, but because they provide sensational topics that overshadow it. Each woman has been either mythicized, canonized, or made into an object devoid of connection to her cultural tradition or landscape.

These essays, which emphasize cultural biography, present a significant panorama of transcendent figures from twentieth-century

Latin American cultural history. There is no doubt that these figures have, or will have, an exceptional role to play, but they are presented here not as strange phenomena but as cultural innovators, subversive dissidents, women who are neither myths nor saints, but simply creators, makers. They are neither angels, prostitutes, nor demons, but a community of artists with a collective vision.

The purpose of this book is to establish a connection between the personality and the work, as well as the challenges encountered in the process of creation. The biographies do not seek to foster unhealthy curiosity, or to mythicize the woman's situation, as has so often been the case. One need only recall how literary critics used the verses of the exceptional Uruguayan poet Delmira Agustini to fabricate a life story even less believable than her art, or how Gabriela Mistral was often dismissed because she was a rural schoolteacher. These essays show that in women's culture, there is a marked connection between private and public life. Viewed together, and not as isolated phenomena, these lives offer an integrated and vital vision of creative work.

By selecting for this book such well-known figures as Delmira Agustini, Victoria Ocampo, and Gabriela Mistral, and others such as Marosa Di Giorgio and Marta Traba, I attempt to present a unified portrait of the fact of their creativity. They are not presented in legendary or mythic terms, but instead belong to the vital tradition within a feminine corpus. Each essay was selected because it elucidates the intrinsic union between life and art, and questions, for example, the impact of woman's work on the literary canon. What does it mean to be a minor or major writer? How have these women managed to lead public and private lives through their creative work? What has been the historical legacy? How have they viewed themselves? And finally, is there a particular shape or form to the literary sensibility of women?

One of the challenges of this book is to present the faces of these notable women vis-à-vis their literary production, not to read them as sanctified figures, but to show them as women of flesh and bone.

The book strives to place their biographies in context and to revitalize their public spaces, not in isolation but in a visibly collective fashion. The anthology also attempts to explore the traditions these writers might have in common, to relate and reflect upon the circumstances under which they lived and developed their art, and to understand the essential anecdotes of the surroundings and the social context in which each of these women led her own, often silenced life.

Despite the fact that the stories of many of these women have been decentralized and decontextualized within the parameters of national cultural history, we will see that by means of their writing, and notwithstanding social and economic obstacles, these women created an essential culture of their own. Only within the last few decades, and only viewed as a whole, has their work begun to be appreciated, and to be reinscribed as a central legacy of a culture that refuses to become masculine, or to enter into what the male critical establishment deems to be the official cultural systems.

The women presented in these texts formulate and celebrate, in alternative ways, their own cultural modules and ways of being. They celebrate their differences as novelists, poets, and folklorists. For the most part they distance themselves from the hegemonic language of their time, as in the case of Violeta Parra, who traveled across Chile to recover the lost oral tradition of popular singers and minstrels, then reworked and restructured the poems and songs, filtering them through her voice for an audience unfamiliar with the roots of its own national identity.

Each of the included artists has "a room of her own" very unlike Virginia Woolf's secret space, where books are devoured in silence. The room of one's own in Latin America emerges from a real context, where genre and culture, social class, tapestries, rags, gardens, and marginality entwine to form a history of women that differs greatly from those of other countries.

Writing in Latin America has been a privilege, both for those who enjoy financial security and free time for creative reflection, and those who do not. Through these women we become aware that the challenge of writing is linked not only to questions economic security or income, but more generally to the problem of how little their work is read.

For women writers in Latin America the struggle to survive as a member of the creative community has always been difficult, fraught with conflict, lacking in any sort of official or government support. At every level the struggle has been arduous. Rich or poor, these women are considered subversives simply because they write, respond to their own way of being in the world, shift perspectives, travel, and record their own images. That is to say, writing becomes, for these women, a totally subversive activity.

The women who make up this anthology form a mosaic of different personalities and fascinating work. Some are popular artists, others are art critics, and others, like Sofía Ospina and Victoria Ocampo, members of Latin America's upper class. Few belong to government hierarchies or work as diplomats. Although none earns a living in higher education, there are some schoolteachers. All of them have forged a visible space for themselves within the world of art and culture, managing to shed their invisibility, and have led fascinating and rebellious lives, challenging the pattern of male tradition as they forge their own cultural identities despite the hostility and silence that engulfs them. One way or another, they have elaborated their own identities with tenacity, perseverance, and creativity. They have granted themselves the authority to be who and what they are. They have knocked down walls in an effort to contribute to the legitimate tradition that for many years ignored them; they have created their own tradition.

The collection opens with those writers who lived at the very beginning of the twentieth century, because it was during that time that the pace of women's social and economic life began to pick up. Large numbers of people moved from the countryside into the cities, and professional opportunities appeared where previously there had been none. It is also a time when many women trained to become teachers, and were able, for the first time, to influence and mold future generations of women, to participate in labor unions, and to legitimize the power that they previously lacked.

An examination of the characteristics shared by these women will certainly show that their idea of "tradition" does not correspond to that held by men. In general, men view themselves as the rightful heirs to certain atavistic signs of society, which they must fulfill, obey, continue, or conquer in heroic style. By contrast, these women artists are pathfinders, inventing new directions, free from the male tradition that throughout history denied them authority and limited them to the alternative spaces of home, convent, school. Their lives are no longer proscribed by male figures such as the confessor or priest, who disappeared at the end of the colonial era.

But if the Catholic priest/confessor who guided women no longer holds sway, his modern counterpart is the establishment that judges or ignores women's work. If the confessor establishes vigilance over authoritative discourse, women create a type of free exchange, without hidden baggage, a discourse motivated by the subjectivity with which she writes. That very discourse disallows male rules and is able to flourish independent of the previous patriarchal tradition.

This anthology not only considers the artistic achievements of women but also deals with their lives. It asks under what circumstances, favorable or adverse, they worked. What did they bring of themselves to their fictional and lyric characters? Were their private and public lives kept separate, or did they mesh? How did these women contribute to the traditions of their respective countries? Would it be possible to forge a relationship between culture, women, and national identity? How did they survive, how were they received at home? Did they travel beyond their own borders?

The essays are presented as a series of inquiries, not answers. Each chapter in the collection responds to some of the issues raised, but more importantly, each raises further questions.

Each of the women in this anthology has her own vivid profile. Above all, the book examines how the experience of being a woman is incorporated into each artist's creative work and then reconstituted in her own life. We observe through these texts that the position of women in art is one of alternativity. The writers themselves adopt ways of representing themselves, and choose different and subversive ways of being. As early as the 1920s, for example, Delmira Agustini eroticized social material in order to set the course for the future of women's poetry. Violeta Parra does not separate the creation of her tapestries from her verses. All of them, consciously or not, voluntarily depart from a phallocentric tradition, declaring themselves free, autonomous from a cultural tradition that always considered them outsiders, found them impossible to classify, and relegated them to the margins of history.

Since the twenties, women writers have participated in the historical processes of their countries, and have re-elaborated a tradition of their own. Such are the cases of Sofía Ospina and Victoria Ocampo, who in iconoclastic ways destroyed the spaces they were denied and replaced them with ties of legitimacy, order, and the structure of knowledge, as well as access to power and speech.

Among the characteristics shared by these figures we must highlight audacity, irreverence, and work on the margins, characteristics that, since the beginning of the century, have been part of the tradition of creative women who forge common bonds and remain outside any system of mass consumption. None of these writers has achieved "best-seller" status.

Certainly the great exception has been the canonical figure of Gabriela Mistral, whose image appears on Chilean currency and postage stamps. But, curiously, she was molded, canonized, and sanctified by the national government. She is the rural teacher who speaks for the poor. She has become "the single mother and humble teacher," and as a backwoods schoolteacher, chose a profession "suited" to women. Nevertheless, many women, including Mistral, maintained a very ambiguous relationship with those in power during the twenties and the thirties. She is the saintly teacher of poverty and apology. In her essays and poems, Mistral writes for and about women in the same subordinate way that Sor Juana addresses the church fathers, begging forgiveness for her limited ability to express herself. Apology, then, becomes a stratagem of the weak, a way of expressing oneself from the margins, a way of living in a world of alternative possibilities.

Given this ambiguity in the face of power and culture, the anthology presents a mosaic of different voices, and at the same time expresses a profound communality. These are women who invented other ways of being and living in the world, created different modalities, reconciled the private and the political, the creative life with their condition as women, and elected in their texts the liberating power of the imagination as a way of life.

These women who, for the most part, never met one another were chosen for their contributions to Latin American culture, but more importantly because together they create a mosaic through which a common tradition, a way of placing oneself on the stage of creativity, can be discerned. Nor are these women strange, unusual people. They are people of flesh and bone, who by means of intense personal struggle and acute self-examination, have entered the public sphere, or chosen the private one, have picked up their pens and have held them in women's hands, have undertaken women's work, and have viewed the world through creative women's eyes.

The reader may ask how it was decided to include or exclude certain figures. This question, faced by all literary biographers and anthologists, centers on what constitutes a life, and what value it contains. It is obvious that the lives of women have not been considered worthy of major biographies, nor even brief portraits. Creative women have not been the focus of the great and heroic stories reserved for male heroes. A revealing survey of Latin American culture turns up only three women whose biographies have been written: Gabriela Mistral, Victoria Ocampo, and the artist Frida Kahlo. The first two already belong to the obligatory hermeneutics of official culture. One received the Nobel Prize, and the other, a grande dame of American letters, was the founding editor of the important magazine *Sur.*

To the lack of biographies one must add the fact that many contemporary women writers, among them Margo Glantz and Elena Poniatowska of Mexico, began to write or publish their own life stories during the eighties. There is a growing interest in reflecting upon identity as it is articulated through autobiographical works.

I believe that this book will provide a guideline for the study and revaluation of key female figures of Latin American literature, how they lived, worked, and wrote. Above all, this book presents the possibility of exploring a common tradition that unites them all.

How does a historical figure become, or make herself into, someone exceptional? Is there something different about exceptionality viewed from the perspective of gender? These are some of the questions to be explored. The criteria for inclusion in the book obviously depends on a personal and arbitrary vision of the definition of success, power, and good literature. Above all else, however, this anthology, so far the only one of its kind, postulates that each of the selected figures belongs to a different, alternative tradition, and not necessarily to a national canon.

From fairy tales to the autobiographies of great political leaders, women who appear in canonical and historical texts are relegated to minor spaces. From La Malinche to Gabriela Mistral, they are the links that help to make history, but rarely the protagonists who operate in visible, public spaces. Again, we must confront one of the initial questions posed by this collection: What is or makes up an inspirational life? How is national identity elaborated in the life of a creative woman? What successes are achieved, what adversities overcome?

As Jill Kerr Conway maintains in the introduction to *Written by Herself,* autobiography clearly reflects gender. Men pattern their life stories on classical models, such as the theme of the odyssey, in which a hero travels and arrives at his elected and privileged destination. Women, on the other hand, tend to prefer the confessional mode, to tell their life stories in an almost circular pattern in which there are no clear goals, but rather the possibility of chance encounters, of creation as an end in itself, without concern for marketing strategies nor the success conferred by posterity.

Jill Kerr Conway's important introduction also serves as a model for this collection of essays, in which none of the women portrayed are conventional. None of them lead a similar life, nor create in a similar way. That is, each of the figures chooses a life in which the personal is intrinsically linked to the creative, and in which her artistic vocation is the prime motivating force.

Despite the many day-to-day demands of their lives, their private situations and roles as mothers and daughters, their poverty or, in some cases, rejection of wealth, none of these women allowed their passion for writing and creativity to wane. They dedicated themselves to creativity and faced the adversities inherent in such a choice. That is to say, all the writers presented are women conscious of an artistic mission, and of the fact that their personal and public lives could be fused, never willing to separate the personal from the public, the intimate from the exterior.

From the powerful and aristocratic figures of Sofía Ospina and Victoria Ocampo to the poverty-stricken Violeta Parra and the social outcast Clementina Suárez, they create alternatives, and live and make art in unexpected, supposedly unfeminine ways. Their nonconformist life-styles constitute a shared, central pattern.

Furthermore, all these writers, from Mexico's Elena Poniatowska to Chile's Gabriela Mistral, possess a deep sense of belonging to their country, a bond to the homeland. An intrinsic connection exists between these women and their country, even though none has been part of "national culture." Love of country is yet another essential text.

Each of these women is characterized by a very deep conviction toward her art, her mission, her presence in the world. Despite obstacles, they work methodically to forge a unique identity that always lies outside the traditional framework of what can be called culture. They participate in cultural life but are never truly accepted by an often intolerant and patriarchal society. For these artists, culture is not to be found in the sacred rooms of museums and universities. It exists in everyday spaces: houses, schools, cafés, markets. Their work appears in alternative, minor publications, in low-circulation magazines.

Another curious phenomenon apparent in these texts is that social class does not determine productivity. Both extremely wealthy and extremely poor women work with the same intensity, and are equally rejected by the official patrimony. Victoria Ocampo was rejected for having the audacity to try to escape from a conventional marriage. Violeta Parra suffered similarly for entering the sacred arenas of culture without the correct sort of background.

Each of the authors selected offers a glimpse of what it means to be a woman writer in Latin America, from the early years of our century to the present. They are an eclectic group. Some have achieved great recognition, some are still quite unknown, others have barely begun their journey. Above all, I have tried to select women whose lives and works shed light on the role of women in Latin America. While they belong to different social classes, they share a desire to escape bourgeois order and norms. For the younger generation, neither the suffrage movement nor feminism alters a perceived need for continued defiance. Although conscious of an earlier heritage and willing to acknowledge their precursors, their texts are nevertheless independent and original. We will see that each of these women, since childhood, felt a need to change, to build a different life. Certain determining factors in their childhoods allowed them to forge new identities, which were later manifested in their writing.

The anthology opens with portraits of women who, coincidentally, were born at around the same time and into the same social class. Some of them built a foundation for future work by others, and would eventually be viewed as the initiators of a cultural tradition that held relevance for succeeding generations.

The collection begins with the figure of Doña Sofía Ospina de Navarro, one of Colombia's most distinguished women, whose work is practically unknown in other Latin American countries and the United States. A number of studies by Mary Berg have reawakened an interest in this remarkable woman.

Sofía Ospina was a woman of many talents, a pathfinder who traveled an as-yet-unrecognized and essential road in Latin American culture, a woman whose work had great repercussions for future generations. Sofía Ospina was the grande dame of Antioquian culture and worked in a variety of areas: a journalist and novelist, she also wrote short stories, descriptions of regional customs and manners, and cookbooks. The editorials she published in the most well known newspapers of her country had considerable impact during her lifetime. Sofía Ospina was one of Colombia's most important cookbook authors at a time when very few people were doing such work anywhere in Latin America. As Mary Berg points out, Ospina can be compared to Eleanor Roosevelt. Her considerable social standing and the prestige of her family's name allowed her to choose a public life, and she was able to devote her energies to women's concerns and issues without jeopardizing her position of social privilege.

Within this space, however, she addressed issues of social welfare by reaching out to less privileged women through her various newspaper columns, editorials, and published recipes. From a position of privilege she assumed the role of benefactor, and donned a socially acceptable mask in order to reach women living on the fringes of Colombian society.

Ospina's cookbooks and other so-called nonserious works, are today seen as more than examples of feminine culture. Indeed, they constitute a valuable facet of national identity. Ospina had the remarkable ability, developed many years later by Laura Esquivel and others, to recognize and convey the true historical value of recipes. Also, in her descriptions of everyday manners and customs, Ospina's concern for women living in poverty, a concern that is the basis of organized social action, was always in evidence. We see as well that Victoria Ocampo would later follow Ospina's example, by using the privileges of her immense social and economic power to bring to Latin American culture an unprecedented sense of international vision.

If Sofía Ospina de Navarro managed to attract the masses through her editorials, essays, and recipes, Victoria Ocampo's mission was to disseminate international culture, and to bring an outside point of view to Argentina through her prestigious magazine, *Sur*. Both Ospina and Ocampo used their social status to teach, to introduce "art." Sofía Ospina, a generation older than Ocampo, educated her readers by describing customs, whereas Ocampo tried to internationalize an isolated nation. Both women forged broad paths within the cultural landscape of their respective countries.

Victoria Ocampo is a link between Europe and Buenos Aires, between writers such as Virginia Woolf and Gabriela Mistral. Thanks to Doris Meyer's biography of Victoria Ocampo, *Contra viento y marea,* the editor of *Sur* is more well known, and perhaps a more controversial figure than Ospina in the United States and Latin America. Nevertheless, Ocampo is still the grande dame of Latin American women's literature, a sort of Sor Juana of the twentieth century, who chooses her own room, not a cell in which to hide, but a place for reflection, travel, and shared knowledge. Her room has a view of not only the Atlantic but also the River Plate.

Through her international magazine, Victoria Ocampo managed to break out of the provincialism of Buenos Aires and Latin America and invite discovery of the great writers of the traditional Latin American canon—María Luisa Bombal, Jorge Luis Borges, Julio Cortázar—as well as outstanding figures from abroad, including Waldo Frank, Ghandi, and Tagore. Later, she would publish the work of a younger generation represented by Alejandra Pizarnik and Griselda Gambaro. Through her magazine, Ocampo clearly established herself as the great divulger of Latin American culture who also provided space for the writings of Latin American women.

Doris Meyer's article is particularly revealing because it portrays a little-known aspect of Ocampo's life: her experiences in India, her visit with Ghandi, and the profound social conviction she brought to her work as a human-rights advocate. Ocampo's passion in this area will later surface in such figures as Elena Poniatowska, Griselda Gambaro, and Rigoberta Menchú.

Both Sofía Ospina and Victoria Ocampo eschewed the life of privileged, bourgeois young women to become the great cultural workers of their time. They were oppressed and punished by society; in Ocampo's case, Juan Perón had her arrested. But both women possessed a spirit of renewal and revolution that enabled them to triumph and, ultimately, claim their rightful places on the cultural stage. They are still remembered, thought about, and discussed at length. Victoria Ocampo's personal life, the fact that she drove a car, led to constant scrutiny and condemnation. As an author of cookbooks, Doña Sofía Ospina was less often a target of gossip because she was regarded as a writer who limited herself to women's matters. Nevertheless, her recipes and descriptions of Antioquian customs are a form of powerful social criticism. Like Victoria Ocampo's essays, Ospina's writings document the society in which she lived.

In Central America, in Honduras, Clementina Suárez is the nation's outstanding poet, yet she is barely known in the rest of Latin America. A member of the aristocracy by birth, Clementina Suárez defied convention when she began to hold dramatic poetry readings, much like those staged today in Uruguay by Marosa Di Giorgio. Suárez's poetry was shocking to her contemporaries. Like Delmira Agustini, she wed an intense poetic vocation to life experience and contributed a remarkable and singular body of work to the erotic poetry of Latin America.

During Suárez's lifetime, "female poets" were confined to certain literary salons, yet even within such narrow circles, their speech was censored. Suárez's poetry is celebratory. She speaks of women's bodies, love, sexuality, and absolute freedom in life. Janet

Gold brings this unique figure to life by studying both her private and public selves. As one of Suárez's poems states:

> *Know that a world exists*
> *without laws or precepts*
> *where everything glows*
> *with tenuous vapors*
> *of stellar rhythm*
> *Understand me now*
> *why fire and water, why wind and earth*
> *fill me with unbearable astral kisses.*

Like Ospina and Ocampo, Suárez could have chosen the carefree life of a society matron, and like them, she deliberately carved out a different, more daring existence for herself. It is important to note that all three women not only carried out their own artistic activities but also were vitally connected to their communities. For example, they each organized women's conversation groups through which individual and collective identities were enhanced. They were aware of their social roles, and of the need to embrace other women's voices.

The spaces created by women's conversation groups were extremely important in the twenties and thirties, as only men had official access to centers of power. Ospina, Ocampo, and Suárez sought and created alternative spaces—magazines, literary salons— through which to promote art and literature. According to Gold, Clementina Suárez was one of the most visible figures in Honduras, yet she devoted much energy to the creation of art galleries. Her pioneering work in this area prefigures that of Marta Traba, who in the sixties would be the most important and controversial art critic in Latin America. Suárez also devoted time to helping unknown women authors publish their work; this, too, was an activity that placed her outside the mainstream. As long as she lived, Suárez was harshly criticized, and her social projects never received government backing. Yet despite such adversity, she was a tireless creator whose untimely death left a deep void in the cultural world of Central America.

In fact, all the poets in this book met tragic deaths. Violeta Parra, Alfonsina Storni, Julia de Burgos, and Alejandra Pizarnik committed suicide; Clementina Suárez and Delmira Agustini were murdered.

Delmira Agustini, a member of Uruguay's wealthy bourgeois, created a scandal of major proportions by writing and publishing erotic poetry. Like Suárez before her, and Alfonsina Storni a few years later, Agustini shocked the establishment. In Suárez's case, art and biography were well integrated. According to Renée Scott, however, Delmira was afflicted with a serious psychological condition that compelled her to create and employ masks in her life and work. Scott presents, on the one hand, a modest Delmira who lived peacefully at home, speaking like a baby, protected and controlled by her mother; on the other hand, there is the Delmira who revolutionizes the language and whose writing is free of all false concealments. As Scott maintains, Delmira's childlike behavior was a mere pretense, a way of living in the world and of protecting herself from the roles assigned to the women of her day.

Of all her possible addictions, an obsessive love of poetry helped Delmira survive. The intense language and the eroticization of her body marked a forbidden path that she followed to her own freedom. A constant use of erotic language served as a mask, a means by which many of these women were able to disguise themselves in order to seek alternative ways of being. Masks have been a way to "describe" and hide the self, an efficient form of disguise used to subvert the established order and play with what has been appropriated. They often represent an irreverent, contemptuous impulse.

In their poetry, both Clementina Suárez and Delmira Agustini express, through highly sensual and eroticized language, a joyful sense of the female body. Both women wrote at a time of profound historical change and participated in the early stages of women's intellectual growth during the twenties.

Unlike Sofía Ospina and Victoria Ocampo, Alfonsina Storni lived and worked during a time of very significant change in the cultural history of Latin America, as illustrated by Gwen Kirkpatrick's essay. The daughter of Italian immigrants, and trained as a teacher, Storni worked and wrote as a way of earning a living and in order to better understand herself. Her journalistic essays profoundly criticized Argentinian society. She fought courageously against discrimination in the workplace, and against other practices that kept women subjugated. Intensely committed to bringing national and widespread attention to women's issues, Storni used newspapers of mass circulation as a forum. Her example remained inspirational for decades, as her presence, biography, and poems, often compared to Sor Juana's early discourses, display a great and subtle sense of irony and power. Storni's life, work, and social position were integrated in a way that would later inspire women like Elena Poniatowska, who, in the fifties, began to produce literature of witness and to speak for those without a voice in society.

Curiously, Alfonsina Storni lived at a time when women, despite their lack of economic and financial resources, began to enter the public sphere. Storni constitutes a significant precedent because she eschewed the type of masks worn by many of her contemporaries, including Gabriela Mistral, the saintly rural teacher who spoke for the Indians and the poor, and Delmira Agustini, the poet who cultivated a split personality in order to write erotic verses.

After Storni, Latin American women obtained the right to vote, and increasingly were able to see themselves as players or creators within a larger, wider community of artists. With courage and greater visibility, several women occupied well-earned places on the national scene. Their new ways of writing and practicing journalism owed much to the great example set by Alfonsina Storni.

We close the first section of the book with Gabriela Mistral and Violeta Parra, women who represent a curious alliance of private and public life, contradiction and status quo, masks and transparency, and who, to a certain degree, reflect the iconoclastic vision of all the individuals in this anthology.

Gabriela Mistral did not belong to the upper class; nevertheless, she acquired power. From an early age Mistral had to work for a living as a teacher. Wisely, she cultivated wealthy and powerful people in order to have an officially viable position from which to work on behalf of the poor.

Educational reform and women's suffrage were the causes to which Mistral was able to dedicate herself. Her struggle for these ideals would not have been possible had she herself operated in, or belonged to, that contradictory sphere in which power and knowledge meet. She speaks and writes from the point of view of a subordinate. Like Sor Juana, Mistral knew the value of apologetic language, and her request for forgiveness disguised the true tonality of her writing. Winner of the Nobel Prize, consul to various countries, Mistral always claimed that her work lacked importance because it dealt with the concerns of women and children. Again, she used a "mask" in order to confront those in power with issues of marginality, recalling Agustini's strategies that enabled her to talk about sexual love.

Mistral's poetry, with its sparse language, pan-American view of nature, and obsession with dispossessed women, expresses the concerns she shared with all women involved in the struggle for social justice: concern for the outsider, and for women's access to culture.

According to Elizabeth Horan, Gabriela Mistral constantly plays with masks, split and multiple personalities, but these disguises are preconceived forms, methods through which she is able to invent and recreate herself and her way of being. We see, through Elizabeth Horan's chapter, how Mistral's life spanned several stages, and how in each of them her persona was grounded and shaped according to the historical moment in which she lived. Mistral cast her lot with the flow of history, and like others, she changed it, becoming a protean and always heraldic figure.

Through Mistral we are able to see that these women defy a common tradition of assigned roles, convention, established bourgeois norms. They share a constant concern for solidarity with other women, and manifest this concern by recovering an essential seat of honor, a place in the world and culture in which they live. They all possess a will to teach and to create spaces.

Mistral writes *Lecturas para mujeres*. Ocampo dedicates numerous essays to the literary works of other women and forges an international network of solidarity. She corresponds regularly and powerfully with Storni, for example. Aware of her own life, she chooses to write her memoirs, her autobiography. Let us not forget that Victoria Ocampo was also the first Hispanic American woman to introduce, by way of a translation of Borges, Virginia Woolf's notion of "a room of one's own." These, then, are the women, the precursors, who created a space of one's own for the next generation.

Violeta Parra is noted for many contributions to the cultural life of Chile, including the compilation of more than three thousand songs, the sculpting of wire figures from cast-off materials, and the museum shows she organized to display her precarious art. Violeta's Parra entire life and work amount to a true cultural phenomenon of singular importance. Her artistic and personal lives were totally fused. Her studio was her home, and her artistic vision corresponded to the life she led.

Much more than the other women in this book, Violeta Parra had to struggle. She had very few financial resources. At the outset of her career, she acted in the most rundown bars of Santiago. She had to fight to create "spaces" in which to perform her songs in public, fight to have her verses compiled. Her intense and defiant life has been much discussed, but as Inés Dölz-Blackburn makes clear in the title of her article, Violeta's fundamental contribution is her "artistic legacy," as well as her conscience and her desire to have the work of artists with alternative, different, and marginal visions incorporated into the official culture of the seventies.

As Dölz-Blackburn points out, Violeta Parra has only very recently been included in the scheme of Latin American poetry. She is the only woman in this anthology who was born into the poverty of a peasant household, worked as a popular artist, and made the official culture of her country accept her. Parra occupies a seat of honor within the popular culture of Latin America. Her legacy is in no way abstract, but rather a true presence within the musical and poetic heritage of Chile and Latin America.

The second section of the anthology centers on a several cultural workers whose talents and achievements are not limited to a single field of endeavor, including Ecuadorian novelist and journalist Cecilia Ansaldo; Costa Rican poet, novelist, and minister of culture Carmen Naranjo; and Mexican journalist, biographer, and accurate witness to reality, Elena Poniatowska, among others.

According to Patricia Varas's article, Ecuador has been of very little interest to literary critics, who tend to focus most of their attention on other regions, especially the Southern Cone. It is therefore significant that this anthology should include an article about Cecilia Ansaldo, one of the most important cultural figures of Ecuador, who has yet to become widely known in Latin America.

A prolific literary critic and promotor of other women's work, Cecilia Ansaldo is fully aware of the central position she occupies within the chauvinistic and culturally indifferent society of Guayaquil. Like Marta Traba, she writes cultural criticism in order to create a space for other women, in this case the so-called Women of the Attic. Cecilia Ansaldo's tireless efforts, her access to public fora, and a powerful insistence on her own privacy are aspects of an interesting intellectual woman of the nineties who still faces, and is confined by some of the same obstacles known to women of the twenties. Like other figures in this collection—Mistral, Storni—Ansaldo has been a member of the teaching profession. She continues the legacy of creative women as educators.

Among all the women profiled, only Ansaldo, Di Giorgio, and Mistral never married, had children, or experienced divorce. Fortunately, as Patricia Varas points out, Ansaldo has been spared the gossip that constantly linked Mistral to supposed lovers and accused her of lesbianism. It is refreshing to report that the literary critic from Guayaquil, like Uruguay's Marosa Di Giorgio, has been free to lead an asexual life as a single woman.

Cecilia Ansaldo is the only woman in this anthology who openly espouses feminism. She is the founder of the Women of the Attic, which, according to Patricia Varas, is one of the most important groups in Ecuador. Cecilia Ansaldo exemplifies the energy with which women have forged a voice of their own in an effort to join together, and lend support to those solitary figures whose access to official culture is constantly denied.

Both Marta Traba and Victoria Ocampo were true achievers and promoters of Latin American culture. Unlike Ocampo, however, Traba always gazed from the inside out. That is to say, her mission was to make the visual arts of Latin America known to the world, to write about Botero, Rayo, Lamas, and to create museums, as well as absolutely memorable literature of witness, including *Conversación al Sur,* a narrative about the disappeared.

All the women portrayed in this anthology are characterized by a profoundly American vision, and by their efforts to rescue Latin American culture from isolation. This is the legacy of Traba and Ocampo. They were great cultural critics, and perhaps the two most singular and versatile intellectual figures of Latin America. Today Marta Traba is still one of the top critics of Latin American art who really began to rescue the plastic arts, to be conscious of their significance. In this way she truly shaped the pictorial culture of not only Colombia but also all of Latin America. Gloria Bautista Gutiérrez underscores Traba's global importance for the region, and emphasizes her contributions as a tireless cultural worker, founder of museums, novelist, and poet.

Just as Victoria Ocampo shaped a style of writing and thought in her magazine *Sur,* Traba's numerous articles in Latin American newspapers introduced a new way of writing art criticism. In addition, she wrote novels, short stories, and poetry that proposed new, important, and original approaches to the topic of women in politics in the Southern Cone. Chief among these works is the outstanding novel *Conversación al Sur,* in which she addresses the theme of authoritarianism and political repression within the generational framework of two Argentinian women who, together in Buenos Aires, talk about the violence, the disappearances, and the Mothers of the Plaza de Mayo.

In Costa Rica, Carmen Naranjo is well known as a social critic, poet, and novelist. Like Ocampo, she is one of the most prominent and important cultural figures of her time, yet her unique contributions also include service in the diplomatic corps and in a variety of official government positions. For this anthology, Patricia Rubio draws a fascinating portrait of Naranjo by outlining her public service and capturing her spirit of commitment within the conflict-ridden world of Costa Rican politics. Indeed, Naranjo has created one of the most extraordinary agendas on cultural policy ever seen in Latin America. Her vision stresses the importance of social justice and democratic education as ways of achieving revolutionary change. Through her literary work she is able to portray the inherent inequalities of Central American society, yet honestly present the shortcomings of both the upper and lower classes. Carmen Naranjo belongs to a great Latin American tradition of writers and political activists who struggle for social change. Like Poniatowska and Gambaro, she has managed to combine politics and a life of letters.

Writers Elena Poniatowska, Rigoberta Menchú, and Griselda Gambaro belong to an essential tradition within Latin American literature. By incorporating the reality of the dispossessed, and expressing solidarity with the poor and underprivileged, their work is linked to a tradition shared by many creative women. Beginning with Gabriela Mistral and carried on by contemporary writers, this tradition opens an important current within American letters for women's claims of solidarity and their communal voice. From Mistral to Poniatowska, the literature of these women is structured to give voice to those who lack one, to identify powerfully with the underprivileged, to make oppression a protagonist. Moreover, the writers forge their own strong sense of culture through an identification with women's issues.

Certainly Rigoberta Menchú belongs to this tradition. Her story, and its treatment by Mary Jane Treacy, offer many more intriguing questions than answers. For example, how might we read a text written by a woman who has had to learn the language of her oppressor? What alternate tools can be employed in order to understand how women write in a society in which the access to speech has been prohibited?

Rather than identifying with a nation, Menchú relates most strongly to a group, to what she has learned about the world around her, and not to Guatemalan culture per se. This point of view is shared by many women writers, who consider the idea of a nation to be merely a point of view or geographic reference having less to do with homeland than with the oppression of certain groups by others.

Mary Jane Treacy's essay suggests ways in which to approach and think about Third World texts. Her questions could be vital to the understanding of these essays as well. For example, what methods are most suited to an understanding of texts written by women? How do women write? With what voices do they value or devalue themselves? For Menchú, socialism offers a new way of seeing the world. Her work is linked to an alliance of oppressed peoples, and her vision is profoundly American.

Literature of witness has been an instrumental aspect of Latin American culture since the seventies. Synonymous with controversy and polemic, it has entered academic discourse under the term "political correctness." But here we must clear up certain transcendent facts. Women who write in Latin America have always worked within the realm of testimonial discourse. Ever since the publication of Gertrudis Gómez de Avellaneda's autobiographical *Sab* in the nineteenth century, women's discourse has sprung from the idea that those without a voice have a right to be heard, a right to speak.

The literature produced by the indigenous movement during the twenties in Peru, and the books set by Rosario Castellanos in her native Chiapas, especially her mother's story told in *Balún Canan,* paved the way for the work of Elena Poniatowska. They sought essential forms of expressing, knowing, and grasping words. Testimonial discourse links us to an historical essence, to the lives of human beings immersed in history.

Long before the famous *My Name is Rigoberta Menchú,* there existed other such books, including Domitila Barrios de Chungara's story of life in the Bolivian mines. Yet for an endless number of reasons, Menchú's book was widely acclaimed by the Western world, and at the same time became the source of great controversy.

Mary Jane Treacy's chapter is revealing and provocative, especially for this section, because it immediately acknowledges the difficulty of writing a biography or portrait of Menchú in the traditional sense of the word. Menchú's work is presented as the collective discourse of a people whose importance resides not in individualism, but rather in the cultural contribution made by the group to the nation. It is interesting to realize that even though many of the women in this anthology have not been political activists like Rigoberta, they have nevertheless fulfilled historical roles and, like Menchú, have been considered controversial.

The passionate life of Puerto Rico's Julia de Burgos, and the legend it has spawned, are still of great interest to the reading public. Her untimely and distressing death places her in the company of Violeta Parra, Alejandra Pizarnik, Clementina Suárez, Delmira Agustini, and Alfonsina Storni, women who, though marked forever by their tragic ends, remain key figures within the history of Latin American culture.

Like Gabriela Mistral, Julia de Burgos made the American landscape a central element of her poetry. The Loayza River and the sea have been immortalized in her poems, which capture the essence of the natural surroundings while breaking with the *criollista* tradition of the island. Burgos was both a poet-in-exile and a political activist concerned about the dispossessed. Carmen Esteves's essay allows us to penetrate the richness of her spirit.

Throughout this introduction, the central role played by Elena Poniatowska in the cultural life of Latin America has been noted often. Her writings include journalism, fiction, testimonials, and novels of love. The product of a privileged upbringing, and raised in a family of the Polish aristocracy, it is in Mexico that she finds a new identity and brings to life stories and individuals relegated to the margins of society.

With the talent and instincts of an excellent journalist, Elena Poniatowska recreates, with skill and originality, the history of Mexico, from the massacre of the students at Tlatelolco in 1968 to the earthquake of 1987, in two masterpieces, *La noche de Tlatelolco* and *Nada, nadie: Las voces del temblor.* Both books weave history and testimonial to capture the reality of these important events.

Journalism and social denunciation, however, have not been the sole genres practiced by this singular woman. She has also cultivated narrative and the short story, as well as certain biographical texts, such as *Querido Diego, te abraza Quiela,* which recreates the lives of Angelina Bewolf and Diego Rivera in postwar Paris, or her monumental *Tinísima,* which recreates the life of Tina Modotti.

In her very descriptive article, Kay García captures for us the lively and gentle personality of Elena Poniatowska, who uses her privileged position in society to speak for the dispossessed.

If Elena Poniatowska's books introduce a new way of facilitating and allowing the underprivileged to speak, it is from literature of witness that she acquires the essential component of her artistic legacy, the very alliance with the dispossessed. Griselda Gambaro establishes this same link in her plays. The only dramatist in this anthology, Gambaro has made extraordinary contributions to Latin American theater. Most of all, Griselda Gambaro has brought to the stage a political component that links her work to texts by Poniatowska, Traba, Menchú, and Violeta Parra.

Like Marta Traba, Griselda Gambaro uses her country's political life as a point of departure for discussing repression through torture. Oddly, Gambaro's earliest works foreshadow what was to occur years later in her country, the drama of the disappearances, the barbed-wire fences that became commonplace. Through her life and her work, Gambaro also came to represent all those writers who were forced into years of exile. During the military regime, she left for Barcelona and did not write plays until her return following the full restoration democracy in the eighties.

Griselda Gambaro and all the writers in this section belong to an important tradition in which the social factor, denunciation, is a central theme. It has consistently been a central concern in the work of women writers who address public issues and the historical record. These women also share a strong connection to the struggle for human rights and the political movements to which it gave rise during the seventies and eighties.

The last section of the anthology focuses on profound experimentation with language, the unconscious, and poetry. The section includes three singular authors—Clarice Lispector of Brazil, Alejandra Pizarnik of Argentina, and Marosa Di Giorgio of Uruguay—whose work exemplifies what many have called surrealist, ambiguous literature. It is, again, difficult to define such terms, but I believe the work of Clarice Lispector best illustrates this approach to language. Giovanni Pontiero, Lispector's translator and perhaps the most insightful critic of her work, says that she sees books as sensations, episodes. In his article he quotes Lispector as follows: "I thought a book was a sensation, an intuition . . . I thought a book was like a tree, like an animal, something that is born."

Rational thought and language play a very minor role in the work of these three writers whose creations fly in the face of a strong male tradition. Giovanni Pontiero states that Clarice Lispector writes from an intuition anchored to a magical language of a discourse made up of fragments and visions, ways of speaking and knowing that are born like certain bolts of lightning, certain fragmented notes, that weave themselves into and out of patterns.

From her first novels, especially *Near the Savage Heart,* and her chronicles about writing, *The Foreign Legion,* Lispector writes as if motivated by a strong intuition that comes from outside herself, and whose central concern is with forms of expression, the structure of language, and the spaces of silence.

During her lifetime Clarice Lispector achieved great critical success in Brazil, but international recognition has come only recently, thanks to the French critic Helen Cixous, who has placed Lispector among the most interesting practitioners of *escritura feminina* of the twentieth century.

If Clarice Lispector defies the convention of rational prose and chooses a poetic language full of symbolic insinuations, Alejandra Pizarnik elaborates her poetry from the subconscious, and from there, maintains a dialogue with poetry. She is considered one of the most important poets of this century, and like Violeta Parra and Delmira Agustini, she died prematurely and tragically.

According to Alicia Borinsky, Alejandra Pizarnik was always a somber and taciturn person, but she made poetry her essential mission, working daily to make her verses some of the most original in the Spanish language. Pizarnik's poetry, like Lispector's narratives, has to do with those mysterious articulations of silence and speech that postulate the impossibility of words in order to truly articulate poetic expression. Both Clarice Lispector and Alejandra Pizarnik struggle desperately to renovate the language, to rid it of rational components and to place it in the realm of the intuitive. Pizarnik's identity, her wanderings, her trips between Buenos Aires and Paris, represent undefined searches, irreducible landscapes in the immense abyss of words, and above all, the impossibility of capturing, through language, a vision of the universe:

> *She undresses in the paradise*
> *of her memory*
> *she ignores the cruel destiny*
> *of her visions*
> *she is afraid of not knowing how to name*

From earliest times, the garden has been a presence and space for communication and discretion. The French impressionists, in particular, made it a place of dreams and random light. Marosa Di Giorgio, perhaps one of the central figures of twentieth-century Latin American poetry, has centered her work on the metaphor and recreation of the garden as the honored site of women's imagination.

Di Giorgio is a poet of great notoriety in Uruguayan literary circles, yet she is little known beyond her country. This is surprising, because Di Giorgio has much in common with Alejandra Pizarnik, and her work has been studied by a number of critics. It is a privilege to be able to include in this anthology an essay about Marosa Di Giorgio by Uruguayan writer and anthropologist Teresa Porzecanski. The chapter is important because it takes us back to a time when poetry was really linked to a way of life, and to a destiny or calling not unlike an absolute passion.

The essay about Di Giorgio describes a woman whose personal and artistic lives are perfectly integrated. She leads a life totally dedicated to poetry and its creation. Porzecanski's article presents a vivid picture of the poet and the unusual image she projects from a stage in Montevideo, and it makes clear that the image parallels the life she has led, completely devoted to poetry. Never employed or recognized in any official capacity, Di Giorgio, like other figures in this anthology, dedicates her entire life to creativity.

Marosa Di Giorgio is one of the few figures of this anthology whose creative work is tied to the rural spaces of the countryside, which she has made the center of her poetics and her poetry. The images and symbolic allusions to these spaces create one of the most unexpected languages of contemporary Latin American poetry. Nevertheless, her work has yet to be translated, and like all the other women profiled in this anthology, Marosa Di Giorgio swims against the current. She does not belong to any of Uruguay's *costumbristas,* or nativist movements, in which the image of the garden is fundamental to many texts. In Di Giorgio's work, the image of the garden is disturbed by means of symbolic language. It is the essential place where the poet finds herself.

This anthology brings together women who led extraordinary lives, members of the aristocracy, the middle and working classes, popular poets, dramatists, fiction writers, activists. What do they have in common, and what unites them? These final pages will provide more than one conclusion, as they allude to not only what these women share but also to the forms that elaborate their common destiny. This is a meditation on their communality.

The socioeconomic class to which Ospina, Ocampo, and Agustini belonged offered no significant support to creative women. Despite the fact that they were from wealthy, upper-class families, they were still marginalized and kept out of the mainstream. As members of the aristocracy, women authors were deprived of means of communication and met with the disapproval of their social peers. These writers saw literary work not as a sideline but as a very serious vocation. As financially independent women, they worked against the roles assigned to them by society. They shared a spirit of defiance and an awareness of their oppression.

All of the figures in this anthology contribute in a notable fashion to the enrichment of their nation's culture. Ocampo opens borders between North and South. Mistral creates vast educational reform. Poniatowska brings to literature the voice of the underclass and stands alongside its members. Pizarnik and Di Giorgio establish a new way of writing poetry, of inventing a language born of each of their particular sensibilities. Nevertheless, widespread recognition and a place in the historical canon eludes them. Neither Mistral in Chile nor Ocampo in Argentina are widely read. Elena Poniatowska, surely the most well known and beloved of all, does not figure in all of Mexico's cultural spaces.

The preoccupation with marginality is another common factor that might form a communal tradition among these women. From Ospina to Poniatowska, the search for and effort to incorporate in women's writing the testimonies of forgotten voices is recurrent, even in the work of writers like Pizarnik and Di Giorgio, who seem to be submerged in an introspective exploration of their surroundings. They, too, approach the voices of women who have been relegated to silent spaces. I believe that this awareness of women's status as outsiders springs from the fact that, as writers, they are all transgressors who cross certain forbidden spaces, challenge their assigned roles, and join their public voice to that of the dispossessed. Alliance and solidarity are the actions that define them.

From Victoria Ocampo at the beginning of the century to Elena Poniatowska today, an essential tradition in Latin American culture has emerged that tries to give voice to, and authentically and collectively validate, the memory of native peoples and the artistic work of women. The overriding idea of providing witness in their work, as well as in life, stems from, more than anything else, the capacity of these individuals to integrate a vision of public issues into their own lives. There is an awareness that they must transgress those public, domestic, and private zones that denounce their experiences as silenced women. This is the case in Ocampo's memoirs, all of Poniatowska's testimonial works, and Mistral's poetry.

These women are also united in their choices of subject matter and themes, which reveal their experiences as women to be central to both their lives and work. Cooking, embroidery, children, love, and memory are not demeaned but celebrated as essential themes. I believe that in these texts it is impossible to separate the flow of history from the women's personal lives. I believe that although many of them have not declared themselves to be feminists, the subjects they choose and the works they create depend absolutely on their womanhood, and on the possibility of offering new spaces in which to awaken an intellectual awareness of women's issues.

There can be no doubt that each of these individuals managed to combine the role of woman and cultural worker in her life. It is interesting that in these essays the influence of lovers and relatives do not seem as important as the profound sense of sisterhood and the valorization of women. The determination to fight for space is apparent from the outset with Ospina and Ocampo. This process of incorporating oneself into the world, of finding oneself, is a common bond and a shared goal.

Through these articles, we can see a clear preoccupation with the forces that make respect for women's contributions difficult. Although society grants women a certain amount of worth, it nevertheless relegates them to the back rooms and denies them rooms of their own. This is why women build their own rooms. They live within themselves, creating and writing. The act of creation supersedes the bounds of gender.

Above all, this anthology represents the life and work of women motivated by a profound creative vocation, by a desire to view the world through and for women. This is the cultural legacy they bestow on us, an innovative tradition of their own.

All the women portrayed in this anthology have made important contributions to Latin American literature. We have not focused on the culture of exceptions, but rather on the exceptional qualities that allowed each of them to live in an autonomous and autochthonous way, outside the rigid and authoritarian culture in which their works were written.

As previously mentioned, only a few of these women—Gabriela Mistral, Carmen Naranjo—serve as government officials. Although the contributions of all have been essential to national culture, they have been, for the most part, invisible to those in power, outsiders vis-à-vis official networks. Only Victoria Ocampo owns a newspaper and is independently wealthy. Yet these women draw creative strength from an alliance based on sisterhood and a deeply rooted literary vocation. The activities of almost all underscores the building of a women's culture, a great desire to be identified as women, and a conscious desire to recover their foremothers, to rethink women's work, to value those arts considered "crafts," and literary forms thought to be secondary, such as letters, diaries. I believe that the tradition of these women is to reappraise what is feminine, not in an alternative or diverse way, but by entering the cultural sphere, the male sphere, in order to universalize rather than defeminize it.

One of the major contributions of these writers is the alliance of their private and public spaces, where there are no hierarchies to separate those who write about domestic experiences from those who focus on intellectual matters. All of them offer broad social criticism in the most positive sense of the word. That is, they further the transformation of an entire culture that has assigned a predominant role to what is rational and masculine. All these women act as a destabilizing force upon certain predominant values that support official culture. Their irreverence and fusion with what is of no apparent importance, such as oral tradition and the voices of the underclass, are an important part of the canon for these creative women.

Each of these women subverts the limits imposed on her gender, is brave, and, above all, defies the establishment. Their families are not the central focus of their work. They are profoundly aware that all the political regimes of the past have forbidden their social imagination, so against wind and tide, against the current, they create a culture, not for the purpose of separating themselves from the nation, but rather to propose a different way of being and living in, of relating to the world, a gaze from and for women.

Each of these women also questions the spheres of power and of knowledge, as well as the relationships between the two, in order to rebel and create their own space where the valorization of affection, intimacy, and sisterhood are the central vehicles of this so-called women's tradition in Latin American culture. All of them are fully aware of their privileged social status, and forge solid alliances with dispossessed women in order to make them a part of history.

Sofía Ospina de Navarro:
WISE ADVICE FROM AN OPTIMISTIC GRANDMOTHER

MARY G. BERG

⌐ WHEN SOFÍA OSPINA DE NAVARRO DIED in Medellín, Colombia, at the age of eighty-one in June 1974, Colombian newspapers and magazines wrote at length of her extraordinary career as a journalist, short story writer, poet, dramatist, cooking expert, etiquette advisor and organizer of charitable enterprises. For several generations of Colombians, she was a combined Eleanor Roosevelt of social causes, Emily Post of the final word on social behavior, Fannie Farmer of culinary strategies, and a popular writer of commentaries and memoirs of a more civilized age. A woman of extraordinary vitality, energy, humor, and curiosity, she shared her insights and common sense with thousands of readers during her decades of frequent editorial essays in such major newspapers as *El Espectador, El Tiempo* and *El Colombiano*. Hundreds of her essays and stories were collected into best-selling volumes that remain a delight to read. Her basic cookbook, *La buena mesa*, which might be translated as *Good Food: A Simple and Practical Guide to Cooking*, has remained a staple of Colombian domestic life throughout the better part of this century, selling many hundreds of thousands of copies in its dozens of editions.

In person, Sofía Ospina was a powerhouse of organizational energy, intense compassion, and emotional warmth. She was dedicated to raising funds for charitable causes, and throughout her life she promoted causes that furthered the education and health of women. She was personally responsible for the university education of hundreds of women. As well as dominating traditional areas of women's literary expression, with her cookbooks, etiquette handbooks, lively memoirs of turn-of-the-century Medellín, plays, and poetry, Sofía Ospina moved like a well-armed battleship into the traditionally male waters of social commentary, sharp critical analysis of current events, dramatic productions of at least six of her plays, and a lifetime of public speeches. She was the first woman to lecture at the prestigious Colón theater in Bogotá, the first woman council member in Antioquia, one of the creators of an important educational task force in Medellín, and a founding member of a literary circle that met regularly and included many outstanding writers, including Tomás Carrasquilla. She was also a painter of some distinction. Sofía Ospina's achievements were widely recognized: she won dozens of awards for public service, culminating with the national Great Cross of Boyacá in 1973, and including the Star of Antioquia, awarded by her home state of Antioquia, as well as designation as the Emblematic Matron of Antioquia in 1961.

Sofía Ospina was born on April 15, 1893, in Medellín, Colombia, where she lived throughout her life.[1] Her family was a prominent one: she was the granddaughter of Colombian president Mariano Ospina Rodríguez, the niece of President Pedro Nel Ospina, and the sister of President Mariano Ospina Pérez. She grew up in a lively household of active participation in public affairs. Her father had returned to Colombia with a U.S. degree in mining engineering and a particular interest in agricultural and industrial development. He was the author of short stories as well as of various historical and scientific works, and he founded the Normal School of Mines in 1895. In 1904 he was named rector of the University of Antioquia.

This was not an era when women commonly received much (if any) formal education, so it was unusual that Sofía Ospina pursued her studies first at the Colegio de la Enseñanza and later at home with a renowned private teacher, María Rojas Tejada. Ospina would later write appreciatively of the educational doors opened to her by this teacher, whose extensive writings on education included a fundamental manual on the importance of preschool education.

Sofía Ospina was married for fifty-five years to Salvador Navarro Misas, a Medellín businessman whom she had known since childhood. They had seven children, and eventually twenty-seven grandchildren and many great-grandchildren, many of whom gathered at the Navarro home every Sunday for decades. When she died in June 1974, Sofía Ospina was front page news all over Colombia. She was mourned and celebrated as a central figure in Colombian cultural life. Many of her books have been reprinted over and over since her death, and collections of her essays have been published. Much-consulted copies of her cookbooks may be found in nearly every Colombian kitchen.

Ospina's passion was education. Early in her married life, when family funds were meager, Ospina taught cooking classes in her kitchen and ran a successful catering service. Her recipes circulated in handwritten form and were soon published as a popular cooking manual. Ospina intended it as an introduction to kitchen and household management for newlywed wives, and she dispenses helpful hints and cautionary advice along with practical lists of ingredients and step-by-step procedures. In a kind, grandmotherly voice, Ospina provides detailed information for brides who, because their mothers may not have shared responsibilities with them, have never had much experience in household management. Ospina sympathizes with their panic as they give the cook orders for the first time, exhorting her readers to self-confidence as well as giving culinary advice. Young brides should never let the cook take advantage of their ignorance and should be firm with their husbands, who may have been excessively indulged by doting mothers and need to be reeducated nutritionally. Along with advice on how much milk to buy and which spices to use only in moderation (an overdose of vanilla can destroy a cake, she warns), Ospina encourages cooks to experiment and vary proportions to suit themselves as she provides clear, easy-to-follow recipes for hundreds of Colombian (and particularly Antioquian) dishes. She extols the merits of local ingredients, of tropical fruits and vegetables, of breads and dumplings and turnovers filled with Antioquian mixtures of sausage, yucca, bananas, and spices. Often she adapts foreign recipes, particularly Italian pasta dishes or Spanish rice mixtures, for local ingredients and Colombian tastes.

Ospina's enthusiasm for advising young women is even more apparent in *La cartilla del hogar,* which might be called *Recipes for Domestic Happiness.* Her declared objective is to create joyful tranquillity on the homefront, a well-fed contentment that can serve as a base for confidence and creative enterprise for the members of the household. This is a menu cookbook and a domestic arsenal of advice and grandmotherly affection. She discusses how to manage domestic help, the importance of interesting conversation during meals, how to appear confident even when the main course has burned, how to dress appropriately, and even how to deal tactfully with your mother-in-law. Along with recipes and menu strategies, Ospina chats about traditional customs and holidays, even including a long poem about turn-of-the-century Christmas celebrations and old-fashioned favorite foods.

Don de gentes, or *Getting Along Well with People: Nuggets of Social Advice,* is explicitly a manual of proper social behavior, and it, too, was a best seller. The 1969 edition, for example, was of sixty thousand copies. In her wonderful voice of the loving grandmother who has seen it all, Ospina gives often humorous advice for every possible situation: how to interact successfully with policemen, doctors, bankers, mothers-in-law, and servants. Presence of mind and self-confidence will win the day, she emphasizes. Keep smiling, and mow down the opposition. "Train your facial muscles," she says, "so that your expression will always radiate happiness and good health, or at least tranquillity" (*Don* 5[2]). It is essential for women to be strong, respected, and sure of themselves; they must insist that in their homes, the personal opinions and wishes of each individual are heard, so that peace and harmony prevail. Ospina scolds those who are lazy, self-absorbed, or too timid to insist upon their rights or to be properly courteous to others. Be careful in conversations, she counsels, so that you don't shock your listeners by being excessively explicit or brusque. When traveling, direct your attention to the new sights and take care that you do not get seduced into spending the better part of your time shopping. Pay your debts on time, do not pester your doctor with imaginary ailments, and, if you are a lady, never smoke in public. When you are dancing, take care that you are not unduly close to your partner, and if a man does not respect your wishes, react immediately and refuse his invitations. Ospina advises moderation in all behavior, and, in her voice of maternal anxiety, discusses her concern that now that women are imbibing alcohol in public, the lines between proper and improper public conduct are often difficult to draw. She worries that after a few drinks, in that carefree and careless state induced by alcohol, women may lose track of the dangers all about them. Take care, she says, or the next morning you may have deep regrets. Ospina's is the voice of the loving, wise, older woman, who, accepting that the modern age is upon us, warns of its perils and yearns to enfold her readers in the simpler, safer times of her childhood.

Many of Ospina's essays are about this childhood golden era for which she feels great nostalgia. She writes with humor, great charm, and extraordinary detail about her memories of growing up in turn-of-the-century Medellín, during that stable period before the War of a Thousand Days ushered in the chaos and turmoil of the modern age. Ospina's *La abuela cuenta* (Grandma's tales) is a collection of twenty-six essays about life in Medellín during the early part of the century, as the town gradually went from being an isolated rural paradise to becoming a still-provincial but much modernized city in close contact with Colombian and world technological development. *Grandma's Tales* is about Ospina's nostalgic memories of childhood, but they also present an analysis of a society in transition, a society caught between its yearnings for stability and change. The book is a compendium of Antioquian traditions and social customs, how holidays are celebrated, religious and domestic practices, how the schools operated, and class interrelationships, especially within households where there were many family members and servants. Vividly, Ospina recalls how things were: what people wore, their vehicles, their amusements, the foods they ate, what medicines they took, and a thousand more details of life. The prosperity of the modern age has brought improved treatments for ailments and greater comforts (she is particularly enchanted with refrigerators and blenders, for example) but has also outmoded or limited some of the old-fashioned pursuits. She recalls playing cards with her cousins by candlelight, fishing for minnows in country streams, wading in creeks, leaping over bonfires, hunting for hen's nests, and "so many other primitive and simple pleasures that we long for nostalgically today" (*AC* 68). Modern scientific farming may produce more apples or cattle per acre, but it precludes some of the simple joys of Ospina's childhood. One after another the harbingers of the new age arrive: the magic lantern, the gramophone, the first car, silent films, and the first airplane.

Grandma's Tales is also an account of the changes in women's lives in Medellín. Ospina describes the very limited formal education provided for girls when she was a child: "It never occurred to us girls that travel abroad was a possibility. For the limited studies that the useless feminine sex needed, the academies for young ladies sufficed, with a year or two at a nuns' school" (*AC* 138–39). But she has to admit that her own education was an exception to the rule, as were the family travels to Europe and the United States. She describes how the limited possibilities for women expanded as the twentieth century advanced. The young married women were no longer content to focus themselves entirely on home and family; they became eager to know more of the greater world, and little by little

> came to believe that there was a place in society for them, that intelligence was not exclusively a masculine attribute, that it might be possible to have wider interests than exclusively domestic ones. And it was then that, without forgetting that they were based within their family circles, and without neglecting their domestic duties, they emerged into the light. Blinking their eyes a bit, and faltering as they took their first steps, but joyful and filled with hopes. (AC 166)

It is this time of first steps, of confused hopes and fears, of traditional roles and new aspirations, that becomes the scenario of Sofía Ospina's short stories. Medellín as it enters the modern age is the main topic of the twenty-eight tales included in Ospina's first collection of fiction and essays, *Cuentos y crónicas* (Stories and chronicles), published in 1926. A detailed portrait of a traditional society in transition is presented; considered together, the stories provide a panorama of individuals, from the most humble, like the poor family of "Ilusiones" (Illusions), to the most prosperous. Each story focuses on an aspect of social interaction, or on one particular social institution: dances, tea parties, women's hairstyles, fashion, the preparation and serving of food (always central to Ospina's perspective on how society functions), child care, or domestic help.

Almost all of the stories examine the institution of marriage. As she scrutinizes an array of matrimonial conditions and tensions and analyzes what kinds of personal alliances are forged between members of a traditional community, Ospina looks in great detail at the lives of women and the possibilities open to them, their behavior at the various stages of their lives, their ambitions, and their limitations. The stories dramatize vivid scenes of tea dances and traditional Catholic masses, formal dinners, romantic rivalries, catty conversations conducted on that most marvelous new invention, the telephone, and endless problems with servants who now have other options, such as going to work in the factories that are beginning to open. Marriage as an institution is examined from many different perspectives. Many of the stories reveal the presence of new financial tensions under the surface of traditional aristocratic respectability. Ospina portrays a series of women who are caught between the assumptions of the old order and the possibilities of the new: women who come to realize (or should realize) that stability is crumbling, and that without self-awareness, honesty, and openness of communication between husband and wife, and a sense of mutual responsibility, entering into the modern age is perilous.

Ospina often deplores the materialism of Antioquian society, although it serves her well as raw material for good-humored satire. In many stories she pokes fun at women who are obsessed with their own appearance or with the acquisition of domestic furnishings. In "Persiguiendo la línea . . ." (Toeing the line . . .), a young woman's efforts to diet herself into physical perfection are depicted as ridiculous; "Sepamos vivir" makes fun of women who spend their lives "tending a beautiful cage full of bored birds" (CC 122); and dozens of stories spoof the obsession with fashionable hairstyles and the fascination with French dresses that swept over the female population of Medellín. Ospina's stories are filled with hilarious depictions of women who are hypnotized by dresses that do not fit them, of women who are ready to kill each other to acquire the latest French marvel, and of women who lie to their husbands about the astronomical costs of these new irresistible treasures. In "En una boda" (At a wedding), the female guests verbally dissect one another's gowns, all of them nearly expiring from jealousy as they

> compliment Laurita, who had the extraordinary good fortune to be just the right size for that 'antique rose' colored dress at Paquín's shop that they had all admired and tried on over and over again hoping it would somehow fit this time, and had finally had their own dressmakers try to imitate so

they could seem to be dressed in the latest fashion from the
most exclusive shop in town. (CC 140)

Of course, they all know one another, and Medellín is just too
small to hide their outmaneuverings, so their silliness is apparent
to them all.

With its detailed and profoundly comic description of a women's
tea party, "En sociedad" (In high society) contrasts the various generations: the grandmothers with their narrow-minded nostalgia
for the old days when people could count on being served a good
cup of chocolate at 3:30 and the two younger generations for whom
the rules have been less clear. The younger married women com-
pete with one another as to who can discover the best new French
pastry shop and who can talk whom into believing that it is really
the height of new French fashion to serve ice cream at 6:00 P.M. or
elaborate, inedible delicacies carried in from a flashy new bakery
rather than the traditional homemade sweets that they would really enjoy eating. The young unmarried girls are trying to deal with
the contradictory messages from their mothers and grandmothers,
wondering what it is they are really supposed to be doing, while
their chatter flashes from fashions to the last dance at the club
to last Sunday's sermon. Ospina captures the symphonic quality of
these layers of voices with their many agendas and confusions, superficial struttings, and generational contrasts. The older women
offer interminable advice, the younger women pretend politely to
listen and then go ahead and do the opposite; they all despair over
each other's ways and love each other anyway. They are proud of
the qualities in each other that most irritate them: the older women
cluck over the spendthrift ways of their daughters, but are secretly
titillated by the giddy new fashionable currents, and the younger
women like hearing the stories of the olden days when butter was
churned and home kitchens turned out traditional dishes.

Most of Ospina's stories are about women of Medellín: old and
young women, traditional and modern, ambitious and timid, lucky

and unlucky. "Un estreno memorable" (A memorable debut) is a hilarious and sympathetic description of Adelaida's passionate desire to impress her friends by showing off a new set of wine glasses she has had sent from France. The story is about the unpacking of the glasses, one by one, as Adelaida frets and muses about just what to serve, anticipating how amazed her guests will be to have different glasses for white wine and red, and then yet another set for champagne with dessert. Melodramatic tension builds as Adelaida worries about getting everything simultaneously perfect: the table setting, the wines, the recipes she has collected from magazines, her clothes. Breathless with anxiety, she almost manages it all, when suddenly the lights go out and Adelaida realizes that the electric bill has not been paid because she has been so extravagant. It is a beautifully orchestrated story, told with suspense and pathos and a lighthearted sense of the ridiculous.

Almost all of the stories deal with a failure of communication between husband and wife. Ospina's belief that marriage should be a partnership of equals is evident, but so, too, is her awareness that this is rarely the case. Throughout her life, Ospina wrote and spoke extensively about the need to educate men as well as women about the necessity of mutual respect and open communication. Abridged freedom, unequal rights, and secrecy are always a basis for matrimonial disaster in her stories. "Los negocios de Paco" (Paco's deals) chronicles the increasing ability of a young married woman to make mature decisions, whereas, in contrast, her husband want his friends to think he is as free as ever despite his marriage. In "El anillo nupcial" (The wedding ring), too, a woman's sincerity is contrasted with a man's inability to be honest. It is an extraordinarily moving depiction of a young woman so lacking in self-confidence that she blames herself when she cannot find her elaborate wedding ring, rather than suspecting that her husband might have taken it to give to a sweetheart. The husband's duplicity is less emphasized than is the excessive innocence of the young woman: she fails to see what is obvious. She would rather blame herself than recognize what is really true.

In other stories, women are at fault in the breakdown of matrimonial communication. Often it is because their perspectives are too narrow, and, like Adelaida and her French wine glasses, they become obsessed with material possessions and short-term social victories because they have no bigger goals in life. Often they are women who have not been educated to be "free" in Sofía Ospina's view, and who have consequently become lost in the baffling mazes of gossip and petty social one-upmanship. Their energies are misused in unproductive and sometimes destructive pursuits. In her stories, Ospina often stops just short of explicit moralizing. She explores the psychology of her women characters, often describing them with affectionate humor, usually sympathizing with their dilemmas, but rarely portraying them as able to step out of the circumstances that limit them. Self-knowledge and enhanced perceptiveness about the motivations of others are always desirable qualities, but they do not necessarily—or even usually—lead to wider opportunities. In "Menos redes . . ." (Fewer tangles . . .), for example, the topic is explicitly changing social conventions of the modern age. The pros and cons of new hairstyles are discussed. Paquita's boyfriend, although an educated man and a poet, is deeply antagonistic to modern changes, and he tells her at great length why he feels modern styles are not for "real women" (CC 72). She explains to him how times have changed and how although long braids and trailing gowns might have been all right for women who sat around looking languid all day, for today's young women who "type ninety words a minute on their Remingtons, and then go right off, in a great rush, to play tennis or basketball" (CC 72–73), it is simply not convenient to have to think about elaborate hair arrangements and makeup. Intellectually he hears this, but emotionally he wants her to be an old-fashioned girl, and she finally accepts that he will not change. She promises not to cut her hair short, and says that, yes, well, all right, "I will henceforth use lotions and ointments to strengthen those chains that imprison my future husband" (CC 74). Her acceptance is ambiguous; it is not clear whether she is simply acknowledging that he is a prisoner of his conception (or misconception) of how a wife should be, or whether she is actively playing the game and welcoming a chance (on his terms) to bind him to her. In any case, he wants her to be the old-fashioned woman who looks after her appearance in order to please him, and she complies. Practicality is a virtue in Sofía Ospina's brisk world; women must choose their battles carefully, get their priorities right, and smile a lot at everyone along the way. Smile brightly, because after all, in a world that is evolving at such a precipitous pace, everything is possible: "Times are changing so fast, that who knows, pretty soon even grandmothers may be out there dancing" (*CC* 144).

Sofía Ospina describes a society in which men may have all of the public power but women have a good deal of control over domestic affairs. She is interested in generational conflicts and often depicts struggles between mothers and daughters, as in "Detrás de las puertas" (Behind the doors), in which an impoverished mother begs her daughter to get an office job but the daughter refuses to work. This is an inversion of the usual tension, which is commonly between a traditional mother and children who want to make what they imagine to be their own choices. In "De luto" (In mourning), for example, a mother forces her daughters to wear black when their uncle dies, but they do so unwillingly, and emphasize that they will only give up their bright fashionable dresses temporarily. It is the mother's victory, and no harsh words are exchanged, but tradition will prevail only briefly, soon to be replaced by modern ways.

Ospina's *Cuentos y crónicas* included four essays, apparently first delivered as lectures, about the roles of women in early-twentieth-century Medellín. She feels that women must insist aggressively on their right to participate in society as equals. In "Feminismo" (Feminism), she expresses her admiration for women who work, and who are useful, responsible, and independent. She makes fun of women who hide behind their husbands and fail to make their own opinions heard. She advocates the recognition by everyone, men and women alike, of the merits of the new feminism, which will strengthen rather than weaken the traditional family. Her "new woman" (CC 177) is dedicated to her family, to charitable causes, and to intelligent progress.

During the half-century that followed the stories and essays of *Cuentos y crónicas,* Ospina's views of Colombian society were made public in hundreds of essays and speeches. Two hundred and forty-nine of her newspaper columns were collected under the title *Crónicas* (Chronicles) in 1983, and reveal her enduring interest in the process of modernization, the differences between men's and women's abilities and roles, and the details of daily social interchange. Everything fascinated her: movie plots and new medical treatments, recipes and airline schedules. The conversational quality of her prose recorded the immediacy of voices of workmen, teachers, dentists, and senators. Neither her sense of humor nor her eager curiosity seem ever to have failed her, although as years went by, her public persona as traditional wise grandmother became more established. For fifty years she lived in the public eye, much interviewed, much photographed, and much quoted by her tens of thousands of regular readers. Her love of good food, family gatherings, and charitable enterprise were legendary. She intended her columns, like her basic cookbooks, to be accessible and useful to everyone. Of *La buena mesa* she wrote: "This is a book to keep in the kitchen and consult daily, and not just one more volume to gather dust on the library shelf." She said often that food is the most important thing in life, and that to eat well is to be happy. Through the years, when newspapers asked her to contribute more and more columns of social commentary, she would insist that they also publish more recipes and articles on nutrition, saying that "people need to be taught how to eat. Well-fed citizens are happy citizens." It seems appropriate that decades after her death, her cookbooks are still consulted, and that well-prepared meals are active memorials to this generous, warm-hearted, charismatic optimist from Medellín, who wrote lovingly of the past and perceptively about the changing times of the present.

Victoria Ocampo:
& SPIRITUAL ENERGY

DORIS MEYER

⌐ IN THE YEARS SINCE SHE DIED at the age of eighty-seven, Victoria Ocampo (Argentina, 1890–1979) has begun to be recognized as the important figure of Latin American intellectual history that she truly was.[1] Often spoken of in her own time as a woman who built cultural bridges between the writers and artists of many continents, she was rarely credited with being more than a cultural facilitator, primarily as the founder and director of *Sur,* a literary journal that was read all over Latin America and influenced the thinking of writers and artists from the 1930s to the 1970s. More recently, Ocampo has been accorded a central role as a feminist writer and activist in an era when Latin American women were beginning to emerge publicly to contest the dominant patriarchal discourse.

Ocampo's literary significance as an essayist—or writer of "testimonies," as a she chose to call them—is also undergoing a reassessment in light of new interpretations of the essay genre and its history in Latin America.[2] A woman ahead of her time in many ways, Victoria Ocampo was, to put it simply, a thoroughly modern individual. Yet her upper-class background, her wealth, her beauty, her cosmopolitanism, and her aggressive intelligence created a kind of smokescreen of misunderstanding that floated around her during her lifetime and even after her death.

I first met Victoria Ocampo in 1962 as part of my senior thesis project, directed at Harvard by Raimundo Lida, who had known Ocampo in Argentina and been on the editorial board of *Sur.* When she greeted me at the door of her hotel room in New York, I had no idea that, within minutes, we would be on our way, in a car my parents had lent me with some trepidation to drive into the city, out to the countryside so she could "see some green" after days of confinement in the cityscape. That introduction taught me not just how essential the contact with nature was to Ocampo's well-being but also how impetuous she could be in the grip of a grand enthusiasm. A dozen years later, when I decided to write a book about her,[3] Ocampo generously invited me to spend time with her in Argentina, where I would also have access to her library and personal papers. In the last years of her life (1976–79), I went for several weeks at a time to stay with her on three occasions in her homes in San Isidro and Mar del Plata. Admittedly, the Victoria Ocampo I knew in those days was more mellow and subdued physically by age and illness. She had become more solitary in her habits and less active in the cultural circles of Buenos Aires and Europe, though no less intellectually engaged if one were to judge by the books she read, the articles she wrote, the correspondence she maintained, and the ideas she continued to generate for special issues of *Sur,* which appeared until her death. She and I would spend hours each day, over meals, walks, teatime, rides to town, and late evening chats, discussing all kinds of subjects. When we weren't talking, she would often send me handwritten notes, from her room to mine, delivered by her *mucama,* Clara. Even in her eighties, Ocampo sustained an intense personal dialogue with literature and ideas—a dialogue that had begun at the turn of the century, when she was a young girl.

By her own testimony, Ocampo was a "voracious and omnivorous reader" and an admirer of writers whose works touched a chord inside her.[4] Like many young females of her time and privileged upbringing, she identified with male as well as female heroes in the books she read in French, English, and Spanish. By the time she was a teenager, she knew that her aspirations would conflict with the life her wealthy Argentine parents envisioned for her. Her intelligence seemed to be a liability rather than an asset. In June 1907, she wrote in frustration to her friend and confidante, Delfina Bunge:

> I'm tired of feeling misunderstood. I'd like people to know me *as I am*. . . . A person "who thinks," a person who analyzes herself and others incessantly, an intensely vibrant and passionate creature can't be happy for more than two minutes . . . if that! To be truly and sincerely *happy* you'd have to be a dullard, have no brains, not think. Or else you'd have to have a rare *courage*, a serene and generous strength of spirit.[5]

The traditional Catholicism of the Ocampo family only served to reinforce her sense of confinement without comforting her restless spirit. A disastrous marriage at the age of twenty-two and a difficult separation a few years later brought Ocampo new anguish instead of the freedom she had desired. In those difficult years of her life, the only spiritual comfort she found was in Dante's *Divine Comedy*, a book that touched her more deeply than any other. After much study and reflection, Ocampo wrote her first published article (in *La Nación*, 4 April 1920, later a more extensive monograph published by Ortega y Gasset in 1924) about Dante's masterpiece through the filter of her own experience as a young woman reader. As she explained years later, "You [Dante] were my Virgil and I was your living soul among the dead. You taught me that Hell was the only way to Paradise."[6]

In the winter of 1931, Victoria Ocampo was in Paris. She was forty-one and on the verge of the most productive stage of her life. On the night of December 5 she went to a lecture given by a frail, bespectacled man in white robes who spoke flawless English with a manner of address that was gentle and disarmingly candid. Mohandas K. Gandhi had come to Paris directly after taking part in the second Round Table Conference in London and was speaking that night to a large and generally skeptical audience about his opposition to British rule in India. The conference had produced no significant change in British policy, and the Mahatma was on his way home to India to continue his resistance to colonial oppression. In the lecture, he explained to his largely European audience the Hindu concepts of *ahimsa* (the renunciation of physical violence) and *satyagraha* (self-purification in the pursuit of truth), concepts fundamental to his philosophy on nonviolence. As Victoria listened, it seemed to her that the strength of the Mahatma's conviction filled the atmosphere of the large hall. Unity and freedom for India could never be achieved, he said, until the divisions and hatreds within each individual were banished in the attainment of inner peace and harmony. Gandhi's message—more spiritual than political—moved Victoria deeply. Years later she recalled that it was "one of the most singular experiences of my life."[7]

The circumstances of this unique evening were, in one sense, not uncommon for Victoria. Her intellectual curiosity, stimulated by her reading, knew no bounds. In fact, being South American and therefore ex-centric to the dominant European perspective of her time, she felt compelled to bridge the gap between the world of the flesh and the world of the spirit by seeking out the men and women she admired in books. More than simple hero worship, it reflected her need for intellectual and spiritual mentors. Only in this way did Ocampo feel she could overcome the limitations of gender and geography in her cultural formation. In the case of Gandhi, the personal encounter had an unusual preamble.

Ocampo first learned about Gandhi's life and work through a biography written by the French author Romain Rolland. Shortly after reading it, she wrote what would be her second published article (*La Nación,* 30 March 1924) in which she praised Gandhi's "moral courage" and defended his crusade against British colonialism in India against those who called him a dangerous agitator. Coincidentally, that same year, India entered her life on the banks of the River Plate in the person of Rabindranath Tagore, the Nobel Prize-winning poet. Tagore was on a tour of South America and had taken sick in Buenos Aires, so Victoria—an avid reader of his poetry in a French translation by Gide—immediately invited him to rest and recover at a villa she leased for him near her family home in San Isidro. The friendship that developed between them during a period of several months of daily contact enriched both their lives. Tagore would write poetry to his lovely Argentine hostess, who became his muse for years thereafter. For Victoria it was the beginning of a spiritual encounter with Eastern philosophy and religion, which would affect her more deeply than she ever suspected.

It was seven years after that encounter that she had hastened to take advantage of the rare opportunity to see and hear the renowned Mahatma Gandhi, whose visit to Paris coincided with one of her own annual trips to Europe. She had wondered if the man himself would live up to the reports she had read of him; her recent experience with the German philosopher Hermann Keyserling had been disillusioning and convinced her that an author's works could only reveal part-truths about him or her. The impact of Gandhi in person on that December night in 1931, contrary to her expectations, was dramatically uplifting:

> His presence radiated a spiritual energy (to use Bergson's words) which some attributed to personal magnetism. Like a powerful current it carried us to the depths of our soul, or rather to the heights—to the heights of which, according to Pascal, man only reaches at instants in his life. Incapable of sustaining them (for saints it would be less impossible), man nonetheless retains the memory of that transparent clarity though he may tumble again into the mist or shadows of his everyday world. The memory endures, unexplainable, unexpressable.[8]

By her own testimony, that evening Victoria experienced something akin to a spiritual rebirth. Since the dogma of the Catholic church had ceased to have meaning for her, she had turned to literature with a kind of religious fervor to fill the spiritual void. But it was Gandhi, a modern Hindu prophet, who by his living example showed her what no book—not even the *Divine Comedy* or the Bible—could convey: the energy of the spirit in action. Thousands of miles from both Argentina and India, her encounter with Gandhi in a Paris lecture hall gave Ocampo a new spiritual direction. Thereafter, she would revere him above all men of his time as a secular saint, and his philosophy of *ahimsa* and *satyagraha,* integrated with the Christian gospels that she admired, became the ideals she most aspired to emulate.

Ocampo's devotion to Gandhi was lifelong and intensely personal; it was manifested by numerous writings and an active involvement with Indian culture until her death.[9] Why this was so is an important key to understanding the conflicts of her character and the leitmotifs of her work.

Instinctively but not orthodoxly religious, Victoria was driven by a need, beginning in her youth, to find personal wholeness. Her physical appetites could be as intense as her intellectual and spiritual needs. At every step, however, she was thwarted by an environment hostile to women's authentic self-expression. The eldest of six sisters, she was the most defiant, the one who chafed most at the restraints imposed upon her by moral tradition and social taboos. At the turn of the century, young women of the Argentine elite were expected to be educated only to a level commensurate with their role as future wives and mothers, that is to say, a level far beneath that available to men. The patriarchal culture of Latin America was a formidable barrier to any young woman seeking freedom of expression. To one with uncommon intelligence and spirit, it was not just frustrating, but agonizing and humiliating. In July 1908, Victoria wrote in another letter to Delfina Bunge:

I want to read Kant, Hegel, Schopenhauer, Spencer, Nietzsche, Renan, Voltaire, etc. I want to read *everything*. I am thirsty, thirsty to swallow everything, admire everything. Oh Delfina, Delfina, I don't know what's happening inside me. You're going to laugh, make fun of me, who cares? *Listen: I feel that I am too intelligent.* I think too much, I understand too much, I feel too intensely all that is beautiful and ugly. And I haven't got enough space, no, I certainly do not. I'm suffocating and it's horrible. Do you understand me? Tell me that you do! No, you aren't *me*. You can't imagine how much I'm suffering.[10]

This confession, never meant for public eyes nor even for her own family, reveals a hunger for intellectual and spiritual fulfillment as intense as the physical appetites that drove her toward romantic love as a possible answer. Ocampo's yearnings remind us of Sor Juana Inés de la Cruz's seventeenth-century testimony about being thwarted in wanting know and to absorb everything around her.[11]

Despite having a loving family, Victoria resented their restrictions on her freedom; she was frustrated by chaperons and oppressive social customs, but her parents' veto of her plans to become an actress and their disapproval of her literary ambitions made her situation as a teenager nearly intolerable. Her aggressive determination to "be herself" even if it meant withdrawing from those close to her is clear in another letter written in October 1908 to Delfina:

I've always been misunderstood; I've been a complex, wild, expansive child . . . but I've closed myself in and learned to keep my slightest feelings to myself with a deathly fear of *feeling* that they would be misunderstood. Little by little this skittish and too-pent-up sensitivity has *torn me up* inside to the point that I've become bitter and moody.[12]

This habit of private rebellion and withdrawal from an uncomprehending world may go a long way toward explaining the tantrums and outbursts of anger Ocampo showed even as a child. Not that she was always moody—the Victoria who confided in Delfina was the brooding, budding feminist, not the carefree young woman who would generally hide this side of her character. Her heart told her that love might be the answer, but her mind foresaw the danger of further entrapment. When she decided to marry, she hoped her husband would treat her as an equal, but she was soon disillusioned. Both of them were quick tempered and stubborn, and their arguments were explosive. After their separation, Ocampo began to reflect more deeply on the way her heart and mind seemed never to agree. She felt that a personal demon haunted her when she would occasionally erupt in violent anger or impose her formidable ego on others. In her twenties, disturbed by inner conflicts and finding no solace elsewhere, Ocampo turned to reading Dante's masterpiece and discovered there the mirror of her own weakness: "You [Dante] stretched out a rescuing hand to me," wrote Victoria in 1965, "and you did so because you know the muddy depths of violence and what it takes to climb out of them."[13]

Ocampo's encounter with Gandhi in 1931 provided a tangible model for moral behavior and a spiritual philosophy she aspired to emulate, albeit with limited success. It could not have come at a more propitious time, as that very year Victoria was undertaking the risks of building her own literary journal and becoming thereby a much more active figure in cultural circles at home and abroad. In the 1930s Victoria became more publicly outspoken in her ideas and opinions; she published articles in her own magazine and in various Argentine newspapers, and she actively supported democracy and human rights both at home and abroad. Her generosity and hospitality to refugees from the Spanish civil war and exiles from Nazi Europe became legendary. Privately, however, she continued to struggle with a tendency to be imperious and demanding. She could throw hairbrushes, slam doors, and give orders like a general when she wanted to, yet she also generously supported those in need, often anonymously and without any fanfare. In an interview with Jorge Luis Borges in 1962, he recalled how Victoria's domineering nature could inhibit him at times: "When she was so filled with enthusiasm for the Laurence Olivier movie of *Hamlet,* I was afraid to tell her that I had only seen it once. She would definitely have insisted that I go again, and I had no such inclination."[14] Generally, Ocampo's close friends accepted both sides of her character as a function of her voracious appetite for life and the enthusiasms she always tried to share with others through *Sur* and her ten collections of essays entitled *Testimonios* (1935–77).

Although she wrote persuasive essays on subjects that aroused her passions, writing was not an ivory tower activity for Victoria Ocampo. She may have had Gandhi's example as a nonviolent resister of oppression in mind when in 1935 she spoke out publicly in defense of women's rights in Argentina. As president of the Argentine Women's Union, Ocampo was widely criticized by the society she had so often defied. In numerous speeches and essays she maintained that women could not be content merely with a political solution to the oppression they suffered. The "masculinization" of society and its worst by-product, war, could most effectively be resisted, she said, by positive acts of self-purification and renewal with the objective of creating a new consciousness in future generations:

> I believe that the great role of woman in history, played up to now in a rather subterranean way, is beginning to crop out at the surface. It is she who can contribute powerfully to creating a new state of things since all her physical and spiritual being is concentrated on the very fountain of life—the child. . . . Therefore, I believe that if today's world [1936], which is turned toward chaos, is going to recover an order, a lost equilibrium it will be the woman who will find herself . . . in the first line of the trenches. . . . Woman is capable of heroism and of understanding the heroism of man. She knows very well that to live life fully and with dignity, it is necessary at times to sacrifice it. But war, today's war, has become so monstrous, so stupid, threatening in such a way the whole human species, that one

cannot now see heroism in it—only the most dangerous and contagious insanity that the planet has ever suffered. . . . As long as man's consciousness is not transformed . . . all the great pacifist declarations, the abstract plans of action, the societies of nations will, in a word, fail. . . . In order that the consciousness of the male child may change or become clearer through the woman, it is necessary that the woman herself rise to the occasion of that task, a task that is hers. We cannot create anything outside ourselves without first having created it inside ourselves. I don't doubt that man will end up becoming what he should vis-à-vis woman. But what is more urgent is that woman become what she should vis-à-vis herself. One will be the consequence of the other.[15]

However much she was devoted to men as heroes, artists, friends, or lovers, Ocampo's first allegiance, when it came to identifying with a cause that interested her passionately, was to women, to their self-development and to their freedom from "colonization" by men.[16] The British writer Virginia Woolf took a similar pacifist, female-oriented position in *Three Guineas* (1938). The two women had met in London in 1934 and had substantially agreed in their attitude toward fascism in Italy and toward war in general, yet, as far as Ocampo knew, Woolf never acknowledged any debt to Gandhi.[17] In the company of Woolf or her books— *A Room of One's Own, Orlando,* and *To the Lighthouse* were Victoria's favorites, all translated and published by Ediciones Sur— Ocampo felt "at home." Few men could understand, as Woolf did, what it meant to be an intellectually gifted woman in a man's world, nor could they give Ocampo the kind of support she needed in her struggle for intellectual existence. If Dante and Gandhi offered examples of spiritual and moral courage, Woolf became the intellectual role model closest to her own gendered experience.

Perhaps because of her adhesion to the principles of Gandhian nonviolence and her perceptions of gender difference, it is not surprising that the subject of men and war fascinated Victoria Ocampo throughout her life.

In 1934, before Italy declared war on Abyssinia, she took advantage of an opportunity to have an official audience with Il Duce, Benito Mussolini. On her mind was the topic of women and the fascist state; the Duce's pronouncements had left little room for doubt that women were to serve Italy as producers of male children to fuel the military machine. Her visit to the Palazzo Venezia confirmed her fears, as she later recounted to Virginia Woolf. Mussolini was, as the next decades proved, merely one in a succession of dictators (Hitler, Franco, Stalin, Perón, etc.) who masked—if often poorly—a profound disdain for women as equals of men behind an ardent appeal to them as loyal followers.

During World War II, Victoria declared her undivided support for the Allies, stipulating that war in this case was justified as a response to aggression and to the atrocities of Nazism. As early as 1939, she called for Argentina to take the side of the Allies: "Whatever the errors and imperfections of countries like England and France may be, their cause today is more than ever ours. To remain neutral regarding their fate is equivalent to remaining neutral regarding our own."[18]

Her appeal fell on deaf ears. Argentina was on the verge of its own fascist experiment. (Several years later, when Perón proposed to grant women in Argentina the vote, Victoria spoke out in opposition on moral grounds, but again to no avail; it was not the vote but the de facto government that proposed to grant it that she opposed.)

A trip to the United States in 1943 gave Victoria the opportunity to observe women at work in the service of war, and this time she heartily approved. To do so was to fight "to preserve the rights that totalitarian nations denied them."[19] But still she had reservations:

> The American woman—in factories, offices, hospitals, laboratories, in the rear guard of the army, and an infinite num-

ber of humble or delicate and difficult jobs—is fighting:
fighting without using weapons, as usual. Of course, she
helps to manufacture them (which is equivalent to using
them). That's the way woman has always fought since remote times. They say that Eve gave the apple to Adam.
Could this be why Adam has tried to keep the monopoly of
forbidden fruit, even that of weapons, to himself? We don't
envy him for it.[20]

If women participated in the war campaign, Victoria wondered,
why weren't they also included in the adjudication of its final out-
come? A brief visit to Nuremberg during the war trials in 1946 impressed her once again with the masculine culture of war and its
aftermath.

The subject of war interested her on a more individual level as
well. Among her close friends, three men in particular—all famous
French authors—were touched directly by war experiences that
deeply affected their lives and their work. Drieu la Rochelle, whom
Victoria met in 1929, had fought in the trenches at Verdun during
the First World War. Recognizing his own inclination to recoil in
fear under fire, he came to worship Force as "the mother of all
things," gradually succumbing to the seduction of fascist ideology.[21]
When Drieu committed suicide in 1945 rather than face possible
prosecution as a Nazi collaborator, he was, in Victoria's opinion,
merely sealing a fate he had chosen for himself years before. By em-
bracing the doctrine of violence and thereby betraying his own nature, he had proven that he could not face the truth of his own
being. "In Drieu's case," wrote Victoria after his death, "the means,
with which I disagreed, were violence and dictatorship. Perhaps
because of my own nature, infinitely closer to violence than his, I
had verified in my personal life how dangerous and damaging that
excess can be."[22] With undisguised regret, she identified Drieu not
as a villain but as a tragic figure, the victim of his own "masculine"
fanaticism.

Another close friend was André Malraux, whom she met through

Drieu in 1933, the year of the publication of *La Condition Humaine*; it was "the best novel of all those I had read in that era,"[23] according to Victoria, who had it translated and published in Ediciones Sur in 1936. In Spain during the civil war, in France as a member of the Maquis, and in Indochina, Malraux discovered the special camaraderie of men at war, facing death and its inexorable mystery. Even though he was an acknowledged admirer of Gandhi, Malraux was fascinated by this social aspect of war.[24] Confessing that she could not unravel the complexities of Malraux's character—why, for example, he left his childhood and amorous relationships out of his *Antimemoirs*—Victoria nevertheless observed the following: when he chose to combat conditions of slavery, Malraux had to go to Indochina. "There he felt the desire to 'right wrongs.' Women [like herself and Virginia Woolf, of Malraux's same generation] were born with the wrong in sight."[25] Indeed, wasn't the spirit of solidarity that women felt in the struggle for their rights and freedom similar to what Malraux experienced on the battlefield? Couldn't it be recreated in future generations under peaceful conditions? Must the threat of death be present for that exalted feeling to exist? It should be noted that Victoria never felt that Malraux considered women inferior to men. The fact that several passages in *La Condition Humaine* were unusually "liberated" for their time in this regard piqued her curiosity even more. After Malraux's death in 1976, she regretted that the subject had never come up in their conversations and that she had been too discreet to ask him about it.[26]

The reticence she felt with Malraux did not apply in her friendship with another French author, also a survivor of the Second World War as well as of the Algerian war of independence. Albert Camus, both African and European, was more open and expressive than Malraux, but he wrote of a similar anxiety, of man facing death and of the horrors of violence. Of the three authors—Drieu, Malraux, and Camus—it was Camus with whom Victoria felt most moral and spiritual kinship. Morally opposed to war,

Camus professed the belief that words could have more power than munitions.[27] Though he recognized no God, Camus believed as she did in another kind of religion: that of truth and intellectual honesty—an attitude, Victoria pointed out, that was comparable to Gandhi's:

> Camus was looking for a term that would suit his lack of belief. What Gandhi calls *truth,* and Pascal, *faith,* Camus calls *the word* . . . With the word he will go into combat against munitions. But what word? I don't believe there exists more than one: the Word [*el Verbo*]. The Word made flesh; if not, of what use is it? The Word made flesh is Gandhi when he cleans what others soil, without sermons, with only his example.[28]

In the final analysis, it is the energy of the spirit, wrote Ocampo, not the religious or moral creed that matters:

> Just as in this century there abound, among people, rebels without a cause (with long or short hair), I believe that there are fundamentally religious spirits without God in sight. How and why this phenomenon happens, I don't know. But there is no doubt that it must have some cause.[29]

After Gandhi, no individual captivated Victoria's imagination and sympathy as did a man whom she never met in the flesh: T. E. Lawrence (Lawrence of Arabia). The Lawrence she admired was not the swashbuckling, idealized movie version of this heroic figure, but the tormented ascetic whose confessional writings touched chords that vibrated in her own being.[30] In an introduction to Ocampo's book *338171 T. E.,* a biographical study of T. E. Lawrence, A. W. Lawrence remarked: "There seemed no other obvious points of resemblance between the two of them except their passion for freedom, with its concomitants (notably a boundless generosity), and the fact that nature had endowed each with a supernormal vigor and forcefulness. And yet," he added, "her book gave the most profound and the best-balanced of all portraits of my brother."[31]

They were more alike than A. W. Lawrence suspected. A decade before she read or wrote about Lawrence, Victoria explained what seemed to her a self-evident truth:

> We can only understand fully those beings whose instinctive sympathies and antipathies are similar to our own; likewise, a book does not illuminate us about ourselves or enrich us about ourselves unless it is in accord with our nature or some of its modalities.[32]

Just as her adolescent heroes, Captain Hatteras and Sherlock Holmes, had been projections of her own character, T. E. Lawrence (not unlike those fictional adventurers) had an analogous effect on her as an adult. Her book about him is therefore a form of specular testimony as revealing of herself as it is of its subject.

What attracted Victoria immediately to T. E. Lawrence was his response to the vastness of the desert—so like the pampas of Argentina—in which he felt: "The pleasure of believing all we see / Is boundless as we wish our souls to be." With this epigraph she began her book:

> T. E. loved the desert in that way. It had won him by its vastness and its suggestion of infinity. As a young man he had quoted those lines of Shelley to explain his feeling for it. I put this first of all because like most such preferences, it is a revealing one. It is a clue which must not be forgotten when we try to thread the labyrinth in which Lawrence himself often nearly lost his way. It is by such preferences, such signs, that the living and the dead make themselves known to us, so that we can tell what they are like, where they will lead us and in what hidden corner of their consciousness they store their purest treasures. But these signs are in cipher. One can

only understand their meaning when one knows the code by heart. The preferences which one shares with another person are the most favorable ground on which to meet him.[33]

There is no doubt that Lawrence was an admirable soldier, fighting valiantly, even recklessly alongside the Arabs whose freedom as a commonwealth under the British Empire he had vowed to win. However, when the Turks were beaten and Damascus taken, he saw that his vow would never be realized, and consequently he suffered inordinate guilt, feeling he had betrayed his friends. But he suffered too, Victoria points out, from an inner moral conflict. He was pursued by a demonic pride that threatened to enslave him; because he had known freedom himself, he wanted to be the one to win it for others. That was why he fought—not because he loved war itself. To punish himself for his failure and his weaknesses, he was determined to live the life of a monk—a monk without a religion. He did not see that neither freedom nor self-discipline was enough for his hungry spirit; in Victoria's words, "In spite of himself he lived on a higher plane than he aimed at. That was why the goal he had envisaged could never satisfy him when he had reached it."[34] What was it, then, that he sought and never attained? Victoria's answer, deciphering the clue she discovered through her own spiritual explorations was this:

> A thirst for the ultimate that no one in the least human could assuage, neither victories in arms, nor those in arts, nor satiated ambition, nor the satisfaction of disdaining the pride which had brought them to birth. A thirst for the ultimate which could only be quenched in the inevitable failure in which every triumph founders; in which every goal reached is not a glorious arrival but a new point of departure. A departure in search of who knows what spoils and conquests for which the need and the chase are even more incomprehensible for those deprived of faith than the eternal silence of infinite space before which faith itself trembles and recoils.[35]

Lawrence of Arabia—famous knight of the desert, later voluntarily disguised as a common airman in the RAF and a private in the Royal Tank Corps—was not the archetypal warrior he appeared to be. To Victoria, he was closer to being an anguished saint, a seeker of the ultimate. His life was devoted to seeking the truth, not only in actions but in words. She understood that for him it was not enough to *live* an event:

> If Lawrence described "horrors" in his mature years [in *The Mint,* reminiscences of barracks life which Victoria herself translated into Spanish for publication by Ediciones Sur], it is because his books are continuous testimonies. Testimonies of the customs of an era, ours, and of the effect which those customs had on a hypersensitive, very talented and in some ways mutilated human being.[36]

Had Lawrence never written his extraordinary testimonies, Victoria has emphasized, the complexities of his character might never have come to light. That he was frequently misunderstood—especially vis-à-vis his attitude toward the wars in which he played a significant role—was something she never tired of trying to rectify.[37]

Victoria Ocampo devoted her life to promoting peaceful dialogues among many cultures in the field of arts and letters. The belligerence she expressed as a young woman continued to be part of her nature as an adult (even as an octogenarian, she was a great slammer of doors), but she consciously sought to transcend her personal weaknesses in the pursuit of the "spiritual energy" she so admired in Gandhi. If *the ultimate* itself is beyond the grasp of human understanding, the highest goal must be the expression of spiritual striving toward it. As Gandhi himself once wrote: "The acquisition of the spirit of non-resistance is a matter of long training in self-denial and appreciation of the hidden forces within ourselves. It changes one's outlook on life. . . . *It is the greatest force because it is the highest expression of the soul*" (emphasis added).[38]

For Victoria, life itself was an unending struggle, a drama that each individual must resolve for him or herself. No larger conflicts, no war among men, could equal the drama of the microcosmic struggle waged on the single, lonely battlefield of the mind and heart. In her own case, the battle had begun early in life and was ongoing. As she wrote in her autobiography in 1963:

> The discovery of spiritual energy . . . was born in me out of the combat between passion and intelligence. Neither one was enough for me. Neither one—located at opposite poles of my being—satiated my appetite for wholeness, that enormous void between the two extremes where my desires, ambitions, aspirations all jostled together like objects in a trunk with too much space inside . . . But the spiritual life (what Bergson called *spiritual energy*) touched another dimension in which there existed no possibility for certain types of disturbances, discords or sufferings.[39]

Perhaps no personal experience brought home to Victoria Ocampo the power of spiritual energy as clearly as the one that took place in May of 1953. Without prior warning and offering no explanation, the police under the dictator Juan Perón detained Ocampo, took her from her home, and imprisoned her. For one month she lived behind bars in one room with eleven other women in Buen Pastor prison in Buenos Aires, unaware of the charges against her or what her fate might be. At first, deprived of all comforts including books and writing materials, Victoria simply felt outrage at the injustice she was suffering; if the dictatorship wanted to aggravate and disempower her, it had done so on a purely physical level. Morally and spiritually, however, her imprisonment had the opposite effect. Gradually, she came to see it as a blessing in disguise; through deprivation she discovered an inner strength she had never known so intimately and completely. A strong spirit of solidarity developed between the women who shared this confinement, women of widely diverging backgrounds and beliefs, not to mention social classes. Jailed against her will, lacking the freedom she had taken for granted, Ocampo understood in her innermost being what Gandhi sought through self-purification and nonviolent resistance to tyranny:

> In those long days, in those dark nights of the month of May, I meditated again on that man born in India who belongs to all of us, the contemporary whom I most admire and whose existence, ever since I discovered it in 1924, was for me a warning, a presence and a balm. He proved to me, by his example, the validity of an aphorism from the *Upanishads:* "A man becomes what he thinks." Desire no other reward, fear no other punishment, said the voice I heard during those dark nights.[40]

Not as an aggressor but as a victim she had glimpsed the ultimate truth. No force of evil can conquer a spirit whose energy transcends its physical condition. As a woman and a South American—separated from Gandhi's experience by cultural distances of body and mind—Victoria Ocampo nonetheless found the true meaning of *ahimsa* and *satyagraha* in those "dark nights of the month of May," briefly but unforgettably, in the voice of her own soul.

Clementina Suárez:
POETRY & WOMANHOOD

JANET GOLD

⌒ I HAVE LOVED BEING A WOMAN. *When I was young I adored having men fall in love with me. I have been vain about my body and my life-style. I have had no complexes whatsoever, nor prejudices of any kind. So you see I have lived to the fullest my life as a woman . . . I have always been in love with love, and not with the person himself. The proof is that I have been able to leave them, to put them to one side of my life. I have been a lover of love rather than of any individual. I have loved deeply, but I have come to understand that more than the person, what I have loved is love itself.*
—CLEMENTINA SUÁREZ, RENÉ PAUCK VIDEO, 1982

The National Theater is packed. In the square outside the main entrance gas lamps illuminate the crowd of curious bystanders. Little Alba and Silvia, dressed as pages, feeling important and shy, hand programs to the citizens of Tegucigalpa as they enter the theater to hear their mother recite her poetry. As she walks onto the stage a murmur ripples through the audience:

All around my body
the primary elements
are stellar serpents
hissing their unbearably
electric caresses.
Fire kisses me,
water kisses me,
wind kisses me,
earth kisses me.

And the shining kiss,
or the trembling kiss,
or the vague kiss,
or the anguished kiss,
ignites my flesh,
ignites my nerves,
ignites my bones,
ignites my soul.

Her small feet glide over the stage. Her arms float, her body sways, her dark hair falls over her face. Her lips and fingernails are painted bright red. She is ethereal in her diaphanous wraps. She is innocent, seductive, pure, and electric and evil:

Begone! Do not judge me
according to your human laws,
I am the golden key
with which you will open the sublime
doors of true
and eternal life,
without the dirty corpse
of social posture your mind creates.

Know that a world exists
without laws or precepts,
where everything glows

with the tenuous vapors
of stellar rhythm.
Understand me now,
why fire and water, why wind and earth
fill me with unbearable astral kisses.

Flesh,
nerves,
bones,
soul.

"Look at the shameless hussy! Why I think she is naked under that thin little shawl she is waving around! Let me by! I refuse to watch this!"

Look at me, I am petals:
Hear me, I am rhythms.
My flesh is your desire
where I see my strength and your misfortune.
My music is written on the breeze
with the rise and fall of my laughter.

A matronly woman covers her eyes in horror, climbs over the spectators beside her, and rushes down the aisle. In her shock and haste she stumbles, falls, bruises her hip. The next day the *Tegucigalpa Chronicler* carries the story of the beautiful young poetess who recites verses of her own creation with nubile candor and exceptional grace. Young girls read her poems and cast soulful eyes to the sky, wishing for romance and poetic inspiration, dreaming of gauzy tunics and flowing hair. Their mothers find *Temples of Fire* or *The Last of My Saturdays* under their pillows and refuse to let their daughters read such trash.

Tegucigalpa's favorite poetess was born in 1902 not in the capital city of this poor and isolated Central American country but in Juticalpa, capital of Olancho, the remote province of Honduras with a reputation for gun-slinging lawlessness and fiercely independent-minded cattle ranchers. Clementina Suárez was the daughter of Amelia Zelaya Bustillo, the pampered offspring of one of those powerful landowners and cattle ranchers, and Luis Suárez, a talented lawyer who arrived in Juticalpa with no land or family, but soon earned the affection and admiration of his fellow Olanchanos. The budding poet spent her youth in a spacious house in the center of town. Hers was a carefree childhood of privilege, unburdened by demands to be anything more than a daughter of the provincial elite.

But Clementina burned with a curiosity for life and ideas. She dreamed of traveling, of making the acquaintance of extraordinary people, individuals who read and discussed art and poetry and philosophy. As a young girl she sometimes made the eight-day trip by mule from Juticalpa to Tegucigalpa when her father was Olancho's representative to the National Congress, and she dreamed of going to Mexico, a place her father had described to her as being vibrant with culture and revolution.

When Luis Suárez died in 1923, Clementina made her first great leap into autonomy, self-determination, and poetry—by traveling. The very notion of a young woman from the upper classes leaving home to live on her own was unheard of in Honduras in 1923. Added to this audacious move was the fact that Clementina now had to pay her own way. The family finances quickly fell into disarray after her father's death and, once she left home, without her mother's permission, of course, she received no monetary aid from Juticalpa. She made her way to Tegucigalpa, living for periods of time with relatives or friends, and supported herself with a variety of jobs—clerk, used book dealer, waitress.

She rapidly became the black sheep of the family when word began to filter back to the province of the unconventional life-style she was creating for herself. For, not long after leaving home, she began cultivating the notion that she was a poet. What's more, she acted as if she had every right not only to call herself a poet but also to live the life she imagined a poet would live. She had always thought that poets were special people, so, now that she saw herself as one, she assumed that specialness for herself. She not only became part of the literary life of Honduras but also pushed the limits of what that life could be.

In its very isolation, Honduras, and here we can say Tegucigalpa, for the centrally located capital city has traditionally been its center of art and literature, has provided an environment that has allowed a rich literary life to flourish, a literary life that serves as its own referent and nourishes its own idiosyncrasies. One of the defining characteristics of the literary life of Tegucigalpa in the twentieth century has been the literary *tertulia,* or gathering of the literati, usually in cafés in the center of town, to discuss everything from politics to poetry. There have been numerous groups that have met at different locales: the Café de Paris and the Jardín de Italia in the 1920s and 1930s, the Café Nuevo Continente in the 1960s, the Cafetería San Francisco and Café Paradiso in the 1980s. Certain cafés have become known as places where writer types are especially welcome, so they return again and again, assured of finding kindred souls with whom to converse about books and ideas. These public gathering places are important because they support the notion of individual and collective identity. Certain people frequent certain places because they are writers. The gathering in a sense makes them writers whether they write well or not. In any case, these gathering places have helped keep literature alive in Honduras.

The late 1920s and early 1930s, when Clementina was testing her poetic wings, was one of the moments in history when café life flourished in Tegucigalpa. There were three major groups that comprised the literary life of the capital, distinguished by age, social and economic class, and ideology, although the fact that Tegucigalpa was a small and introverted community meant that members of the various circles saw one another regularly, and there was much exchange and camaraderie, as well as competition and an-

tagonism, among the groups. In one group there were the older, established writers, respectable men of letters such as Alejandro Castro, editor of the *Revista Tegucigalpa* (Tegucigalpa magazine), and Alfonso Guillén Zelaya, a well-known poet and director of the newspaper *El Cronista* (The chronicler). When they left their offices at the newspaper or the Ministry of Education, they would stop in at the Café de Paris or the Jardín de Italia. The collective impression they created was of refinement and seriousness.

A second group was formed of young men of literary inclinations, although not necessarily dedicated exclusively to this pursuit, such as Antonio Rosa, Arturo Martínez Galindo, and Guillermo Bustillo Reina. These young men tended also to be dashing and handsome, sophisticated and international, and their writing reflects their savoir faire. They were young and energetic—literary professionals in training, but determined to sow their wild oats before settling into respectability. They were young entrepreneurs, diplomats, and dandies. Most of them had family money and connections, and literature was one of their many refinements. They met at the Tegucigalpa Club and the International Club. They wrote verses in praise of Tegucigalpa and its irresistible young women. They formed a bachelors' club and vowed to let no women rob them of their freedom and independence. Some of them died young, leaving behind the promise of talent; others grew old and published their memoirs of those years of love and sport and literature.

Finally, there were the Bohemian writers, the youngest group, intensely committed poets such as Daniel Laínez and Claudio Barrera. They were generally younger than those of the other groups, or, if not actually younger, they were more youthful in their idealism. They were either not of the ruling class or rejected or disregarded class as a determinant of their self-concept. They described themselves as Bohemians, which meant to them that they were different from the rest of their society, driven by higher passions and nobler ideals; they were dreamers, lovers of art and literature, in pursuit of the chimera of Beauty. Their proclivities leaned to the popular as well as the arcane, so their most cherished moments were those spent reciting Baudelaire in Mamá Yaca's *estanco,* a dirt-floored tavern with rustic tables in a poor section of town. Many of them later became established, known, and respected for their writing, and in retrospect have come to be classified by Honduran literary historians as the Generation of '35.

It is not an editorial oversight that the names offered as representative of these groups are all men, for indeed these gatherings were male-bonding sessions as well as literary get-togethers. How then was Clementina to live a poet's life in an environment that provided her with no role models? But she was clever, tenacious, and brave. She brazenly gave herself permission to sit in cafés with the writers and artists of Tegucigalpa, the only woman in the group. She waited tables at the Jardín de Italia, assuring herself visibility among the literary clientele. She frequented the Café de Paris and laughed and talked with the illustrious gentlemen of letters who gathered there. She had affairs with some of the debonair and handsome young professionals of the Tegucigalpa Club. She even spent many raucous hours drinking and reciting poetry with her Bohemian buddies at Mamá Yaca's watering hole.

Not satisfied to follow the example of Tegucigalpa's other poetesses, who occasionally sent lovelorn, languid, or innocent poems to the local newspapers, often signed with coy pseudonyms, Clementina disdained the term *poetess,* choosing to call herself a poet. Like the other (male) poets, she valued her own work, talked about it, publicized it, published volumes of it. Her first book, which was also the first book of poetry by a Honduran woman published in Honduras, was titled *Corazón sangrante* (Bleeding heart, 1930). The prologue was written by Alfonso Guillén Zelaya, one of her mentors from the Café de Paris. Uncommonly shrewd in a way that many traditional Tegucigalpans considered unladylike, she understood the importance to her career of acquiring the protection and approbation of prominent cultural figures, so Guillén Zelaya's laudatory and supportive prologue was just the first in a lifelong collection of prologues, essays, character sketches, and portraits with which she surrounded herself.

Having these defenders was indeed important, for her critics were numerous. Many thought she had taken things too far when she set up housekeeping with the dashing Antonio Rosa without being married to him, and when she proceeded to have two children out of wedlock. Her unconventional poetry recitals, her refusal to act like a married woman during her brief and colorful marriage to poet Guillermo Bustillo Reina, her carefree child-rearing practices—all were cause for general disapprobation and for ostracism from some of Tegucigalpa's social circles.

In 1930 Clementina visited Mexico. It was her first trip outside of Honduras, the first in what would become a series of journeys too numerous to count or even remember, wanderings that took her to New York, Cuba, Panama, Costa Rica, Nicaragua, Guatemala, El Salvador, the Soviet Union, China, Spain, Argentina. She walked in and out of many identities, in some ways a postmodernist before her time: she thought of herself as a citizen of Honduras, as a citizen of Central America, of Latin America, of the planet, of the universe.

In Mexico she associated with Mexican writers as well as writers from Central America who were living there as political or cultural exiles. She published two volumes of poetry in Mexico in 1931: *De mis sábados el último* (The last of my Saturdays) and *Los templos de fuego* (Temples of fire). She also made the acquaintance of a number of artists there, among them Diego Rivera, who is said to have admired the candor of her expression and painted two portraits of her. There was something about the art world that enthralled her: she loved visiting her artist friends in their studios, watching them paint or sculpt for hours. She herself never pursued the craft, but a love of color, form, line, and texture, coupled with a growing commitment to the social themes prominent in Mexican art at the time, drew her ineluctably to this world.

As she followed her vagabond instincts, staying two months in

Managua, three weeks in San José, six months back in Tegucigalpa to spend time with her daughters (who had to get used to the idea of having a glamorous but often absent mother), her life took on contours that were flamboyant, intense, and unique for the time and place. She gave poetry recitals, visited with friends, appeared at public gatherings and ceremonies, had love affairs, fostered friendships with artists and writers. Still cognizant of the need for friends in high places, she cultivated relationships with everyone from ambassadors and military and government officials to bankers, businessmen, and prominent intellectuals. She sent letters back home to the Tegucigalpa papers detailing her cultural activities, and her poems and lyrical prose pieces appeared in newspapers and literary journals throughout the region. In 1934 she published six issues of a literary/cultural magazine she called *Mujer* (Woman), walking the streets of Tegucigalpa in a bellhop's uniform to publicize and sell copies of her first editorial venture.

Youthful and attractive, energetic and ambitious, Clementina continued to compose poems that publicized her sensuality, flights of joy, and descents into melancholy, such as "Engranajes" (Gears) in San José, Costa Rica, in 1935. But while in Cuba in 1936–37, inspired by the political activism of many Cuban writers and intellectuals as well as by news of the popular struggle against fascism during the Spanish civil war, a cause that captured the imagination of many Latin Americans, her poetic expression underwent a profound transformation. *Veleros* (Sailboats; Havana, 1937) and *De la desilusión a la esperanza* (*From disillusion to hope*; Tegucigalpa, 1944) reflect the turmoil of a consciousness awakening to the suffering and injustice of a world much larger than the self, much larger than Honduras or even Central America. Like numerous other Latin American writers and artists, Clementina Suárez entered the compelling and ongoing debate concerning the role and responsibility of the intellectual in the fight for peace and justice. Several poems from this period experiment with this new commitment:

Firm in the ranks,
I await the hour
that will free all obstacles
and hurl me into the sea of struggle
with the joyful will
of one who defying death
conquers life!

I was a desperate butterfly
imprisoned in the walls
of useless hours.
But the new battle cry
has finally reached my ears
and I have opened my arms to it
as to a horizon of light
that shows me the way
to hope's only harbor! . . .
("The Cry," from Sails)

But for all her revolutionary zeal, Clementina never lost her commitment to her own sensuality, or her fascination with romantic love. For a long time, she tried to combine these two enthusiasms, looking for a lover who would also be a "comrade":

The paths have separated
and the plows left behind.
I have begun to call you "comrade"
and have sewn my poverty to yours.
I one stitch, you another . . .
("Plows," from Sails)

During the 1940s Clementina took up residence in Mexico City. She was by now a well-known, some would say notorious, figure in Central American cultural circles. She became more and more committed to "culture," not only promoting her own work but also concerning herself with the promotion of Central American art and literature. She rented a large house in Colonia Roma and, to earn money, but certainly also because she enjoyed their company, she rented rooms, mostly to artists, writers, and Central Americans in exile in Mexico. Her house soon evolved into a unique space, the first of several attempts to create an environment where her commitment to culture could find outlets for expression.

Art galleries were a novel phenomenon in Mexico City in the 1940s. Indeed, Mexico's first gallery, Galería de arte mexicano (Gallery of Mexican art), was opened by Inés Amor in the basement of her home in 1935. Perhaps reacting to the fervently nationalistic bias of this gallery, Clementina called her home "Galería de arte centroamericana" (Gallery of Central American art). Central American artists in Mexico at that time were mostly poor, happy to be in an environment where art was vital and visible, but struggling to make ends meet. So the space Clementina created was a kind of oasis, a Bohemian "Casa de la Cultura," anarchic, open, unofficial. There are stories of Mexican poet Guadalupe Amor walking around the house barefoot, of Guatemalan novelist Miguel Angel Asturias doing one of his numerous revisions of *El Señor Presidente* at her kitchen table, of Nicaraguan poets conspiring in her parlor to negotiate secret purchases of weapons to mount an attack against the Nicaraguan dictator. If an artist needed a place to sleep, there was always a sofa, but he might have to share the parlor with an impromptu poetry recital or a group of Clementina's friends drinking and talking late into the night.

As Clementina came to see herself more and more as a kind of matriarch of Central American culture, she dreamed of a flourishing art gallery, a publishing company, a cultural center where poets and artists could come at any time of the day or night, knowing they would find kindred spirits with whom to share ideas, poems, a place of spontaneity and informality, free of the false pomp and illusion of official culture. Her Galería de arte centroamericana was a first attempt, a rehearsal of that dream. The walls of her house became crowded with art work exhibited for guests and potential buyers, some of the pieces she purchased, others were exhibited and sold, some were given to her as gifts or in appreciation for her efforts to promote someone's work. Her collection grew. Among her most treasured pieces were the many portraits of her that her artist friends executed.

A typical example of the kind of cultural nurturing that took place at the Galería de arte centroamericana is the case of Costa Rican artist and writer Francisco Amighetti. After several years of traveling through Central and South America, often on foot, painting, drawing, engraving, and writing poems and travel memoirs, as well as spending time in Taos, New Mexico, and New York City, he had come to Mexico to study mural painting. He had come without any kind of scholarship or government support, so he got a job working with Nicaraguan poet and publisher Pablo Antonio Cuadra, who had started a publishing venture in Mexico. He received a salary only sporadically, so he was unable to pay the rent at his pensión. He and Clementina had known each other since the mid-thirties, when they met in San José, and their paths crossed with a certain irregular frequency, given their equally nomadic lifestyles. When he made his plight known to her, she offered to let him have a room at her house. When he could, he paid rent; when he couldn't, he gave her one of his woodcuts or painted a watercolor or drew a sketch of Clementina.

One day he showed her the engravings and the accompanying prose text that he had produced during his stay in Harlem. She responded with a characteristically ambitious and generous gesture: she went out and raised the money to publish, in 1947, *Francisco en Harlem*, Amighetti's New York memoirs with thirty-one accompanying woodcuts. In her travels around the city distributing copies of the book and talking about future plans to publish an anthology of Central American poetry by young writers, she one afternoon knocked on the door of an apartment shared by a group of artists. José Mejía Vides opened the door to find before him an attractive woman dressed in black, wearing a single red rose, offering him a copy of Amighetti's book. It was love. The courtship was brief; they were married the next year.

Mejía Vides, an artist from El Salvador, had, like so many others, been drawn to Mexico to study the then-fashionable art of mural painting. Like Amighetti, he and Clementina had met years before when Clementina was visiting his country. Perhaps something about cosmopolitan Mexico City fanned their previous acquaintance, turning it into a more powerful attraction. Shortly after their marriage in 1949 he was asked to take on the job of director of the National School of Graphic Arts in San Salvador. Hoping to reproduce her flourishing if somewhat anarchic cultural matriarchy in this new venue, Clementina agreed to accompany her husband.

Besides her own energy and notoriety, she now had the respectability of being married to the director of a prestigious art school. Using every weapon at her disposal, Clementina, by now quite adept at convincing potential patrons of the arts to donate to her causes, established and ran throughout the 1950s the Salvadoran version of the Galería de arte centroamericana, calling it El Rancho del Artista. It was not in her home this time, but in a rural setting on the outskirts of San Salvador. There were bedrooms where visiting writers and artists could stay, as was the case when Costa Rican sculptor Francisco Zúñiga spent several months in residence while he was executing a monumental sculpture commissioned by the Salvadoran government. There was plenty of wall space for the young artists, such as her friends Luis Angel Salinas and Camilo Minero, to exhibit their work. There was space for poetry readings, concerts, lectures, and, of course, for the frequent get-togethers that often lasted well into the night, after everyone had emptied their pockets for that last bottle of rum. It was a Bohemian hangout, but it also possessed an aura of official respectability, particularly for those occasions that Clementina hosted as cultural attaché for the Honduran embassy in El Salvador, a position she held from 1955–57.

But this was the same Clementina who had scandalized Teguci-galpa with her sensual poetry, her flirtatious manner, and her re-fusal to hide her love affairs or her unwed motherhood. So even though she was married and held an official title, these to her were the legalistic trappings of hypocritical social mores and bureau-cratic nonsense, and she more often than not disregarded their strictures, taking delight in the reputation she earned as an enfant terrible. Stories abound of her tendency to speak her mind, re-gardless of the power or position of the object of her scathing hon-esty. She was known to have insulted everyone from the Spanish ambassador in El Salvador to the good ladies of the Tegucigalpa Club. Nonetheless, she continued to move in high as well as undis-tinguished social circles, plotting and maneuvering the promotion of Central American culture. She was responsible, for example, for organizing weekly open-air art exhibits in a centrally located park in San Salvador. These exhibits gave young artists a chance to show their work and to exhibit collectively; they also made art accessible to people of all ages and social classes.

Her years in El Salvador were full and rewarding to her, are in many ways the centerpiece of a long life of working hard to forge her own poetic voice and to nourish and stimulate other artists and writers. She has been an example to many women of the satisfac-tions as well as the difficulties of living one's life in accordance with one's own instincts and desires, and of daring to be a woman writer in a male-dominated world. She has been nurturing to cre-ative individuals, although not necessarily in stereotypically femi-nine ways. Sometimes she coddled, reassured, encouraged. Often she pushed, prodded, organized, challenged, criticized. She has left a unique legacy, indeed she had become a legend in her own time and continues to be one after death.

During those years in Mexico and El Salvador of creating her unique cultural spaces and filling them with friends and art, Clem-entina composed what is perhaps the central work in her lifelong poetic project of learning to speak with a voice that is sensual and gloriously female as well as socially and politically aware. *Creciendo con la hierba* (Growing with the grass) was published in 1957 by the Ministry of Culture of El Salvador after being awarded a national prize for poetry. A single long poem divided into eight sections, it is a plea to the poet's lover to become her comrade as well:

> *My friend, you may say:*
> *your heart, for you to love me,*
> *is not where it should be.*

> *It is too wide,*
> *a harbor,*
> *limitless dawn.*

> *It is listening to*
> *man's lament*
> *and his urgent desire*
> *to be free . . .*

> *You must waken.*
> *Raise your bones*
> *from their sleep.*
> *Leave yourself naked,*
> *voluntary,*
> *changed . . .*

> *Before,*
> *in our daytime,*
> *I was only one.*

> *Now,*
> *in our night,*
> *I multiply in my wounded*
> *flesh*
> *the voices of spent women,*

of mothers
their furrows ripped
by daggers
and
of young girls with hands
full of thorns . . .

And you, tell me,
are you with me
in this circle of my blood . . . ?
(*Growing with the grass*, stanzas 7, 8)

Clementina always felt that she was least appreciated in her home-land. She had been criticized so maliciously in Honduras, and her efforts to gain government support for her cultural projects so often ended in frustration, that she was content to do her work in Mexico and then in El Salvador. But in 1957, responding in part to her inner restlessness, in part to an invitation from Ramón Villeda Morales, who had recently been elected president of Honduras and had plans to stimulate culture and public education, she left her husband and traveled to Honduras with an exhibit of Salvadoran art and literature. Villeda Morales had indeed inspired many Honduran intellectuals with the hope of government support for the arts, so Clementina was convinced to stay and participate as cultural coordinator for the Ministry of Education. In this role she initiated and supervised numerous projects, such as the establishment of mobile libraries in the parks of Tegucigalpa and the publication of easy-to-read and beautifully illustrated books on Honduras' national heroes. She wrote the culture column for the newspaper *El día* (The day) and opened Honduras' first art gallery, Galería Morazánida, in 1959. She encouraged young artists who had never done so before to exhibit their work, and proved to be extremely resourceful, if unconventional in her methods as a fund raiser. Understanding the artists' practical need to earn money from his work, she became very successful at convincing local banks and businesses to purchase the works of Honduran artists. This in itself has been one of her major cultural accomplishments: to professionalize art in Honduras and convince Hondurans of the value of their own artists.

In 1958 she published *Canto a la encontrada patria y su héroe* (Song of the found fatherland and its hero), a single long poem divided into thirteen sections, in which she resolved her long-standing love-hate relationship with her homeland. It is a beautifully sculpted challenge to anyone who would criticize her or deny her her birthright. It is Clementina on the stage of the National Theater announcing that she has come home and that no matter what the small-minded gossips say, she has an inalienable right to be there:

> *I cannot come home . . .*
> *Because I never left.*
> *You are a country constructed*
> *inside me.*
> *You flow within me*
> *like an open river.*
> *You come from a distant past*
> *rebellious and vegetal,*
> *everything in you is new and old*
> *a land for childhood*
> *and to immortalize time.*
> (*Song of the found fatherland and its hero,* 1)

But governments come and go, and with them their plans and hopes. By 1969 Clementina was weary of trying so hard at home and feeling she was accomplishing so little. She was tired of corrupt politics and tired of being criticized. When she returned from a visit to Cuba in 1961, glowing with praise for the revolution; when she participated in public protests against government repression; when she began reciting openly combative poetry, she became persona non grata with the military government. Plans to return to El Salvador and revive the Rancho del Artista came to a grinding halt when, in July of 1969, Honduras and El Salvador entered a short but intense confrontation referred to in the foreign press as the "Soccer War." Although the period of actual fighting lasted scarcely a month, bitterness between the two countries persisted to the extent that borders were closed for almost ten years.

Unable because of her Honduran citizenship to return to El Salvador, Clementina stayed in Tegucigalpa, but with an attitude of sharp-tongued irascibility rendered flippant by her obvious disrespect for the government. Despite her increasingly vocal criticism of what she considered to be the falsities and weakness of her countrymen, Honduras came to recognize the worth and accomplishments of its prodigal daughter. In 1970 she was awarded the Ramón Rosa National Prize for Literature, Honduras' highest literary honor. Around the same time the National University published an anthology of her poetry, *El poeta y sus señales* (The poet and her signs), and *Clementina Suárez,* a compilation of biographical sketches, literary essays, reviews, interviews, and poems composed in her honor, as well as reproductions of the many portraits painted of her over the years.

In 1975 she purchased a house in an old, centrally located neighborhood of Tegucigalpa. She unpacked her books and her impressive art collection for the last time, and hung a sign on the front door that read Galería Clementina Suárez. She hung the portraits of herself by artists from all over the world in the hallway, the kitchen, in her bedroom: sketches by Francisco Amighetti and José Mejía Vides, a caricature by Augusto Monterroso, paintings by Francisco Zúñiga, Luis H. Padilla, Dante Lazarroni. Her folk art crucifixes and sculptures decorated the gallery space, which was also her parlor. Like it or not, she was home to stay. Except that she continued to travel, exhibiting works from her own collection as well as organizing shows abroad for local artists. It seemed that the older she got, the feistier she got, and the more adamant in her opinions.

She remained loyal to the Cuban revolution and supported the

Sandinistas in Nicaragua. She frequently attended literary conferences and peace conferences, always shocking and delighting the younger generation of writers and revolutionaries with her outspokenness, her stamina and her willingness to criticize repressive governments and denounce U.S. intervention in Central America. She became a living emblem to them of a previous generation's spirit and commitment. When she was killed in her home in December 1991, by an unidentified intruder, Honduras realized it had lost a national treasure.

Her life and now her memory are many things to many people. She is remembered for her unconventional behavior, but also for her courage and persistence. She was a woman of firsts: the first woman to publish a book of poetry in Honduras; the art gallery she opened in 1959 was the first one in Tegucigalpa; her efforts to professionalize art in Honduras were pioneering; they say she was the first young woman in Juticalpa to wear pants and to refuse to ride side-saddle, that she introduced the "New Woman" to Honduras. It would not be an exaggeration to call her the matriarch of Honduran culture.

In addition to the value of her bold, sensual, woman-centered poetry, and the importance of her life-style as a role model for women with creative aspirations, Clementina Suárez contributed to culture in Honduras as well as in the larger Central American context in what might be called an ephemeral way, for it was through a series of lived moments, of shared spaces, of envisioned opportunities. It was places that were lived in, moved out of, spaces full of people coming and going, full of paintings and poetry, alive with the energy and hope of projects. It was also having the private, inner resources to be a very public person, with social goals and grandiose vision. It was marching into any traditionally male arena and acting as if she belonged there. It was loving being a woman, and through her self-acceptance, opening the door for other women to redefine creativity and femininity for themselves.

The Creation of
Alfonsina Storni

Gwen Kirkpatrick

⌒ THE ARGENTINE POET Alfonsina Storni (1892–1938) has become a legend in Latin American literary history.[1] Socially defiant, professionally ambitious, gifted with talent and early fame, she was nonetheless limited by her social origins, her training, and restrictions for women in the public realm. As an unwed mother, she encountered legal and social barriers in her struggle against these obstacles. Her bittersweet triumphs have created a dramatic aura around her poetry and her biography.

Generations have read her poetry and identified with it, and her story has served as the inspiration for movies, television programs, women's magazines, and songs. She was not among the first women to clamor for greater rights for women, but her voice was certainly one of the most eloquent and direct. Her famous poem "Tú me quieres blanca" (You want me white) is a vibrant and rebellious rejection of the masculine double standard. Another much-anthologized poem, "Hombre pequeñito" (Little man) leaves no question as to her views on society's idealization of the caged female: "Ábreme la jaula, que quiero escapar; / Hombre pequeñito, te amé media hora, / No me pidas más" (Open my cage, I want to escape; / Little man, I loved you half an hour, / Don't ask me for more).

These poetic pronouncements in the first decades of the century were not met with universal acclaim. Because her poetry was often openly erotic and added anger and rebellion to the usual stock of topics for women's poetry, most literary critics typecast her with the negative qualities assigned to female expressions of anger and desire—shrill, strident, dangerous, and destructive. Yet she was a popular poet, and her wide readership and public visibility have stimulated ongoing critical debates about her work.[2]

Not only Storni's writings, but also her life, have been the focus of a great deal of speculation and legend making.[3] As a woman from modest immigrant beginnings, she was teacher, a poet, dramatist, and journalist who aspired to public prominence. Her status as mother of an illegitimate child made it more difficult for her to move within the social and professional circles in which she fought hard to forge a place for herself. A dramatic figure in so many ways, Storni even heightened the public effect of her suicide in 1938 by writing a poem about her death and mailing it for publication the day before she died. Unable to struggle further with the recurrence of cancer, she chose to walk into the sea at Mar del Plata.

As would be expected with such a compelling biography, a great deal of the critical commentary on her writings has been intertwined with speculations on its origins in her personal life. Much of this commentary has centered on society's victimization of Storni and of women in general, a viewpoint that could be defended by reading her poetry. Nonetheless, it is difficult to stereotype Storni in so limited a role as that of victim. Her energetic defiance, lively creativity, high productivity, and stubborn striving add up to a curious tale of triumph. Although many of her critics have been left behind in the dust of history, today young readers discover her poems with the shock of recognition, marveling at their personal boldness and acute vision, finding her absolutely contemporary.

These are poems that need no footnotes to explain abstruse allusions and that speak, though not without irony, of the age-old questions of love, family, the body, women's lot, and life in the city.

Storni was associated with a "middlebrow" public and considered to be "outside the vanguard" because of her use of conventional poetic techniques, like rhyme and meter, in much of her work. Her most important writings were in lyric poetry, a genre usually associated with the private realm, that space where the soul's musings are transformed by verbal artistry. It is also the genre, along with autobiography, most associated with women's writings, at least until recent decades. Yet Storni made this realm a more public sphere. Not just the nature of her poetry but also its presentation in widely circulated magazines and periodicals opened up the private realm of lyric poetry to new readers, the readers of women's sections in newspapers and popular magazines. She seized on the elemental appeal of the standards of melodrama and sentimental literature. Combining these traditions with her own unsentimental eye and her acute sense of social justice, she put a public and decidedly female stamp on her poetry. She understood her readers; they were her social peers. Her own experiences, both in the provinces and in Buenos Aires, had educated her in the desires and strivings of a burgeoning group of middle-class women, eager to enjoy the benefits of what promised to be new horizons for women in the public sphere.

Alfonsina, as a young child, emigrated with her parents from Switzerland in 1896 and witnessed enormous changes in Argentine society. Waves of immigration, an expanding prosperity based on agricultural exports, and an ambitious public educational program made the nation a center of commercial and intellectual life. Its capital, Buenos Aires, was recast architecturally with the country's riches and was transformed from a neocolonial outpost into the fashionable Parisian model of wide boulevards. Storni's immigrant beginnings did not set her apart from the general populace, since by World War I Argentina's population included a majority of immigrants, mainly from Italy and Spain.[4] Raised in the provinces, she studied in a teacher training institute *(escuela normal)* and at eighteen years old received the title of *maestra* (teacher), a profession she would practice with great energy for most of her life, especially in a school for the dramatic arts. Teacher training was the gateway to involvement in public life for women of her generation and class, and a step up the ladder of social standing. Public education was in Argentina, as in many other parts of the Americas, the route of access for non-elites. The country's strong focus on immigration and public education, developed earlier primarily by President Domingo F. Sarmiento, promised to lead to an expanding economy, population growth, interior development, and the democratic participation of its citizenry. Some of these promises came true for Argentina, though not without great social costs for those who were considered less than citizens. Broad social and economic changes engendered debates about the category of citizen itself, and universal suffrage (for men) was a heated topic.

The women's movement, in its many variants, had been active in Argentina from the turn of the century.[5] It shared alliances and goals, and sometimes leaders, with other social movements, including socialism and anarchism. Not only leftist movements organized women, but conservative groups such as pronativist societies and religious organizations also stressed the importance of women in the public sphere, based on their maternal and familial roles. Storni moved to Buenos Aires in 1912, where her son was born. She emerged into the public spotlight with the publication of her first book, *La inquietud del rosal,* (The restlessness of the rosebush) in 1916. The enormous changes that swept the world during World War I did not leave Argentina unaffected. The appearance of the "New Woman," visible in movies, magazines, and on city streets, stirred anxieties about women's roles in fast-changing societies.

Although the popular appeal of Storni's legendary career has made famous some of her poetry, other aspects of her life and career have been ignored in the necessary shrinkage involved in myth making. Her activities were not limited to the message of her poetry and to the rebellious gesture. In her career as poet, journalist, teacher, and speaker, Storni exhibited an uncanny eye for social topics directly affecting women's lives and was able to publicize them through her prose writings.

As an inheritor of a vigorous feminist movement in Latin America, Storni used the "women's page" of major daily newspapers and magazines to set forth her own version of feminism. In many respects, her efforts exemplified the rise and decline of women's activism during her lifetime. More traditional than some of her feminist friends and associates, she nonetheless championed many feminist concerns of her day. On a more personal level, we can see her sense of social urgency wane as she received wider critical acclaim and was accepted into influential literary circles.

Given her symbolic role, it is not surprising that most studies on Storni separate her from the public sphere, choosing to examine her only in her role as an isolated and sentimentalized figure. A study of some of her journalistic writings can help to move this legendary poet back into the context of her lived history.

Storni's life dramatically illustrates the rise of a new class of activist professional women, often immigrants or first-generation citizens, whose emergence in Argentina was affected by a growing women's involvement in the workplace outside the home and by labor movements in urban areas. These women often entered the public sphere through the classroom, through journalism, or through community organizing and service fields. Storni herself noted the striking surge of middle-class women in intellectual life, and in 1936 she singled out the connection with the teaching profession. Calling many women writers "feministas a pesar suyo" (feminists in spite of themselves), she pointed out the number of teachers among them:

Vienen en parte, de la cultura normalista: el mayor número de las escritoras sudamericanas son maestras y más están,

por vía de la fermentación intelectual, contra su medio social
que sirviendo sus formas tradicionales.[6]

(They come, in part, from the schoolteacher culture, the
greatest number of South American women writers are
teachers and, via intellectual ferment, more are against their
social milieu than are serving its traditional forms.)

A passionate defender of women's and children's rights, Storni
took a visible position in women's activities, especially in the early
stages of her career. She used her assignments of the women's column in various periodicals, such as *La Nota* and *La Nación,* to
make acerbic and penetrating commentaries in favor of social reforms, especially in the areas of women's legal status, workers'
rights, the civil status of unwed mothers, and the role of the church.
Although the more overt political tone of such writings changed
as Storni moved more completely into certain literary circles of
Buenos Aires, the abundance and nature of the early journalistic
writings may surprise the reader accustomed to a more private vision of her life.

In Buenos Aires she first worked at various jobs, in a glove factory, as a cashier, and as an office worker in an importing firm. In
a speech given in Montevideo in 1938, sharing a platform with the
two other major female poets of her time, the Chilean Gabriela
Mistral and the Uruguayan Juana de Ibarbourou, Storni related
the beginnings of her literary career, with her first poems at the age
of twelve years:

> Desde esa edad hasta los 15, trabajo para vivir y ayudar a
> vivir. De los 15 a los 18, estudio de maestra y me recibo Dios
> sabe cómo. La cultura que en la Normal absorbo para en
> Andrade, Echeverría, Campoamor. . . .
> A los 19 estoy encerrada en una oficina. . . . Clavada en
> mi sillón, al lado de un horrible aparato para imprimir discos
> dictando órdenes y correspondencia a la mecanógrafa, es-
> cribo mi primer libro de versos, un pésimo libro de versos.

¡Dios te libre, amigo mío, de *La inquietud del Rosal!* . . .
Pero lo escribí para no morir.[7]

(From that age until 15, I work to live and to help others
live. From 15 to 18, I study to be a teacher and graduate,
God knows how. The culture I absorb in Normal College
stops with Andrade, Echeverría, Campoamor. . . .

At 19 I am enclosed in an office. . . . Stuck to my chair,
beside a horrible apparatus that prints records dictating orders and correspondence to the typist, I write my first book
of verses, an awful book of verses. May God spare you, my
friend, from *La inquietud del Rosal!* . . . But I wrote it so I
wouldn't die.)

Citing from the poem "Bien pudiera ser" from her third book,
Irremediablemente, which she judged "también malo" (also bad),
she contrasts the poem's message of the ancestral and silenced pain
of women with the more personal nature of her early poems. She
states that her presence at the gathering in Montevideo signifies

un homenaje a la uruguaya y a la chilena; a Gabriela y Juana,
y en ellas mi adhesión a la mujer escritora de América; mi
fervor por su heroísmo cuya borra conozco y mi recuerdo in-
clinado para las mayores desaparecidas y las que, ausentes
corporalmente en esta tribuna, están en ella por el valor
magnífico de sus obras.[8]

(a homage to the Uruguayan and the Chilean; to Gabriela
and Juana, and my adherence to the woman writer of America; my fervor for her heroism, whose erasure I know, and
my remembrance of the disappeared older ones, and those
who, physically absent in this tribunal, are in it because of
the magnificent value of their works.)

The solidarity with other women, especially women writers, is
a constant trait often noted in histories and testimonies of Storni's
life and work. Rachel Phillips points out that 1916 to 1925, when
her first four volumes of poetry were published, "were the crucial
years of establishing herself and fighting for a living."[9]

Storni's collaboration with other women in the public sphere began very early in Santa Fe, where she contributed to periodicals and was named vice-president of the Comité Feminista de Santa Fe.[10] In Buenos Aires in 1912, where she found work and began to publish her first articles in *Caras y Caretas*,[11] she also participated in feminist activities. One of her friends, Carolina de Muzzili (1889–1917), was director of the *Tribuna Femenina*, one of Argentina's first feminist periodicals, and in 1914 Storni participated in a benefit recital for Muzzili's publication and her crusading work in behalf of working-class women and child laborers.[12] Muzzili, a self-taught socialist from the working class, was the first woman official of the Departamento Nacional del Trabajo, a position earned by her work in child labor and women's labor rights.[13] In 1916 Storni and Muzzili again appeared together in Rosario, where Storni spoke on women's education and gave poetry recitals, as she did in Buenos Aires at meetings sponsored by the Socialist Party.

In Argentina, feminist organizations directed themselves to women's suffrage, especially after the first elections in 1916 under the Saénz Peña Law, which granted universal male suffrage.[14] The Argentine Socialist Party was a long-term ally of women's rights and since 1903 had included a platform supporting women's equality.[15] Alicia Moreau de Justo (1885–1986), a doctor, teacher, and founder and director of several organizations and magazines, was unquestionably the central figure in the women's movement within socialism, and her lifework became a symbol of leadership and service.[16] When the Socialist Party decided in 1918 to centralize the fight for women's suffrage, Moreau served as president of the new Unión Feminista Nacional. In 1919, the Partido Feminista Nacional came into being under the direction of Julieta Lanteri-Renshaw. Although without much hope of winning elections, the party made an important symbolic impact by bringing women's suffrage, civil rights, and labor issues directly to the public's attention. In the same year, Storni published articles on both suffrage and civil rights. The year 1919 also witnessed the first number of *Nuestra*

Causa, a monthly journal founded by Alicia Moreau to serve as a forum for feminist groups and as the organ of the Unión Feminista Nacional. Storni participated in events sponsored by the journal and the organization; in 1921, *Nuestra Causa* recorded a program in her honor given by the union after she won the municipal prize for poetry.[17] Storni's efforts in the relief effort for victims of World War I in Europe led to an association with Moreau. According to Storni, World War I marked the end of an epoch for women, initiating radical changes in cultural and social values because of its revelations about the bankruptcy of patriarchal culture.[18] Although she was not an active member of any political party, it is clear, given her participation in feminist activities and labor-rights meetings, that she was fully aware of the political questions of her day and was outspoken in her support of these causes.

In 1918 Storni was one of the leaders of the Asociación pro Derechos de la Mujer, initiated by Elvira Rawson de Dellepiane (1867–1954), a physician, an educator, and one of the founders of the early Centro Feminista.[19] Among the goals of this group (whose numbers grew to eleven thousand) were the abolition of laws that established different standards for men and women, the advancement of women to directive positions in the educational system, the enactment of laws protective of motherhood, the eradication of prostitution, and equality of jobs and salaries. On this last issue Storni is especially vehement in her journalistic writings, often pointing out the reality of numbers of working women in the nation and their inequality in salary and in job opportunities. Some of these articles, such as "La perfecta dactilógrafa" (The perfect typist) in *La Nación,* 1920, and "¿Por qué las maestras se casan poco?" (Why do few teachers marry?) in *La Nación,* 1921, use satire and humor to raise serious issues. Her "Bocetos Femeninos" (Feminine sketches) in *La Nación* found space among the recipe columns, fashion photographs, society notes, church news, and items of general cultural interest. Without neglecting the constraints of this journalistic medium, she inserted a record of the less-visible aspects of a large, low-salaried group of female employees. Reaching a group of readers who might not read specifically feminist publications, she presented her opinions. In this series for *La Nación* she wrote under the pseudonym "Tao Lao," whereas in the series of *La Nota,* "Femenidades," and in other publications, she signed with her own name.

By 1920, having published in some of the major periodicals of her day (*Caras y Caretas, Atlantida, La Nota, Nosotros*), Storni began to work as a regular contributor to *La Nación,* the major daily newspaper, where she continued to publish articles until her death in 1938. At the same time she was writing poetry and working as a teacher in public and private schools. Her journalism often returns to certain central issues: working women and their occupations, the relationship of women to national and cultural tradition, the role of the church, single mothers, marriage, good and bad models of motherhood, female poverty, migration to the city, fashion, and discussions of the "innate" characteristics of the female nature. Observations on class distinctions and references to the role of the teacher recur with regular frequency.

According to Storni, religion, poverty, and patriarchy are closely linked. For example, in "La carta al Padre Eterno" (Letter to the Eternal Father), she relates existing legal structures to church doctrines:

> Sabemos ya que desde el punto de vista moderno, filosófico, diré, las Sagradas Escrituras son anti-feministas, y las leyes por las que nos regimos, inspiradas en gran parte en aquellas, anti-feministas también.
>
> Pero toda mujer que entrara a considerarlas, en pro o en contra se volverá feminista, porque lo que por aquellas le está negado es pensar con la cabeza y por algunas de éstas, obrar con su voluntad.[20]
>
> (We now know that from the modern, what I would call philosophic point of view, the Sacred Scriptures are antifeminist, and the laws we rule ourselves by, inspired in great part by them, are also antifeminist.

But every woman who might begin to consider them, either for or against, would become a feminist, because what
they deny her is thinking with her head and, because of some
of these laws, acting with her own will.)

The topic of patriarchy and moral standards returns in articles
concerning women's poverty and the status of the unwed mother
in "La complejidad femenina" (Feminine complexity), in which she
outlines the psychology of the roles of dominator and dominated.[21]
Other articles, such as "En contra de la caridad" (Against charity) in *La Nota,* 1919, and "Derechos civiles femeninos" (Women's
civil rights) in *La Nota,* 1919, are more straightforward in their
vehement criticism of social norms and legal sanctions involving
women. In "Derechos civiles femeninos," Storni calls for not only
the vote for women but also equal protection under the law, so that
such a vote might have practical worth. Both of these articles are
related to women's struggle to reform the Civil Code—a major fea-
ture of Argentine feminism until 1926, when the reforms were won.
Saying that women lead "una vida colonial" (a colonial life), she
notes especially the necessary duplicity of the unmarried mother:

> Sabido es que esta mujer, madre de un ser humano, que ha
> de servir a la sociedad en igual forma que los llamados hijos
> legítimos, no tiene protección alguna de la ley, ni del con-
> cepto público, ni de la tolerancia social.
>
> La mujer en estas condiciones, si quiere educar al niño,
> mantenerlo a su lado, ha de usar de subterfugios, recurrir a
> falsedades, envilecerse de cobardía. . . . Para el hombre cóm-
> plice en la vida de un ser no hay sanción ni legal, ni moral.
> Hay más; ni siquiera está obligado económicamente a nada.
>
> Esto es un resabio del Cristianismo mitificado.[22]
>
> (We know that this woman, mother of a human being,
> who must serve society in the same way as the so-called le-
> gitimate children, has no protection whatsoever under the
> law, or of public regard, or of social tolerance.

The woman in these conditions, if she wants to educate
the child, keep him at her side, has to turn to subterfuges
and falsehoods, and vilify herself with cowardice. . . . For
the accomplice male of this life of a human being there is
neither legal nor moral sanction. Even more; he is not even
obligated economically for anything.

This is a leftover of mythified Christianity.)

In another article of 1919, "El movimiento hacia la emancipación de la mujer en la Republica Argentina: las dirigentes feministas" (The women's emancipation movement in Argentina: the feminist leaders), Storni also points out that the Socialist Party was the only one that currently included the vote for women as part of its platform. Tracing the history of the feminist movement in Argentina, she describes the movement's leaders, outlines the goals of the different branches of the movement, and gives statistical evidence of women's participation in the labor force.[23] In her discussion of political support for the movement, she states that the Socialist Party has played an important role in spreading the suffrage movement throughout the working class.

Storni speaks out against the institutionalization of charity and the social structures that force the creation of such institutions in the article "En contra de la caridad": "Sabido tenemos que hay un concepto bien generalizado en las organizaciones sociales defectuosas: crear el pobre para darle la limosna" (We know that in defective social organizations there is a well-generalized concept: create the poor so you can give them charity).[24] Storni called for wiser legislation that would oblige society to create means to provide for the needs of its citizens.

In "Un tema viejo" (An old theme), Storni calls feminism a collective transformation, a sign of the defeat of masculine directives, and a natural state of human evolution:

Reírse del feminismo, por eso, me parece tan curioso como
reírse de un dedo porque termina en una uña. Para llegar a

lo que llamamos feminismo la humanidad ha seguido un proceso tan exacto como el que sigue el embrión para llegar a ser fruto o el fruto para transformar sus elementos en embrión, a pasos sucesivos.[25]

(Therefore to laugh at feminism seems to me as strange as laughing at your finger because it has a fingernail. To arrive at what we call feminism humanity has followed a process as exact as the one an embryo follows to become a fruit, or for a fruit to transform its elements into an embryo, by successive steps.)

Arguing against those who attack feminism and who cite "authorities" such as classical precedents and biblical teachings, Storni counters that feminism is "una cuestión de justicia."

In her writings Storni claims that she is not a militant feminist, even though she supports many proposed legal and social changes regarding women. The writings for *La Nota* (especially in 1918 and 1919), where she directed the column "Femenidades," as well as her other journalistic writings of that period, are notable for their partisan stance. Besides dealing with the civil status of women and other social issues, Storni gives ironic commentary on female fashion—the corset, "suicidal" high heels—in articles interspersed with sketches, poems, and short stories that generally reflect a more sentimental type of popular literature, with their intense appeal to "el desengaño en el amor" (disillusionment with love) and to elaborate backdrops of interior setting and dress.

With some striking exceptions, the column "Bocetos Femeninos" in *La Nación* responded to the needs of the commercial press. The form of the "sketch," which Storni often used, makes few claims to permanence. These pieces are often impressionistic observations with highly personalized judgments. In a kind of urban adaptation of the travelogue, they record vignettes of daily life in Buenos Aires—the subway crowds, shoppers, female "types" (the domestic employee, the provincial, the secretary, the schoolgirl, the shopper, the mother)—in a chatty tone with frequent asides to the reader. The tone of these short essays varies widely. Some are breezy and humorous; others are straightforward accounts of noteworthy topics concerning women, such as the recent census figures on occupational divisions for women or the marital status of the citizenry. They gain their appeal by mixing trite feminine stereotypes with issues of basic economic and social concern to women.

In some of these articles it is easy to see Storni's own personal issues, especially in her concern for the financial and professional insecurity of schoolteachers ("La maestra" and "¿Por qué las maestras se casan poco?"), the hypocrisy surrounding virginity ("La novia"), and society's excessive emphasis on female beauty ("La impersonal" and "Las crepusculares"). Although she is often eloquent in her defense of women, she can be aggressively disparaging of many aspects of women's culture. Pretense, slavish imitation, and obsessive romanticism, specifically the fixation on marriage ("Las casaderas" [Marriage brokers] and "El amor y la mujer" [Love and the woman]), are targets of satirical exposés.

In "Las casaderas" (*La Nación* [8 August 1920]: 4) Storni calls for reader responses to her hypothetical marriage agency, which would solicit unmarried men (even from other planets) to match with husband-seeking women. Her reaction to the responses she received serves as the starting point for "El amor y la mujer" (22 August 1920: 6). With tongue in cheek, she salutes her readers as eternal romantics:

> Regocijáos por lo pronto, de ser todavía las celosas vestales del romanticismo (es muy lindo ser vestal; el tul blanco cae divinamente y lame el rosado pie con delicada gracia).
>
> Vuestra imaginación se interpone así entre la realidad y el sueño como un elástico de poderosa resistencia que apaga y suaviza los choques.
>
> (Rejoice, meanwhile, for still being the jealous priestesses of romanticism [it's very nice to be a priestess; white tulle falls divinely and licks your rosy foot with delicate grace].

    Your imagination inserts itself between reality and dream
like a rubber band of powerful resistance that stops and soft-
ens blows.)

Thus they compare the voluptuous condition of woman to that of
certain inferior races that live only to love and satisfy their passions, and they even claim that the lofty maternal sentiment is pure
instinct.

    As in so many other articles, here Storni speaks from several dif-
ferent angles, using a highly embellished rhetoric common to many
columnists. Addressing her female readers as "mis dulces amigui-
tas lectoras," "oh divinas," "adorables mujeres," and "pequeñas
amigas," Storni as Tao Lao tackles many of the popular myths
about women without running too much risk of alienating the casual reader.

    One of her favorite topics was fashion and women's devotion to
it. Here she reveals contradictory impulses, or at least plays on
those of her readers. Although she denounces fashion's excesses
and the often pathetic and ludicrous lengths to which women will
go to serve this master, she shows a keen eye for details of dress
and, more revealingly, what these details show about their wear-
ers. Dress is the code to which she most commonly refers when discussing the ascent up the ladder of social class. Street scenes of
Buenos Aires and commentary on social customs reveal her ambivalence toward Buenos Aires, as do many poems of her early period. References to the city's sacrifices to impersonal norms, its
rapid movement, the rule of "vanity and pride," and a scale of values based on money and class—complaints registered by most
urban observers of all periods—alternate with expressions of clear
delight in the variety of human types and idiosyncrasies. The frequent idealization of provincial life is countered by depictions of
the movement, color, and freedom of the city.

    Storni's eye for the ridiculous and the pathetic often fastened on
the cult of imitation that circulated in "la pequeña ciudad que de

gran ciudad oficia" (the little city that acts as a big city), as in "La impersonal" (27 June 1920: 4). Here she scolds the female who is devoid of originality and "real sentiment":

> Y si la impersonal es completamente pobre, caerá en la ridiculez de dar las formas más novedosas a telas viejas y ajadas, arrastrando así, sobre su propio cuerpo, la tristeza de su pobre alma expuesta a la mirada aguda del que pasa.
> (And if the impersonal one is completely poor, she will be so ridiculous as to give the newest forms to old and worn-out fabrics, dragging along, on her own body, the sadness of her poor soul exposed to the sharp gaze of the passerby.)

In "Las crepusculares," she records the late afternoon pilgrimage to the downtown fashion stores in the Calle Florida. The "damitas" (little ladies) referred to by the synecdoche of their "zapatitos" (little shoes) cluster together, reverently awaiting a fashion show. Her use of diminutives is telling, as is her coy address to her feminine readers in the satirical articles—"oh divinas." Her sharp jabs at class and economic distinctions are hard to miss, and their juxtaposition to the society notes makes them especially ironic. Alternating a highly embellished rhetoric with a spare, direct style, she usually makes her point in no uncertain terms.

In "La emigrada," Storni gives a sympathetic portrait of the young women who arrive alone in the city from the provinces to make their way "en las grandes ciudades como criada familiar o en los institutos de salud e higiene como mucama" (in the big cities as a domestic maid or in health and hygiene institutes as a maid) (*La Nación* [1 August 1920]: 2). She recounts a newcomer's growing awareness as the "María, Juana, Rosa, etc." begins to adapt to a new setting. In a short but richly detailed piece, she captures a scene so common to her day and to ours, the migration to Latin American cities of women alone or with their children. Such a young woman, reared in a rural setting without reading or writing skills, accustomed to turning her wages over to her elders, arrives in the city with a sealed envelope, whose contents she cannot read. The limitless possibilities of the city dazzle her: "La ciudad produce en la emigrada rapidos efectos: como una planta transplantada que no sabe qué hacer con la exótica savia que recibe, se resuelve de golpe por dar un estirón hacia arriba" (The city produces rapid effects in the emigrant: like a transplanted plant that doesn't know what to do with the exotic sap it receives, she suddenly resolves to grow straight upward).

The most common initial transformation of the transplant is superficial—fancy shoes, costume jewelry, and flashy clothes. The second phase is one of growing pains, as she begins to observe and to imitate not her peers (her roommates) but the family for whom she works. She learns to search not for the trappings of prosperity but for the means to a better income, and she asks for a raise. The "emigrada" learns the lessons of the city, unlearning the lessons of her place of origin, whose "árboles del camino podrían decir: la que pasa se llama María, o Juana, o Rosa, pero los árboles de Buenos Aires sólo dicen que la que pasa es una libreta de ahorros" (trees along the road could say: that one going by is María, or Juana, or Rosa, but the trees of Buenos Aires only say she is a little bank book).

The marks of class and social categories are nearly always present in Storni's journalistic writings. Even though most of her articles focus on personality or character types, economic and social status is the thread that unites her writings. Occupational divisions among women are a frequent theme of her journalism, especially in *La Nación*. For her it is no surprise that most domestic employees would be women, or that the great majority of educators are women. Some occupations receive special attention in these articles, like the secretary, the teacher, the doctor, and the domestic employee, and even the watercolorist (singled out for her irregularity of salary) constitute part of the gallery of contemporary portraits. Storni's own profession through her adult life, that of teacher, receives special treatment. She devotes two articles in *La Nación*,

"La normalista" (13 June 1920: 1) and "¿Por qué las maestras se casan poco?" (13 March 1921: 4), to this topic. In the second, the *normalista* defends herself against her "cowardice" in bucking the system, because she fears expulsion if she criticizes the educational administration. As further justification of an apparent immobility, she ends with clear logic: "Y por último: mi madre es viuda y mis hermanos están desnudos" (And finally, my mother is a widow and my brothers and sisters are naked). Teachers are the one group that almost never provokes ironic commentary from Storni. It is clear that her own work as a teacher, and her admiration for other women teachers, is a matter of great pride. "¿Por qué las maestras se casan poco?" is another version of the traditional story of "la mujer que sabe latín," a topic still debated in contemporary society. Storni definitely sees this situation as a problem worthy of serious attention. Her analysis of economic, intellectual, social, and moral factors ends with no solution, but with a vindication of the superior qualities of the profession's members. Education marks a step up on the social scale, but offers little economic advancement or acceptance by more highly paid professionals. The serious discussion she devotes to the topic shows her concern for this emerging class of women, and perhaps a preoccupation with her own situation: "Por lo que está en condiciones de leer, de adquirir, aspira a más de lo que su medio social le permitiría" (Given that her condition allows her to read, to acquire things, she aspires to more than her social milieu will allow her).

Although she is a staunch defender of women's rights, Storni is not always tolerant of all aspects of women's culture. More traditional in her approach to women's roles than some of her feminist colleagues and friends, she sees biological destiny as the major force for women. Instinctive motherhood, an innate sensitivity to human emotional needs, and a capacity for sacrifice are traits she attributes to her sex. Certain behavioral patterns associated with women, however, come under sarcastic attack. Sentimentalism and superficial rigidity in moral standards are two of her favorite

topics. These two traits impede women from taking a "philosophical" view of their roles, inhibiting them in their search for self-
development. Articles from *La Nación* such as "La mujer enemiga
de la mujer" (22 May 1921: 4) and "La mujer como novelista" (27
March 1921: 4) illustrate her position.

Even though she was insistent about making a place for herself
and for other women in literary circles in Buenos Aires (a fact
never omitted from her biographies is that she was the first woman
to attend literary banquets there, an action that met with no little
resistance), she claimed that women had not evolved sufficiently to
be effective in certain spheres. In both these articles she cites lack
of experience as the determining factor in women's incapacities. In
"La mujer enemiga de la mujer," she says: "A falta de educación del
carácter, y a carencia de buena disciplina mental, hay que achacar
tanta enemistad de mujer a mujer" (So much enmity from one
woman to another must be attributed to a lack of character training, and to absence of good mental discipline). Women's lack of
generosity with one another could be remedied by attention to
their training, by forming a type of sisterhood that would train
them to uphold standards of virtue with more compassion and less
hypocrisy. The price paid for rigid adherence to uncompromising
standards indicates to her the female's greatest weakness, for "si la
virtud ha costado tanto para conservarla que endurece el alma y la
cierra para comprender cualquier error, entonces tanto valía no
tenerla" (if virtue costs so much to conserve that it hardens the
heart and closes it to understanding any error, then it is not worth
having). Despite the measured tone and appeal to reason that she
creates, it is apparent that Storni speaks from the most acute personal awareness. Although she gained growing acceptance as a
writer, was sought after as a speaker, and became known as a successful teacher, this kind of acceptance did not always transfer into
the social sphere. As many of her contemporaries have recorded,
she could not be welcomed into many "respectable" homes, even
though she might associate with the same families in the public

sphere. Her condition as unwed mother created barriers that not even her talents and energetic efforts could overcome.

"La mujer como novelista" is a troubling article for readers who might search for a consistent and unequivocal defense of the woman artist in Storni's work. Her remarks on the recent proliferation of novels by women lead to the conclusion that she saw a dubious future for women as novelists. Not only does she find women lacking the range of lived experience necessary "para observar el mundo con ojos claros y penetradores" (to observe the world with clear and penetrating eyes) but she also implies that the very sensibility that is their greatest gift can bring about their undoing as novelists: "Si la sensibilidad femenina es rica, la sensibilidad pura no basta para la obra de arte" (Even if feminine sensibility is rich, pure sensibility is not sufficient for a work of art). Granted, women with fortune may be permitted to live the sort of life that permits them to break with expected norms and experiment more fully with other types of existence. Yet the same liberty robs them of their most treasured possession, their feminine nature: "Luego, una vida extraordinaria destruye en la mujer lo que la hace más preciada: su feminidad" (Then, an extraordinary life destroys in woman the very thing that makes her most prized: her femininity).

Here Storni appears to go against many of the ideas in other articles. Woman is limited by her narrow range of experience, but breaking these limits makes her less womanly. In this respect the article shows a notable shift in her writings, forecasting some of the positions she would adopt later. Even more interesting, it reveals a link between her journalism, outspoken in defense of women's liberties, and her short fiction pieces of the period, which largely cling to the sentimental romantic plots that she finds to be the inescapable lot of the woman novelist. Nonetheless, sentimentality and an unrealistically romanticized view of reality (two of the main criticisms leveled at her early poetry) are targets of derision many times in these columns.

The image of woman as a mother and as the anchor of the family unit serves Storni as her rationale for the ethics of sexual equality. Such a position reflects that of many feminist activists during this period. She embraces the exaltation of motherhood, even though it leads her to some contradictory approaches. Many of her arguments find their logic by recalling women's importance and contributions in traditional roles, such as those found in rural societies. Storni often refers back to a golden age of tradition, where women were accorded their rightful place. In "Sobre nosotros" (*La Nota* 94 [26 May 1917]: 1865–66), she proposes to analyze why the crowds of Buenos Aires are rude and why women suffer such discourtesy. Her thesis rests on the fact that, as a city of immigrants, Buenos Aires has not had time to develop a collective spiritual culture, because "la cultura colectiva descansa en el cariño a la tierra, a la historia, al hogar, a la ley, al porvenir" (collective culture rests on affection for the earth, history, the home, the law, the future). She likens the development of a civic consciousness to the cohesion of the family unit:

> ¿Exigiríamos de él [el pueblo] las consideraciones espon-
> táneas que las mujeres recibiríamos si tuviera cabal concepto
> de la familia como institución primera de la colectividad,
> como asiento y fundamento de la raza?
> (Would we demand from the people the spontaneous con-
> siderations that women would receive if we had a full con-
> cept of the family as the first institution of collectivity, as the
> basis and foundation of the race?)

At the same time that the family unit serves her as the basic metaphor of a healthy society, it is an almost mythic family, one she finds hard to reconcile with the facts of a newly created society in constant flux and change.

In other articles the family in particular raises uncomfortable issues. The image of the mother can be a problematic one, especially when she drops the straightforward analytic tone and veers toward fictional recreation.

In "La dama de negro" (*La Nota* 4, no. 191 [4 April 1919]: 427–28), Storni combines a vignette of life in Buenos Aires with moralizing on the mother's role and the baleful effects of a society obsessed with artifice and appearances. Here an excessively elegant lady with her five-year-old daughter is seated facing the narrator in the subway. On a second look, the narrator notices that the child has been transformed by her mother into a rather dirty and "cheap doll." With her bleached hair and painted cheeks, the child reflects a pathetic case of the vanity and dislocation of values the city so often presents. The scene brings to mind the case of a woman on trial who tried to commit suicide by flinging herself into the water with her two children; she succeeded in killing them but not herself. The narrator finds the attempted suicide more honorable than the subway child's deformation at her mother's hands. Like the obsession with matrimony, the relentless search for beauty and appearances, at great social loss, is highlighted constantly in Storni's articles. Whereas the forms vary, from direct moralizing to sentimental tales with tragic endings, her aim is clear.

In reading her prose, in addition to her well-known poetry, it becomes evident that Storni's journalistic texts reveal unexplored facets of her personality and professional life and also cast light on the cultural and social milieu of her time. They give us an entrance into the coexistence of several versions of feminism and show the interrelationships among women, the popular press, literary movements, and the emergence of a middle-class female reader. As Storni moved more into the mainstream of intellectual life in Buenos Aires, the topic of feminism became a less-persistent theme in her journalism. Her writings in general reflect the tensions facing women of her class who found themselves in the midst of a rapidly changing society, where the realities of women's lives could no longer correspond to the reigning mythologies. These mythologies, so often reflected on the same pages of the newspapers and journals where Storni published her pieces, are brought into higher contrast by their juxtaposition to Storni's articles.

Many of the women for whom Storni wrote came from a background like hers—children of immigrants who worked outside the home, some of whom were able to move into a growing middle-class sector via the teaching profession. And like her, many must have sensed the incongruities between their everyday realities and the weight of tradition. Although Storni herself is well known as a public figure and as a poet, her links to the history of women of her lifetime deserve to be explored. New approaches to history, biography, and literature, making use of the extraliterary writings of prominent women writers, can offer a way to return such isolated figures to a lived history. In doing so, we not only discover neglected genres but are able as well to rethink our canons of literary and social history.

Gabriela Mistral:
LANGUAGE IS THE ONLY HOMELAND

Elizabeth Horan

⌐ GABRIELA MISTRAL'S LIFE (1889–1957) can be divided into four eras, each articulating distinct phases in the extraordinarily wide-ranging production of this ever-restless poet-essayist-cultural critic. Her witness to all the social turmoil of this century pushed her into and beyond the predictability of literary success. The first era spans her residence in Chile, from her birth in 1889 until her departure in 1921 to work in postrevolutionary Mexico. From 1906 onward she was publishing in provincial newspapers, then in magazines affiliated with the rapidly growing school system, then in other literary magazines, writing and revising the material partially included in her first major volume, *Desolación* (1922; revised and reprinted in 1926).

Her departure for Mexico in 1921 initiated a new era in Mistral's life: from 1922 to 1938 she rarely stayed in one place for more than a few months. Her addiction to travel and her dependence on the income that lecture tours and journalism brought contributed to her fame as the continent's leading authority on popular education. Wherever she went, her opinions were sought and quoted, for Gabriela Mistral was regarded as a kind of oracle or prophet, and throughout Latin America, enormous crowds greeted her. Big, solid, ignorant of makeup, oblivious to coquetry, racially and sexually ambiguous, she was the distracted centerpiece of official homages and empty social events. With her origins in unpretentious rural schools, she was something of an anomaly among literary celebrities, and not just because she was a woman. She was forward-thinking yet suspicious of fashion, a wholly self-taught verbal genius who endlessly revised her work, before and after publication, a writer of multiple uncertainties and thus the very antithesis of the effortless brio that characterized peers such as Lorca and Neruda.

The catastrophes of the civil war in Spain initiated a new era for Mistral, as for all writers in Spanish. While Mistral's exile had begun some two decades before, this was for her and for most of her contemporaries the end of Europe as they had known it. The war forced the onset of a new self-consciousness among Latin American writers, who, like Mistral, had to focus and reevaluate their aesthetic practices and political allegiances. With the fall of France, Gabriela Mistral moved to Brazil after having published *Tala*, her second major volume of poetry, under the auspices of Victoria Ocampo in 1938. The disasters of war turned suddenly personal: in 1943 the apparent suicide, in Petrópolis, Brazil, of her adopted son, Juan Miguel Godoy, precipitated the mental and physical decline that eventually led to Mistral's death.

The fourth and final period of Mistral's life, from 1945 to her death in 1957, has about it an odd sense of belatedness and unreality. When in 1945 she became the first Latin American Nobel laureate, neither the ceremony or her now-international fame acknowledged the central preoccupations of Mistral and of other Latin American intellectuals. Although she, like Neruda, was seeking new forms for merging poetry with history, the Nobel Prize celebrated her for poems she had written more than two decades earlier. Long since weary of protocol and regalia, she nonetheless boarded the boat to Stockholm to stand before the white-haired king of Sweden, wearing the famous black velvet dress, receiving the gold of armaments manufacturer Alfred Nobel. Facing yet another crowd, another promotional appearance, another ceremonial function, she as ever spoke of the honor being directed not to her person but to her status as a representative of a distant literature utterly unfamiliar to this once-dominant Europe now exhausted, in ruins.

Despite ill health in the last thirteen years of her life, Mistral continued writing. Putting aside the journalism that she had so long used to supplement her income, a great part of her energies she devoted as always to travel. She also continued work on the two volumes she had begun in 1938, finishing neither in her lifetime. By now her poetry was a memory book in which she daily assembled herself and a Chile populated by ghosts, and thus she shored against the losses of the near and distant past. Gone were the complex meters and enjambment of her youth. Long, assonantal lines and the skipping beat of romance were balms to a body and spirit racked by rheumatism, diabetes, and cancer.

Somewhat scandalously awarded Chile's National Prize for Literature in 1951, five years after the Nobel, the picture we have of Mistral during these years could be clearer. Gabriela Mistral's letters, one of the most important indices to her thought, give some evidence of dementia. As was the case throughout her life, she relied on others to see her work through the press, and some of this material from her last years was published as *Lagar* during a trip to Chile in 1954. Her writings in the last years of her life were not as arduously polished as was her wont, yet much of it, posthumously published in *Poema de Chile* (1967) and *Lagar II* (1992), is of the very highest order.

Coexisting with the possibility that "La Vieja" was by 1950 slipping in and out of dementia is the possibility that she took advantage of the latitude allowed an older woman of whom little was expected. Rather than allowing herself to be trundled out for ceremonial appearances and oracular pronouncements, she increasingly spoke or kept silence as she pleased. In her "elder statesman" role she could certainly embarrass the authorities, as for instance when she spoke from Chile's Presidential Palace. She happily announced to the assembled multitudes a land-reform act that existed only in her mind, while the right-wing ministers at her flank blanched with horror and tried to get someone to shut her up.

If Gabriela Mistral was protean and unpredictable in her life, death turned her into an empty yet readily available sign, a message that could be variously filled with meaning, depending on the circumstances. Mistral's death and funerals in 1957 became the opportunity for yet another series of mass public gatherings. It was as if after receiving "for Chile" the 1945 Nobel Prize, Mistral's next most important duty to her country was to die and thus effect a final return, forever affixing her in the frieze of public events. In the scramble to appropriate her figure following her death, the Foreign and Education Ministries, the pedagogues and church bureaucrats, the grainy photo spreads and glossy magazines slid over the difficulties and contradictions of her personality. With death and return the anarchic originality of her poetry, prose, and speech seemed at last containable, no longer embarrassingly corporeal. As a ghost she could be a permanently virgin mother representing all that the national institutions of church, state, and school would ostensibly honor. Motivating the hot air of official homages following her death was a tremendous sigh of relief among those institutions who had always sought, with varying degrees of success, to appropriate her to their own ends. Now that she had slipped away, her image could be fully co-opted without fear of her querulous, unpredictable interruption. Honoring Mistral thus became an empty ceremony of false tenderness, ostensibly recognizing but actually dismissing impoverished children, agonizing mothers, scorned schoolteachers, godforsaken Indians, penniless refugees, rural workers. Her death tells us something of why this woman who was one of the twentieth century's greatest poets preferred the anomie of exile rather than to live, trapped, accepting constant affront as her daily bread in a so-called homeland.

The worst aspect of the public recognition accorded Gabriela Mistral is that her writings are subordinated to a life and "character" fitted to a preexisting code of feminine saintliness. Only a few scholars have even begun to examine her in the context of intellectual history—most notably Vargas Saavedra, but also Concha, Villegas, Scarpa, and Fernando Alegría. Most of the commentary that would pretend to scholarship is in fact an endlessly fascinating, daunting compendium of qualities specifically associated with sanctity in women. The attributes the commentators would discover in Gabriela Mistral—personal modesty, secret suffering, a gift for prayer, concern for less-fortunate others, the purification of debilitating sexuality, renunciation, self-abnegation—are presented to "explain" the subject's eccentricity. Making Gabriela Mistral an anomaly reinforces the stereotype of Chilean femininity (coquettish, yet devoted to home and family) that Mistral's figure flatly contradicts.

We need to rummage among the circumstances linking Gabriela Mistral with an "exemplary" femininity in order to identify components the homages suppress. The hagiography most amply covers her early years in Chile, from her birth in 1889 as Lucila Godoy Alcayaga, in the provincial town of Vicuña, some four hundred kilometers to the north of the capital. Her father was an unemployed schoolteacher and former seminarian, Jerónimo Godoy, who had been married for a year and a half to Petronila Alcayaga, thirteen years his senior. Petronila, euphemistically termed a "widow" in many accounts, was forty-four years old and had a teenage daughter, Emelina, from an earlier relationship. Much ink has been split on this father whom the poet scarcely knew (for he abandoned his wife and infant daughter before the latter turned three years old), and many writers like to assert that Jerónimo Godoy exerted an indelible influence on the future Nobel laureate. His erratic employment as a schoolteacher, his penchant for composing and singing verses, the trees he planted, his Bohemian character are all called forth to account for his daughter's (otherwise inexplicable) wandering, writing, and interest in the natural world. Averring that the father's absence forever marked his daughter effaces the very real and palpable presence of the women with whom the young Lucila Godoy, later Gabriela Mistral, chose to spend her life. Her household from birth to age twenty-seven consisted of her aged mother and, intermittently, her older sister and niece. Her subsequent companions were the sculptor Laura Rodig in Chile, then Mexican educator and diplomat Palma Guillén in Mexico and Europe, then Puerto Rican educator Consuelo Saleva during the years of the war, then writer Doris Dana in the years after "that thing from Sweden," so that each of these women corresponded to one of the four eras of Mistral's life.

The young Lucila Godoy spent her childhood and adolescence in the Valle de Elqui, an agricultural and mining area located on the edge of the desert to the north of Santiago. The idealized description of this valley forms an emotional center of her later work. Most accounts of her youth work from Mistral's suggestion of Elqui as a quasi-biblical locale, but unlike Mistral, most outsiders markedly dehistorize that setting in order to state Mistral's origins in terms of a remote and mythical, national past, and similarly to assign her a racial heritage that has varied according to the interests of the time.

A principal theme of the poet's youth is her perseverance in battles with the devil. Closed-minded clergy, blind and incompetent teachers, uncomprehending and jealous supervisors all worked against her. A primary factor in her favor was her sister Emelina, fifteen years her senior. Gainfully employed in the local schools, Emelina supported the household on her earnings and taught the young Lucila to read and write. The family's circumstances were marginal. They often moved from one site in the valley to another, hoping to improve their lot. The young girl was unfavorably regarded by her teachers, who thought of her as peculiar and self-absorbed. When her formal schooling ended by age fourteen, the young writer commenced a series of low-wage jobs close by the provincial cities of Coquimbo and La Serena. By this time she was publishing poetry and prose in local newspapers.

The record of Gabriela Mistral's publications, appearing from 1905 on, stands in contrast to the hagiographical accounts. From the very onset of her appearance in print, what Gabriela Mistral wrote was shaped by the secularizing interests of liberals and radicals seeking to supplant the traditional authority of the church. Her early publications are intimist essays, typical of the times. She had a particular inclination to write short meditations on social topics, on female friendship, on women's education, and on the revolution in Russia. She wrote for provincial newspapers where she was living, in Vicuña, then in Chile's northern port cities of Coquimbo and Antofagasta. Her base of readers expanded with her transfer to teach in the city of Los Andes, keeping her close to the rural environment that she preferred, yet within a morning's journey from the bookstores of Santiago.

These first two decades of the twentieth century were an extraordinary time in Chile. These were years of social movements that increasingly coalesced in Santiago, with women mobilizing for education and the vote, with the rapid politicization of the urban proletariat and of newly formed student groups, with organizations of theosophists and vegetarians, of Tolstoyan communities and formidable Masons. Within this commotion previously belletristic pursuits such as writing and editing were suddenly opened up to relative outsiders. Even the scions of the Chilean oligarchy were impatient with the conservative provincialism and essentially eighteenth-century institutions that had so long held sway. In contrast to the restrained, fourth-handed imitation of pale European models, Mistral and her contemporaries championed emotion and originality. Even so, Chile's established writers were generally male, moderately successful urban professionals who discovered in the countryside a source of renewal. How and why Gabriela Mistral, an outsider and a female with no beauty, no formal education, no family connections, almost no money, was singled out amid so much artistic and intellectual talent is a phenomenon worth extended consideration. Despite her lack of any academic degree, she moved from teacher's assistant to headmistress of Chile's most prestigious public school in scarcely fifteen years. That advancement was tied to the expansion of the Chilean educational system and to her prolific record of publication.

Although Gabriela Mistral's national reputation dates from 1914, when her "Sonetos de la Muerte" took first prize in a literary contest in Santiago, she had been published since 1912 in Theosophical Society magazines, literary journals throughout Chile, and periodicals read by schoolteachers. In 1917 fifty-five items by Mistral were included in a series of school texts or *Libros de Lectura,* edited by Manuel Guzmán Maturana, distributed throughout Chile and other Latin American nations. In these prose poems, parables, and didactic verse she offers art as an anodyne to social and economic injustice, the latter becoming a more visible concern from 1918, when she went to live and work in the harsh circumstances of Punta Arenas on the Magellanic Straits, the southernmost city in Chile. It was a bitterly divided city, between fantastically wealthy landowners on the one hand and the large population of recent immigrants from southern and eastern Europe on the other.

Like many of her female contemporaries, Gabriela Mistral justified her social concerns as an extension of the schoolteacher's role that in itself expanded on the idea of women's moral superiority to men. This attitude was consistent with a critical establishment and secular educational system that sought some way of registering "woman" within the discourse of the nation, of acknowledging the need for reform without actually calling for any changes. Although the national press attacked women's reading groups as "descabelladas locuras unnaturales," a figure such as Mistral, presented as an isolated voice in the wilderness, offered something of a palliative, a nod in the direction of an increasingly literate pop-

ulation of women and men thrown back on their own meager resources despite the tremendous revenues flowing from Chile's mines,
forests, and industries.

Mistral was no isolated figure. The Liceo de Niñas, or state-
sponsored girls' school, was another factor crucial to her fame, le-
gitimating her presence in an otherwise all-male public sphere.
Within the worlds of the Liceo de Niñas and the normal schools
Mistral and her female contemporaries were figures of absolute authority. These were far more egalitarian organizations than were
the overwhelmingly urban and married, middle- and upper-middle-
class constituencies of the Women's reading circles, the Women's
Club, and the Professional Women's Association. It is worth asking how far the various women's political action campaigns of the
1930s and 1940s would have progressed without the girls' liceos as
a common ground on which the collective emphasis on reform
would be built, through the enactment of protective laws preventing
the exploitation of women and children. Whatever the differences
among Mistral and her sundry colleagues, they were all committed
to the education of women as the starting point, and women's economic self-sufficiency as the goal.

Feminists must recognize that Mistral, like others in her generation, was to some extent complicit in repressive versions of femininity, the only difference being that Mistral's texts are even today
being called to serve those myths. Gabriela Mistral's possible com-
plicity in the construction of her public image could be traced to a
rhetorical stance that she shared with other Chilean protofeminists
in the first quarter of the twentieth century: as they did in positing
woman as a center of moral righteousness, she invoked the preexisting code of female sanctity as a means of countering informal
and institutional misogyny. The de-sexualized figure of the saintly
rural schoolmarm enabled Mistral to express alienation and outrage at a culture that registered "woman" solely in terms of the
ability to entice male desire. That quasi-parental, semireligious figure of the schoolmarm led, in turn, to Gabriela Mistral's becoming

a register for the construction of "woman" within the discourse of nationhood in Chile, for the religious idealism attributed to the "teacher" answered the secular state's need to bolster its authority.

If Gabriela Mistral was complicit with the state-sponsored monumentalization of her figure, such strategies of accommodation would be a means of coping with her vulnerability as a self-educated, lower-middle-class woman from the provinces who lacked any family or marital advantages. The complex and contradictory relationship between Gabriela Mistral and the Chilean government did not end with her retirement form the public schools. In her decades of service representing Chile and/or Latin America in various international organization, and in her intracontinental lecture tours, newspapers and local intellectuals greeted her as a semi-official speaker on behalf of education. Yet the categories of "normalista" and "lyric poet," which permitted her access to literary life, scarcely correspond to the identity as a rural Latin American woman that she emphasized after she left Chile. In the end she was an autodidact rather than a "normalista," and her writing career was as anchored in journalism as in the lyric.

Mistral was living in Mexico when *Desolación*, her first volume of poetry, was published, bearing a prologue (probably written by Federico de Onís) that represented the poet as an "unknown" rustic. This characterization, combined with the fictions of the poet's personal modesty and devotion to children, enduringly established the terms of Gabriela Mistral's fame. Although she was indeed "known" and well-recognized among educators, the "unknown" characterization played down the possibility of any threat to the status quo. It was in this context that her praisers and promoters described her in terms overtly intended to recall the Virgin Mary, and her male contemporaries honored and recommended her aesthetic as suited to women readers. For all their enthusiasm for Mistral's work as based in a strict moral code, Federico de Onís and Pedro Prado praised her work without adopting that aesthetic in their own writing.

More than any other aspect of the poet's lifelong production, a single section of less than two dozen short lyric poems (out of some 120 items in *Desolación*) has constituted the base for the narrative construction of the poet's life that has continued up to the present day. Drawing from the group of poems subtitled "Dolor," which are dedicated "a su sombra," that pseudobiographical narrative reads the poems as an "historieta," a soap-operatic account of how the poet, an innocent country girl, is betrayed by a young man, first after he degrades their chaste love by engaging in a consensual physical relationship with another woman, and subsequently when he kills himself in despair over what he has become.

It is impossible to underestimate the impact, extension, and durability of the "historieta" narrative, which, as Palma Guillén observes, derives from male fantasy:

> Los comentadores (no sé cuántos libros y artículos se han escrito sobre G. M. machacando sobre esta imagen que tan satisface el orgullo varonil) nos imponen la silueta simplificada de una mujer haciéndose pedazos al borde de un sepulcro en un amor único y terrible. Seguramente esos comentadores han soñado con un amor así para ellos mismos y han querido una mujer así—parecida a una fuerza de la Naturaleza—que se destroza en un nudo fatal de amor y muerte del que ellos mismos son motivo y objeto.[1]

The "historieta" narrative holds that the anger and bitterness of *Desolación* arises from the poet's frustrated longing for womanly fulfillment, because the suicide of this young man to whom she is eternally pledged denies her the (male) child for whom she longs. Here the clichés of feminine sanctity enter to counter the image of a barren, old maid with no sexual interest in men. To account for the various positive depictions of rural women in the countryside, which stand in contrast to the poet's first-person allusions to suffering and a generalized, unspecified desire, the conventional interpretation stipulates that Mistral's social consciousness is an attempt to transcend the visceral pain, "the melancholy sting of infertility" (Díaz Arrieta 1946). The evidence of Mistral's early journalism indicates, however, that the 1909 suicide of her real-life acquaintance, Romelio Ureta, had little if anything to do with Mistral's supposed "turn" to writing on behalf of children and mothers.

The topics of education and childhood, as well as the inclination to melancholy, are hallmarks of her writing from as early as 1905. One wishes for more careful studies like Scarpa's, of the extant multiple drafts of poems: he shows the author of *Desolación* as having deliberately constructed a "single love" bio-mythography. When further paired with the external evidence of the personal correspondence, the internal evidence of the drafts indicates the fictiveness of the "autobiography" of *Desolación*. The poetic representation of a "single love" therein is a unifying element permitting an extended commentary on desire, suffering, and death, viewed from a perspective resolutely outside and beyond heterosexual engagement.

Seen in this light, the prose poems of *Desolación* present a consciously elaborated statement of the poet's aesthetic and moral intentions that further belies the simplified historieta and its supposedly leading the poet into a quasi-maternal "renunciation." As in *Tala* ("Muerte de mi Madre") and *Lagar* ("Locas mujeres," "Hospital") Mistral puts together poems in series that posit the confluence of desire and pain. Like the "Locas mujeres" of *Lagar,* the prose poems in *Desolación* depict a variety of situations that pose the origins of speech in the quality of woundedness. Suffering is key to the ability to apprehend beauty. Her "Decálogo del artista" is explicit: whether male or female, artists are a special caste. The artist's immersion in the life of the imagination offers a sensory experience vastly superior to the grotesque impersonality of heterosexual desire:

Una canción es una herida de amor que nos abrieron las
cosas. A tí, hombre basto, sólo te turba un vientre de mujer,

el montón de carne de la mujer. Nosotros vamos turbados,
nosotros recibimos la lanzada de toda belleza del mundo,
porque la noche estrellada nos fue amor tan agudo como un
amor de carne.[2]

More than the capacity of suffering sets Mistral's aesthetic universe apart. As in the writing of so many women in the early twentieth century, the narrating or speaking voice is situated outside, looking in on, witnessing scenes of passion and betrayal. This stance, which critic Alberto Sandoval Sánchez and others in the feminist collection *Una Palabra Complice* describe as "voyeurism," emphasizes the speaker's or speakers' conscious psychic distance and dissimilarity from those they watch. Like others in the generation of Chilean writers to which she belonged, Gabriela Mistral anthropomorphized the natural world, but she differs from them in that her concentration on suffering, evident in *Desolación* and constant throughout her work, stipulates that love takes the whole body and soul, and hungry for more is synonymous with pain.

The series *Poemas de las madres* (written in 1920) hints at the possibility of erotic satisfaction. Rather than the generalized pantheism so often attributed to Mistral, these prose poems individually and as a whole propose a specifically female sensory experience of "infinite sweetness" that the poet associates with a creativity antithetical to the patriarchal family, marriage, and heterosexuality. The language of semimystical speech is Mistral's language of love, minus the threat of violence. Like so many of her contemporaries, Mistral's interest in theosophy and spiritualism made of these an alternative space, an arena for philosophical conjecture independent of the entrenched conservatism of the church.

Multiple references to suffering and "the intimate wound" are the most definitive aspect of Mistral's poetic production, as Jaime Concha has pointed out. Guzmán and others have wanted to take these as symptomatic of female jealousy toward the philandering male lover, with feelings of guilt and betrayal intervening consequent to his suicide. Such a "biographical" approach diminishes to "individual neurosis" the poet's multiple expressions of rage.

Some aspects of Mistral's poetry, such as her ongoing preoccupation with femininity as a visceral experience of blood and breast, entrails, flesh, bone, and milk, pose the very deepest challenge to feminists, as does her vehement insistence on desire as a wound. In *Desolación* her concentrated attention to the physical traces of that wound is bound up in specifically feminine self-representations. Yet in *Desolación* and *Ternura,* Mistral's seeming preoccupation with the theme of motherhood, her evocations of gestation and the mother-infant relation, show her claiming those aspects of the female body that least interested male writers of her day. Her celebrating maternity is among other things a pretext for an eroticism concentrated on the female and utterly devoid of masculine influence. At her most utopian, Mistral evokes the body of the mother to construct "woman" as an identity at once subsumed by, yet radically separate from, the corporeal experience of maternity.

After *Desolación,* the emphasis on the female body continues in the major aesthetic statements appearing in the introduction to *Lecturas para mujeres,* and in "Colofón con cara de excusa" (printed in the 1945 edition of *Ternura*). In her "Recuerdo de la madre ausente" (1923) as in her lullabies, the female body is named—breast, arm, milk—as the source for women's authority as namers, readers, singers, and tellers of subversive tales. The verses that she chose for *Ternura* (1925, 1945) continue to assert as primary the physical experience of woman as depicted from a female subjectivity. *Ternura,* the most widely reprinted of Mistral's volumes, is in some sense directed toward children even as that "writing for children" offers a pretext for positing a sensibility at times erotic (in the lullabies) and at times political (in the rondas). The erotic and the political frames Mistral's explicit statement that her lullabies are intended, first and foremost, "to serve the emotion" of other Latin American women: "Love without words is a knot, and it strangles."

After the flourishing intellectual scene in Chile, the next significant context for Mistral's intellectual development occurred with her participation in the educational reform program of José Vasconcelos in postrevolutionary Mexico, from 1921 to 1923. Palma Guillén, whom Vasconcelos designated to assist Mistral on her arrival in Mexico, is a reliable source with respect to Mistral's activities touring the Mexican countryside, setting up rural schools and libraries, and compiling *Lecturas para mujeres*. Guillén avoids the impressionism of other contemporary accounts of Mistral's activities, even as she declares her solidarity with Mistral against a relentlessly hostile world: "Pobre Gabriela, tan maltratada, tan injustamente atacada y tan sola siempre!" (Poor Gabriela, so mistreated, so unjustly attacked and always so alone!)

Leaving Mexico following the furor of her having a school named after her with her statue in the courtyard, Mistral traveled to Europe. From Europe she sent some essays about writers and artist she had met, which were published in Chile's leading newspaper, *El Mercurio*. Following a visit to Assisi, she also started, at this time, a series of *Motifs of Saint Francis*. On her return to Chile in late 1924, she found that her relations toward many of Chile's leading intellectuals had substantially changed. In letters to Eduardo Barrios and statements to the press she indicated a desire to distance herself from Santiago and any kind of regular contact with the literati. She resigned her position in the school system, having served it twenty years. She also returned to La Serena, and bought a house, where she intended to start a small escuela-granja, along the Rousseauian principles of Belgian educator Decroly. But she received in late 1925 an appointment to serve in Europe as a representative to the Paris and Geneva-based League for Intellectual Co-operation, a division of the League of Nations. She would be a key member of the Latin American section, and would work alongside other internationally renowned writers in producing publications, translations, films, and the like. It is not clear that Mistral went with complete willingness, and that she might have preferred, as she later put it, to stay with her aged mother. Feeling unable to decline the post, she left Chile at the end of 1925 with no idea of when she would return.

This departure was definitive: from 1925 onward, she only returned to Chile for two very brief visits. Working in international organizations was not particularly remunerative, and at one point the government suspended her pension entirely, a situation that probably motivated her trip, in 1930, to the United States, where she taught at Barnard College. Her new and growing consciousness of a specifically Latin American identity, which might have begun during her first stay in Mexico, took on an additional dimension as she prepared to teach about pre-Columbian civilizations and about Alfonso Reyes, whose work she admired immensely. From New York she went on to a highly successful lecture tour of Central America and the Caribbean, where she further consolidated her increasingly anticolonialist, anti-imperialist posture, writing in favor of Sandino and in defense of Puerto Rico, for example.

In letters to Alfonso Reyes she complained about having to write essays for periodicals, to support herself, but Mistral's journalism of the late twenties and early thirties is a valuable index to her continuing intellectual development. The study of this journalism, along with various collections of letters and documents, is necessary for filling in the gaps in what is known about the day-to-day details of Mistral's life from the time that she took up residence in France in 1925. By contrast, the letters dating from her residence in Chile are valuable for showing the writer experimenting with varieties of prose. Present-day readers tempted to discern in Mistral's correspondence some "truer" version of the self will find that the self depicted therein is as wittingly "constructed" as in any of her poetry or journalism, as Mistral's so-called love letters, primarily to Chilean poet Manuel Magallanes Moure, written from about 1914 to 1921, strongly indicate. She engages a variety of self-representations—poor but honorable country girl, shy poetess, distant intellectual, stood-up date, to name just a few—which all lead away from physical intimacy with the male addressees.

In contrast to the heavily edited, yet fascinating letters that Mistral wrote to Magallanes Moure, the letters that she wrote during the years of residence and travel in Europe and the Americas present a rich portrait of the writer as having built a life beyond the familial boundaries that defined the lives of the vast majority of women. Her extensive correspondence is of particular interest for understanding her relation to other writers, her letters to Cuban writer Lydia Cabrera being a case in point. Her letters deal primarily with the failing health of their mutual friend Teresa de la Parra, a Venezuelan writer who was Cabrera's inseparable companion. In contrast to Mistral's published correspondence with famous men—Mexican writer Alfonso Reyes, the Costa Rican editor García Monje, and Chilean novelist Eduardo Barrios—the letters to Lydia Cabrera present the poet's unstinting adoration of the dying Teresa de la Parra. Absent from the letters to Cabrera are the feelings of mistrust and betrayal that appear in Mistral's correspondence with other writers, who published or permitted third parties to publish her letters without her consent, with consequences occasionally disastrous to Mistral. It seems that Cabrera knew to protect that trust, but not others: Mistral's attempts to maintain friendship with Cabrera were strained by her bitter disappointment with the Cuban-born writer's upper-class milieu of society ladies, and by Cabrera's failure to answer Mistral's letters.

In 1933 a special act of the Chilean legislature mandated for Gabriela Mistral a consular post with the right to choose her own residence. This somewhat regularized her financial situation. Although the position was unsalaried, she was able to collect a percentage of the various fees paid to the consulate, which allowed her to slow the frantic pace of her journalism and devote more of her time to writing poetry. Initially she went to live in Naples, but either her antifascism or her gender made her unacceptable to the Italian authorities. Her residence in Madrid came to an end with the publication in Chile of a private letter in which she had expressed opinions highly critical of Spain's people and politics. Following a move to Lisbon and the disastrous impact of the Spanish civil war in the Basque country, Mistral in 1938 published *Tala,* her second major volume of verse. Fascism, the civil war, the hostilities in other parts of Europe, all contributed to Mistral's return to Latin America, but Mistral's tour of Argentina, Chile, and Peru, her first in thirteen years, convinced her that the situation there was not much better: as she described in a letter to Marta Samatan, "hunger and filth I saw, Marta, to make you cry."

The publishing house Sur, directed by the Argentine Victoria Ocampo, underwrote the costs associated with *Tala.* Ocampo's contribution through subsidizing the enterprise, and Palma Guillén's, in editing the volume, which Mistral dedicated to her, contrast with the Instituto de las Españas publication of *Desolación* sixteen years earlier. Where Mistral had appeared under the auspices and through the agency of various men—Pedro Aguirre Cerda, Eduardo Barros, and Federico de Onís—now she was brought forth by women.

In *Tala* the death of the poet's mother in 1928 becomes the occasion for a series of "nocturnos"—that is, night poems—dealing with death, and of grave-side meditations. The last of these, "Lapida Final," ranges over the body of the dead mother, putting the memory of breasts, eyes, lap, and hand in the context of a "vast and holy symphony" of old mothers. Mistral's notes, published as an appendix to *Tala,* suggest that the last poem of the series, a plegaria, redeems the series as a whole, which she sees as representing the "fruits of pain." Where earlier interpretations have settled on the image of the pious, suffering daughter, Sylvia Molloy convincingly argues that matricide, linked to the poet's self-representation as a wanderer, establishes the condition of exile and haunted return from which the poet speaks, not just in *Tala,* but in nearly all of Mistral's later work. The project of creating a consciously female-authored poetry proceeds from the necessity of escaping or abandoning the physical world. Poem after poem moves past a range of female ghosts into a dream world of liberatory solitude ("La Fuga," "La Flor del Aire," "Todas ibamos a ser reinas.")

Mistral's pre-1938 publications from Europe suggest some of the other, diverse subjects that she took up in *Tala*. She drew from those aspects of European culture that she saw as particularly relevant to Latin Americans. Popular education was one such preoccupation; the development of crafts and folk culture was another. She was drawn all her life to "heroic biography" and thus in her travels sought out, often to her disappointment, those writers, artists, and intellectuals whose work appealed to her conviction that art and education could bring transcendence.

The clarity and occasional colloquial language of Mistral's prose from the late 1920s and 1930s, and of the poetry in *Tala,* form a strong contrast to the tendency to archaism and twisted syntax in *Desolación.* It could be that writing for the complex audience of children, teachers, and school administrators made her surer of her prose, or that journalism was a means of exploring, outside of the trance that meter can impose, what most passionately involved her. These years found her utterly absorbed in the poet's most pressing task of positing the construction and fragmentation of identity, which Mistral approached from her perspective of an outsider working around an often indifferent or hostile medium.

Although Mistral's international and diplomatic activities were a significant aspect of her fame, the dialectic of personal with national and continental identity is in Mistral's work a very complex problem. With a well-founded suspicion of nationalism in *Lecturas para mujeres* and elsewhere, she came close to declaring that the spirit of patriotism did not exist, as such, in women. Nostalgia not for the "patria," but for the "patria chica," for the land of her birth, motivates much of her verse. In distinction to her verses, her prose was often effectively a form of public relations, part of her job as a professional writer and Chilean consul at a time when Chile had a leadership role, a high visibility, among Latin American nations.

Mistral's compulsion to travel is a quality that some writers have regarded as particularly Chilean. Even if that were the case, her restlessness was tied to definitive aspects of her personality, whether hypersensitivity to negative feelings toward her or her delight in landscape. Her pleasure in walking strange streets and being a guest in borrowed rooms gave her new eyes with which to look on an unfamiliar horizon.

Although Mistral in 1939 had intended to establish her residence in Nice, amid the deteriorating situation in Europe and her departure for Brazil she had already begun work on two collections of poetry, *Lagar* ("Wine-Press") and *Poema de Chile* ("Poem of Chile"). Each of these collections signaled wholly new directions, not just within her work, but for writers throughout Latin America. In consequence of her relative isolation in Brazil, her being able to maintain contacts with friends through her always prolific correspondence, and an editing project she undertook for a U.S.-based publisher, she returned to the wide and serendipitous reading that was central to her creativity. Living in Brazil when she became the first Latin American to receive the Nobel Prize for literature, Mistral's acceptance of the 1945 prize "on behalf of all workers for Latin American culture" acknowledged her immersion in that culture as the determining condition of her work.

During her final years (1945–57), Gabriela Mistral worked simultaneously on two books of poetry, her volume *Lagar* and the posthumously edited *Poema de Chile* (1967) while she moved between Mexico, California, Italy, and New York. As the last volume that the poet published in her lifetime, *Lagar* was barely noted when it first appeared, in 1954, coinciding with her final visit to Chile. The enormous number of homages published at the time of that visit and then following her death in 1957 concentrate on relating the poetry from prior to 1938 to Mistral's public figure. Prior to the advent of feminist criticism in Chile, critics who mentioned *Lagar* at all generally described it as willfully hermetic and excessively difficult. Interpretations of *Lagar* in the earlier mold of Mistral's personal piety, spirituality, and vague philosophical leanings are, for the most part, inadequately theorized, or follow ideological convenience. The tragic self-representations of *Lagar,* particularly in the very powerful series *Locas mujeres,* are very different from the didactic, strongly narrative romance of *Poema de Chile.* Yet both are premised on speech that begins with a shedding of identity. That loss of self is the premise for Mistral's asexual stance as a prophet of destruction, in *Lagar,* or ecological doom, in *Poema de Chile.*

Although the figure of Gabriela Mistral was adapted to a range of political exigencies during her lifetime, with her death in 1957 her image became a fixture in public art. The "floating Gabriela" that appears in Chilean stamps, murals, bank notes, and photo homages is a disembodied head in profile, or a transparent, tutelary spirit superimposed over or against that of an adult woman with one or more children. In the appropriation of Gabriela Mistral's figure for explicitly political, nationalistic purposes, she becomes a site for positing a timeless, inborn identity—national, racial, sexual, with the specific image being a function of the target constituency. In distinction to the somewhat youthful, populist image of the "saintly schoolteacher," regimes seeking to shore up their prestige abroad invoked her as "Latin America's cultural ambassador, the Nobel Queen." In more unstable or transitionary regimes she is especially liable to appear as a loyal traveler who roams the world while remaining mindful of her origins. In these referents of the schoolteacher, the ambassador-queen, and the loyal citizen-at-large (all reified in the verses and mini-biography that some four generations of Chilean schoolchildren have been assigned to memorize) "Gabriela Mistral" is, as Soledad Bianchi has wisely put it, "almost a synonym of sexual ambiguity, with her cropped hair, her long robes, and her seldom shaving." That sexual ambiguity is less an acknowledgment of lesbian possibility than a negotiated space in which the de-sexed queen is a female man. The Mistral of nationalist reduction mediates between the state and Woman as producer of future citizens.

Depicting Mistral as a secularized Madonna grew less attractive with age. Some ten years after a death that otherwise sober chronologies describe as an "apotheosis," critics published evidence of her paranoia and suggested that she was arteriosclerotic. The later 1970s saw an ambitious program of publication of several volumes of Mistral's prose, less because Gabriela Mistral was popular than because the right-wing dictatorship sought in her a safe contrast to the political inconvenience of Chile's "other" Nobel laureate, Pablo Neruda, affiliated with the Communist Party. By the 1980s, cultural critics seeking to escape the perceived limitations of the "poetess" were turning to the rich, complex body of Mistral's prose. With the turn toward her prose, the cult of Gabriela Mistral may be coming full circle, but returning her to a more-inclusive notion of the historical. Assertions of Mistral's mestizaje and her complex political and class allegiances are replacing earlier characterizations of Mistral as a remote "descendant of conquistadors." Her seemingly strange political pronouncements are being reread as her shrewd manipulation of her later image as a distracted old lady. These explorations of ideological issues in Mistral's intellectual development establish a precedent for the interrogation of sexual identity in Mistral's public figure. Just as it took critics and historians with allegiances and identifications marginal to those of Chile's cultural status quo during the Pinochet era to pinpoint Mistral's mestizaje, it will take a feminist criticism likewise working from a consciously "minority" or dissenting perspective to challenge the tendency to locate Mistral in relation to a male desire that is patently irrelevant to her stated primary interests and to her positing a specifically female subjectivity.

A way of getting beyond the limitations of traditional life-and-work approaches, and to avoid as well the reduction that results from trying to pin Gabriela Mistral to a given cultural milieu, is to emphasize instead the immensely protean quality of her practice as an artist. Having become proficient, while yet in her teens, at writing long, meditative, intimist poetry and prose, she went on to work at length in the sonnet, a form in which she excelled, taking

Agustini's cue and twisting the language of Darío to its limits. Even as she was perfecting intricate rhymes and rhythms in the sonnet and in other lyric verse, she was writing didactic poetry for use in the schools. Preeminent as a writer of seemingly simple lullabies, she also excelled in historical biography, whether in her colloquial prose "Recados" or in the elegiac verse portraits grouped under this same title. At the same time as she was developing the lyric personae of the series *Locas mujeres* in *Lagar,* depicting the length and breadth of various possibilities of absolute loss for women in the twentieth century, she was writing the almost medieval *Poema de Chile,* a narrative, didactic poem with extended characterization, dialogue, and description. No sooner did she become accomplished in one form did she move on to another.

In contrast to taking the life and work of Gabriela Mistral as a pretext for positing various clichés about what is feminine, it is useful to observe Mistral's verse as manifesting a transgressive consciousness. Recent feminist interpretation explores in Mistral's work the possibility of multiple, coexisting identities in women, identities that the Chilean Raquel Olea and Argentine Sylvia Molloy both link with the "unspeakable" identity of the lesbian. With Olea and Molly I would argue for bringing to the surface what is glancingly implied about Mistral's sexual identity in a variety of print insinuations. It is certain that the poet's friendships with women were at the center of her daily life, and that her emotional intimacy with women sustained her through her deepest crises, whether the invidious attacks in Chile, her mother's death and the suspension of her pay which left her fundless in Europe, or her adopted son's apparent suicide.

Rather than seeking to uncover a hidden or private Mistral, we need to interrelate the diplomat and this woman who witnessed firsthand some extraordinary and important transitions in the intellectual history of Latin America, and to correlate these with the woman who joked, drank scotch, and smoked cigarettes endlessly, who raised from infancy an adopted child and prescribed herbal cures to exceedingly cerebral men and women of letters. I like to think of her as a guest comfortably taking tea with Unamuno in Hendaye and maté with Victoria Ocampo in Mar de Plata, of her sitting in silence, unfooled by the posturings of Diego Rivera, of her towering disheveled and hatless alongside the well-coifed and girdled Storni and Ibarbourou. I am melancholy with how the would-be biographers worked her over and admiring of her patience with the readers who unwittingly brought her pirated editions for her to sign for them, which she did. Above all I like to see her writing atop a board stretched across her knees, scrawling in pencil on the cheapest grade of paper, endlessly revising, transforming the material legacy of the language that would be her only homeland.

Violeta Parra:
SINGER OF LIFE

INÉS DÖLZ-BLACKBURN

⌒ BORN: OCTOBER 4, 1917, San Carlos, Ñuble, southern Chile. *Died:* February 5, 1967, Santiago, Chile. *Father:* Nicanor Parra, elementary teacher and musician. *Mother:* Clarisa Sandoval, homemaker and seamstress. *Brothers:* Nine, the most famous one, Nicanor Parra, a poet who won Mexico's Rulfo Award for Literary Excellence, 1991. *Children:* Isabel (1937), Angel (1941), Carmen Luisa (1950), and Rosita Clara (1952–54). Divorced: 1948, Luis Cereceda; 1949, Luis Arce. 1960, meets the Swiss minstrel Gilbert Favré, a companion of many years. *Activities:* Poet, folklorist, composer, singer, folk collector, potter, painter, teacher, entertainer, weaver, producer, scriptwriter, etc. Author of *Décimas de Violeta Parra: Autobiografía en versos* (1970), innumerable song-poems, *Poésie populaire des Andes* (1965), and *Cantos folklóricos chilenos* (1979). 1964: Louvre Museum in Paris, a solo exhibition of *arpilleras* (original embroideries with social motifs and paintings and wire sculptures).

THE LEGACY

*Violeta has not died. She only
took away her life*

*. . . write as you wish. Use all the rhymes which come to your
mind, try diverse instruments, sit down to the piano, destroy
the metre, liberate yourself, scream instead of singing, blow
the guitar and tune the horn. The song is a bird which will
never fly in a straight line; it is a bird without a flight plan: it
hates mathematics and loves whirls.*
—Rodríguez, *Cantores*

On February 6, 1967, on the front page of all of Santiago's newspapers, sensational news stirs the city: Violeta Parra, the woman
of the people who conquered Paris and revived the Chilean folklore, unburying melodies and old lyrics, has committed suicide,
shooting herself in the left temple.[1] Acquaintances and family members make remarks about the tragedy. A magistrate in La Reina declares that only Saturday the artist mumbled: "I am sick with sadness." Her current companion, Alberto Zapicán, affirms with
bewilderment that they were planning to visit Argentina the following week and then tour Europe, where they had a series of engagements. Eduardo Parra, a brother, believes that Violeta was suffering from some kind of a nervous breakdown aggravated by
financial problems, and the fact that the La Reina tent, the artistic, cultural, and commercial center in which the artist had invested
all her energies and economic resources, was a failure.

Since her return from Europe eighteen months earlier, people
had noticed in her a tendency to isolate herself and a profound re-
verse in her personality in the form of sudden mood changes. Frequent allergies and rashes all over her body, insomnia, sudden impulses to disperse her creative energy, followed by apathy and
lethargy, worried her friends and family. The breaking up of a
cherished relationship with the Swiss minstrel Gilbert Favré, whom

she had met in 1960, was believed to be one part of the problem. Another factor was her belief that she had lost the popularity she had enjoyed for so long. Besides, her neighbors in La Reina antagonized her and wanted her tent to be moved away, thinking it was a source of fights and commotion in the new, respectable suburb. Finally, it worried her that the place, far away from downtown, had a fluctuating audience. Rage and frustration possessed the artist. In the meantime, Isabel and Angel, two of her children, succeeded with a downtown Peña Folklórica in which the chic and the powerful got together steadily.

In the following weeks and in the years after her death, the Chilean newspapers continuously covered details of her successes in Europe, where she sang, painted, composed, sculptured, and experimented in pottery and *arpilleras*. Also, articles focused on the solo exhibit of her art in the Louvre Museum in Paris (1964); on the substance and impact of hundreds of her folkloric songs and volcanic political ones; and on her recollection of folklore throughout Chile (she assembled about three thousand samples taken mostly from rural informants).

However, February 8, 1967, newspapers pointed mostly to her impact as a singer and folklorist. An impressive crowd attended the burial: artists, popular singers, the circus and folklorists unions, guitarists from all over the country, Centers of Mothers, a delegation of the Central Committee for Young Communists, her mother, her three children—Isabel, Angel, and Carmen Luisa—her brothers, relatives, and friends.

Also among the people in the cortège are actors of theater, radio, and television; the president of the Senate and the future president of Chile (1970–73), Dr. Salvador Allende; the poet Pablo de Rokha; the writer Ariel Dorfman; and union workers of all trades. In later editions, reviews of tributes in her memory appear adorned with references to her legacy to the Chilean folklore, her autodidaxia and the incompatibility of exceptional beings with their milieu. At the Catholic University, her brother, the world-renowned poet Nicanor Parra, officially donates to the institution seventeen of her *arpilleras,* six of her oil paintings, her guitar, harp, bass drum, some manuscripts, photos, and posters of her Louvre exhibit. Round tables, discussions of her work and contributions, recitals of her poetry, exhibits of her art flourish, especially around cultural institutions.

For the past ten years, the phenomenon of Violeta Parra has been an important topic in universities in Chile, Latin America, Europe, and the United States. The studies are centered on her cultural legacy and her decisive and important contribution to contemporary Latin American literature and women's rights. She is considered a leader for effective political and social changes, even in the rigid and intransigent patriarchal society to which she belonged, and at a time when a woman's voice and activism in a leadership capacity is still supposed to be ignored, and perhaps chastised.

For the masses, her figure has become a cult object, a myth equivalent to the one exercised around Eva Perón in Argentina. As Eva, Parra is considered the revolutionary voice of the voiceless, a miraculous being who listens, understands and gives, a powerful spirit who can be reached from beyond. Tearful pilgrimages to her grave by adoring followers are commented on by the media each February 6, along with religious gatherings and television and radio programs in her honor.

Among her literary production, the *Décimas autobiográficas en versos chilenos* (1970), with a dazzling and engaging introduction in verse form by Pablo Neruda, Nicanor Parra, and Pablo de Rokha, stands out. This work has been compared to *Martín Fierro,* the epic poem of José Hernández. As in this poem, so in *Décimas,* an individual of poor and humble origin defends eloquently and essentially her origin, authenticity, and right to be free and respected. In *Décimas,* Violeta is the rebellious being, the marginal woman struggling alone against injustice and the callous ignorance of her genius. Also, this work defines her as a social activist in function of the rights of women, education for children, struggle against alcoholism and corruption, and the affirmation of human and equal rights.

Her most popular musical compositions, *tonadas, cuecas, parabienes*—love songs most of them—are published in an anthologized form by Alfonso Alcalde in *Toda Violeta Parra* (1974). An eloquent and stimulating personal reflection about the artist (15–53) and a well-researched chronology of her life and work make this publication a must for the Parra scholar.

Juan Andrés Piña, in *Violeta Parra 21 son los dolores* (1978), accomplishes a similar task in skillfully assembling seventy-five of the most significant of Parra's love songs. In 1965, Maspero publishers in France had printed a few of them in bilingual form. Piña's anthology is more complete, more carefully researched and chosen, and with incisive and important notes for each song. This work, I believe, marks the acknowledgment of Violeta Parra as an important literary figure in contemporary Latin American letters. Some of the song-poems are Violeta's; others are arrangements, imitations, or have been corrected by her through an initial version collected in the country.

Cantos folklóricos chilenos (1979) is another posthumous publication. Parra interviews rural minstrels and collects from them traditional lyrics and melodies. This work is key to understanding her interaction with people she feels are close to her soul. The texts of the interviews describe how she relates to them, how she accepts and respects them. The approach is personal, casual, teasing, and affectionate. She records the songs given by the informant and records the encounter with a simple, colloquial, and easy-reading language portraying with fidelity and tenderness the singer and his/her surroundings. This book is fundamental for the evaluation of her prose and appreciation of her hidden warmth and humble traits of personality in her otherwise tempestuous, complex, and difficult character. "The submissive lamb disguised as a fox," as her brother Nicanor calls her in the famous introduction to *Décimas,* is perceived forcefully and comprehensively, and even poetically, in these descriptive vignettes.

Bernardo Subercaseaux and Jaime Londoño reconstruct the life and personality of Parra in *Gracias a la vida* (1981), basing their story on testimonies of people who knew her. Her emotional turmoils, difficult personality, inexhaustible creativity, and prodigious energy are commented on and discussed. Also evaluated and interpreted are her political and social activism, marriages, affairs, dislikes, and hates.

In the eighties, in the circles of artistic composition, her decisive role in the creation and growth of the "New Chilean Song" and the "New Song" in general is solidly reaffirmed. In this type of composition, the song is perceived as a social compromise focused on the problems and concerns of the marginal and dispossessed. In the filming world, music written by the artist for four film productions is analyzed, and a documentary made in Switzerland about the artist is promoted. Parra's paintings are extensively reviewed by renowned critics and art professors in *El Mercurio*, the leading Chilean newspaper. The comments are based on "Casamiento de negros," "Le Cantante calva," and "La cueca," among many others. Photographs of the paintings are shown. The reviewers consider them skillfully portrayed, and they call attention to the fact that Parra never had any training in this type of art. The paintings constitute a serious pondering on the same themes that permeate the rest of her work: tradition, men's and women's conflicts and concerns, peace, humanity, pain, joy, human rights, justice, etc.

Patricio Manns in *Violeta Parra, la guitarra indócil* (1986), remembers in numerous vignettes the friend of many years and the vital woman lightly and rapidly wandering throughout the world with the heavy burden of an uncontrollable creativity and an ardent passion for life.

Isabel Parra, the eldest daughter of Violeta, publishes in Spain another enlightened book on her: *El libro mayor de Violeta Parra* (1981). Numerous letters of Parra to the greatest love of her life, Gilbert Favré, appear in this work. Their trips and recitals in Chile, Latin America, and Europe, and the details of their feuds and reconciliations add new dimensions to the understanding of Violeta, the woman. These letters to Favré, relatives, and friends have allowed the critics to study in more depth her distinctive prose. A detailed chronology of Parra's life and work, a discography, and a compressed anthology of her most popular song-poems—including two in French—complete this important book, one of the closest and most intimate approaches to Violeta's personal and artistic crisis. *El libro mayor* defines her identity as artist, wife, mother, and lover and clarifies her social and political manifest.

Coming back to this past decade, we must ascertain that the sensationalistic, morbid, and melodramatic notes in the media about this extraordinary woman, so prevalent for many years, are less frequent. However, every now and then there is a proliferation of commentaries of some people's favorite themes, such as: the suicide and possible causes; the scrutiny and interpretation of her numerous love affairs; her grief over the death of her youngest daughter, for which she blamed herself; her beginnings as an artist in circuses and second-rate cantinas; her incursions in the country searching for traditional folklore; her first steps as a singer and composer in Radio Chilena, etc. Yet, having repeatedly exploited and squeezed, they no longer produce great impact or make "big" news. The picturesque and anecdotal vignettes about her unconventional behavior are also too well known; so are the testimonies of people who were close to her and the details of her eccentricities, real or invented.

Unfortunately, the political "vampirism" or the use of the Violeta phenomenon by many self-serving persons or entities in order to reach personal goals still persists. The magic of Parra's name persuades, inflames, and inspires the masses, and the politicians know it. The hysteria surrounding the myth produces *violetomanía*. For the *violetómanos*, Parra is the object of a true cult, and they identify themselves with this victim of a system struggling against it tenaciously, without ever conquering, to be finally defeated and destroyed by it. They perceive her as a lonely and solitary gifted being carrying constant sadness as a companion while paradoxically trying to perpetuate and spread joy and happiness to others. She is also the *animita* (spirit) from whom favors are usually granted.

A solid and contradictory profile, through the decades always the same, continues intriguing and perplexing old and new adepts: obstinate, generous, mutable, irascible, amiable, self-destructive, neurotic, and of a depressive nature, she loved Life but constantly was dazzled by Death.

As a composer, Violeta's song "Gracias a la vida" (Praise be to life)—a true ode to joy—included in the hit record "Las últimas canciones" (The last songs), is the song that has consolidated her fame in music. It is one of the most famous Latin songs ever recorded. The American-born Joan Baez, the Argentinean Mercedes Soza, and Violeta herself have communicated through the delicate and sensitive lyrics about the joy of living and loving. The record was cut twenty days prior to her suicide.

In the eighties and nineties, well-recognized intellectuals and critics from America and Europe[2] have carefully focused their attention on the sociohistoric significance of Parra's work, and have integrated her into the literary canon as a writer of foremost importance. Not neglected by these scholars, either, is the discussion of her legacy to the national and Latin American culture, and the projections of her art and genius, which have broken stereotypes and conventional parameters. The consensus is that she was born when she died. Her social conscience, they declare, emerges through a strong and irreverent voice that is, nevertheless, not dogmatic or in the domains of the pamphlet, because she skillfully universalizes and essentializes the humanitarian protest, in spite of the fact that her stance arises from her own world.

The influences on Parra's *Décimas* are perplexing. The critics discover connections with Francisco de Quevedo, San Juan de la Cruz, Federico García Lorca, the medieval minstrels, and the court's

"Cancioneros" from fifteenth- and sixteenth-century Europe. How could this self-taught rural and wild woman who lacked a formal education and was not a reader capture in her poetry the vein of this extraordinary literary corpus? That corpus, according to Parra's scholars, rests in the folkloric tradition she easily absorbed, collecting thousands of song-poems from the lips of humble depositaries in lost villages and hidden hamlets in her native Chile.

The scholars go even further, affirming that the stature of the artist is comparable to that of Gabriela Mistral and Pablo Neruda, both winners of Nobel Prizes for literature (1945 and 1971, respectively). On evaluating many of her musical compositions, they find tone and style similar to the folkloric melodies of Béla Bartók and Igor Stravinski.

In relation to the "Neopopulism Song," she is considered the creator. The Neopopulism Song is alien to the cute, sentimental, and stereotyped typical Chilean song, focused in the postcard figure of the peasant and its surroundings, that tries to incite patriotism. Although the New Song has the same objective, it adds a component of harmonious engagement and compromise between the worker and its milieu. Justice and humanity must be at the center of this fragile relationship. Violeta has promoted this creed, the essence of her social conscience, in the political songs.

When we come back to Parra as a literary giant, recent scholarship asserts that she belongs with the best in the panorama of twentieth-century literature in Latin America. There are extensive references to her original and distinctive voice and lyrics, her difficult simplicity, and the easiness and effectiveness with which she expresses the problems and concerns of people from all over the world in our times. Her voice not only illuminates and produces a deep awareness but also moves to act and/or to take a solid stand on the matter.

The first two books that have concentrated exclusively on Violeta Parra as a literary master in poetry and prose are: *Violeta Parra: Santa de pura greda. Un estudio sobre su obra poética* (1988) and *Violeta Parra o la expresión inefable. Un estudio de su poesía, prosa y pintura* (1992), by Marjorie Agosín and Inés Dölz-Blackburn. These studies are in-depth initiations into a virgin and complex field.

The power of Parra's word, her combative journey on behalf of "the other," her feminism and the conflicting profiles of her adepts and fans might be more perceptible with an extensive discussion of three of her works: *Décimas,* her letters (in Isabel Parra's *Libro Mayor de Violeta Parra*), and songs of love and social conscience, all with a strong, although different, aesthetic and emotional impact on the man of the street, the home, the factory, the cantina, and the university and artistic circles.

Nowadays, academicians, scholars, journalists, feminist groups, politicians, and social activists ponder from many angles the dimensions and value of these works. A historical and cultural context of great significance in the history of Chile is gleaned through these writings.

THE WORDS AND THE WORK
THE SONGS

The lyrics of the musical compositions of Violeta Parra vary in their message and tone.[3] A few are centered on fulfilled love, the most famous of these being "Gracias a la vida" and "Volver a los diecisiete" (On being seventeen again). There are hymns to the joy of life. Love is the force that makes the poet feel invincible, radiant, and playful. She absorbs and gazes with new eyes upon the world around her in these compositions.

The most numerous song-poems are the ones that focus on lovesickness, abandonment, despair, and grief. "La lavandera" (The laundress), "La Jardinera" (The jardinière), and "Run-Run se fue p'al Norte" (Run-Run left toward the North) are the better known in this group. The moaning and lamentation of the woman in pain are not strident or weeping. Mostly, they are a dignified, restrained, and somber monologue. Faith and Hope seem to prevail in spite of the present darkness in the soul. The singer/poet perceives in the distance the promise of a new dawn. The beauty of the verses relies mainly on the difficult simplicity and the skill for condensing the emotional turmoil in rich verses of universal appeal.

The poetical expression of social conscience is masterfully developed by the poet in a solid and powerful corpus. In these political songs, Parra attacks, denounces, and uncovers the wickedness of societies and systems in order to produce changes, reform, and awareness. Her instruments are humor, sarcasm, and occasional witty virulence. The verse is easy and fluid. The most popular political songs are: "Ayúdame, Valentina" (Help me, Valentina), "Me gustan los estudiantes" (I like students), "La carta" (The letter), "¿Qué dirá el Santo Padre?" (What is the Pope going to say?), and "Arauco tiene una pena" (Arauco has a sorrow). The poet, in these songs, is the voice of the voiceless, that is, the voice of the marginal people and the dispossessed. Priests, bureaucrats, lawyers, doctors, the indifferent rich, and the corrupt politician are hit with the powerful hammering of her verses.

All these song-poems are revealing of the cultural and historical context in which they were created, especially in relation to the situation and condition of the Chilean woman, and even the Third World woman. In their compressed and lyrical demureness, the verses express, with essentially conveyed beauty, the sorrows, problems, and grief these women carry as a daily burden. Joy in their life is rare and ephemeral. Pain does not defeat their spirits.

Men are portrayed in this important body of Parra's work either as mere shadows or as powerful forces. Nevertheless, in both cases, they unilaterally control the present and future state of affairs related to women and other social problems.

DÉCIMAS

In this autobiography in verse, we observe the socioeconomic and marginal structure of society through the eyes of a liberated woman of humble origins struggling to be recognized and heard by a patriarchal society.[4] As Gina Cánepa affirms, we also contemplate a forceful Parra trying to lighten a double marginality: the poor rural woman transferred to the city and the one of the ugly woman trying to triumph as an artist in a society that esteems beauty over the person.

In *Décimas* Violeta tells her life story up to the death of her daughter Rosita Clara in 1954. After a happy and idyllic childhood in a village close to Chillán, the family suffers a series of misfortunes. To name a few: one of her brothers dies; the father is fired by the fascist government of Carlos Ibáñez and becomes an alcoholic, a condition which contributes to his death; and Violeta becomes marked for life by a virulent smallpox that shows mostly on her face. The family is destitute, and its members go in separate ways. Violeta goes to the city and earns a living singing in bars after doing the same, for some time, with some of her siblings in itinerant circuses in small country villages.

Poverty and hunger teach young Violeta to be resourceful and self-sufficient. It shows in the *Décimas,* along with the beliefs, traditions, experiences of her life in the country, and some of the songs that she took from the family's repertory or learned while visiting peasants. With a simple and forceful voice, she expresses her solidarity with the feminine experience of the marginals: alcoholism, unwanted pregnancy, prostitution, single motherhood, physical and verbal abuse, workers' discrimination, children's victimization, abandonment, the conflict of the mother-worker-wife, women alone struggling for survival, etc. *Décimas,* in the light of this perspective, is an important social document.

In 1954, Parra is invited to the Festival of the Song in Poland. She goes, leaving behind a second husband and a small baby. In this section of the *Décimas,* in tormented verses, the poet describes an internal crisis: the one of a mother leaving children behind while trying to achieve personal fulfillment. Her anguish can be understood by any working mother. The trip signals liberation and the personal recognition of her talent as an artist.

When she returns to Chile after two years, the process of re-affirmation that she has been experiencing comes to a halt. There is guilt on facing the death of her baby daughter in her absence and a sense of defeat: her second marriage fails. Moreover, the memories of the first one, in which she was battered and tormented, are still with her. She immortalizes both of these experiences in the *Décimas*. The autobiography is interrupted here. A few poems deal with her mother, as a rock of ages, and her brother Nicanor, as a mentor and friend.

In essence, *Décimas* show Violeta Parra as an autonomous, self-made woman and artist and proves her literary stature as one of the most important individuals in the cultural field of the Hispanic world. A pioneer in so many artistic endeavors, she influenced vastly the core of the city while keeping her rural identity. Her works and her words are a painful journey into the feminine psyche, bringing revelations from a marginal point of view. These revelations are significant for the understanding of the Hispanic woman in Latin America.

THE LETTERS

The letters portray the pain and schism of a tortured and sensitive spirit harassed by many and contradictory demands.[5] Most of these letters are addressed to Gilbert Favré. Others are to her children, some friends, and members of her family.

On reading them, along with the personal vignettes by her daughter Isabel, we witness the poet's deep depressions, the torment of allergies that immobilized her, and the emotional conflict produced by the demands of men whom she loved but who attempted to separate her from the creative forces that ruled her life.

The feminine epistolary genre is considered by many critics a subgenre. It is not in the case of Violeta. The letters are a lyric and powerful journey into pain, anguish, and the insecurity produced by the belief in her own ugliness. The expression becomes universal in its eloquent essentiality. The *woman* is again the main subject, not in her doings and goings, but in the complexity and delicacy of her spirit and soul. The shadow of Death is cast throughout the fluid lines. Lyric metaphors, original imagery, and symbolisms, colloquial language and a certain naïveté reveal an extremely vulnerable being surrounded by a circle of solitude in a world she understands but *cannot* accept.

CONCLUSIONS

In Parra's song-poems, *Décimas,* and the letters, the liberated woman is the main character. Deep emotional and spiritual wounds are the price for attempting to break the secret code of the patriarchal society that cannot accept this liberation. Mother, wife, worker, friend, and a visionary empowered with social and political responsibilities, she is overwhelmed by the weight of so many roles and the overt ignorance of her creativity and genius. This forceful portrait of a tormented, gifted woman stirs and inflames the reader and generally forces us to reexamine postures, sense of values, and beliefs and attitudes conducive to the establishment of new rules of fair behavior and action. Through this redeeming journey, a new perception of women's psyche and conflicts emerges. Once again, the power and the magic of the Word leads to new and higher elevations; in this case, deeper understanding and compassion for "the other" and others.

Violeta seemed to live for Truth and Love. Death caught her after a joyful envisioning of a new day conveyed through some refreshing and premonitory words written on the day prior to her end. Truth and Love are the central motifs in the brief passage, along with her passion for Life:

> . . . the essence of Truth is what I have tried to convey for so
> long and now I am going to sing with all the strength I am
> able to project from Geneve to Til-Til, from Helsinki to
> Montevideo and I shall pursue that singing as long as the

morning-star sheds light . . . I'll see you tomorrow, partner, I can hardly keep my eyes open; the ink is almost announcing that everything has an end . . . only three more lines, the lights are disappearing within my head, curtains shadow my mind I'll see you tomorrow or perhaps the day after tomorrow, because today is Saturday and it is raining tomorrow will be another day we shall see what is in the making.
  —(PARRA, *LIBRO MAYOR,* 145–46)

Violeta wrote this poem on a Saturday. On Sunday, she took her life away. The first line of the poem, perhaps unconsciously on her part, announces her intention:

Ordeno la despedida, señores y caballeros
(I am ordering a farewell, ladies and gentlemen).[6]

7

Cecilia Ansaldo:
WOMAN BETWEEN THE PRIVATE
AND PUBLIC SPACE

PATRICIA VARAS

⌐ ECUADOR IS A SMALL AND SELDOM-HEARD-OF COUNTRY on South America's Pacific coast. Rich and diverse, it has four distinct regions: the Oriente, or Amazonic region, to the east; the Andean region, or Sierra, in the center; the Coast, or Costa, to the west; and the Galapagos Islands. These regions are so different that you get the feeling you are visiting four countries with little in common.

The port city of Guayaquil, on the south coast, is the main commercial city of the country and, today, it may be larger than the capital, Quito. Guayaquil is a hot, frenzied, and even violent city. Life is hectic and difficult, and at the same time dynamic. Guayaquil traps its citizens in a way that is difficult to understand. A young chronicler of the city, Jorge Martillo Monserrate, has said:

> Eres tan hermosamente cruel que cuando te quiero odiar, asesinar, darte las espaldas y escapar de tus feudos, me atrapas y obligas a escribirte esta pública declaración de amor (*El Universo* 1992).
>
> (You are so beautifully cruel that when I want to hate you,

kill you, turn my back and run away from you, you entangle
and force me to write to you this public confession of love.)

It is in Guayaquil that Cecilia Ansaldo has lived, studied, and
worked all her life. She claims that "Guayaquil is a superficial and
aggressive city" in which she lives and has developed her career
and self, which manage to survive because she is also aggressive.
However, Cecilia is not superficial at all, and here is where the
struggle to gain a public and private space begins.

Cecilia, today, is one of Ecuador's key literary and cultural critics. Of course, this did not come easy. Cecilia teaches and is the
principal of the Alemán Humboldt School. Among other administrative and teaching positions, she also teaches Spanish, literary
theory, and Spanish American and Ecuadorian literature and has
been dean in the Faculty of Philosophy, Literature, and Educational Sciences in the Catholic University, her alma mater. She has
taken various postgraduate courses and traveled to Spain with a
scholarship, where she acquired her degree as professor of Spanish
language and literature.

Considering her time constraints, the quality and quantity of
her work as a writer and speaker in the cultural life of the city is
surprising. Cecilia has written many essays, anthologies, and in-
troductions, primarily on Ecuadorian literature. Today there are
many writers who ask her to launch his/her books or to comment
on them. Newspapers and magazines gladly give her space for
book and cultural reviews. She has been writing since 1990 with a
group of women, Mujeres del Atico, an editorial column in Guayaquil's oldest newspaper, *El Telégrafo*. Cecilia has also organized
many cultural programs. Among them, Dialogues with a Writer, a
successful series carried out with the Alliance Française. Once
again through this effort, Cecilia showed her commitment to in-
crease the Ecuadorian public's knowledge of Ecuadorian literature.

Her passion for research and thought is complemented by her
love for teaching both at high school and university levels. She en-

joys teaching advanced grammar because she believes that it is a tool for knowledge and that "getting into the labyrinths of grammar has given mental order to my thoughts, and swiftness to my expression."

Cecilia's commitment to her work, her rigorous training, and her demanding attitude toward all who surround her are qualities that have left an imprint in the work of this critic, teacher, academic, and administrator. This is the most visible side of her public persona. Another side, which is there to be discovered because she does not pretend to hide it, is her informal and candid self. Cecilia is up-to-date on rock music, comics, and soap operas. This makes her very popular among her young students. Her knowledge on soap operas, especially Brazilian ones, is part of her interest in popular culture and how it takes a form that ia attractive to so many. Cecilia likes to break the dress code as much as possible, she prefers jeans over anything else, and she has a huge t-shirt collection that keeps growing.

Her public persona is eagerly sought by all, exercising pressures that have meant sacrifices. The main one is her time. Cecilia writes poetry, though it has not come to light. She reads at late hours. In one of her columns she writes that it took her three months to finish a book. She likes to travel, but this must wait. Time is her ally and her enemy: her intellectual interests must take place in an "anguished struggle with time." Furthermore, the need to juggle all these jobs and activities respond to an economic need that is not always rewarded. To be a critic, a writer, a cultural promoter is an unpaid profession in Ecuador. It is impossible to live off these activities, therefore Cecilia must take on many chores to make ends meet. And "luxuries," such as buying books and records, are ill afforded.

Cecilia's choice of work is not the easiest in a city where cultural life is minimum, where people are concerned with surviving and making money, where society is very conservative and wants "things to be as we were told they should be"—that is, there is no revision or questioning of cultural patterns or traditions. Cecilia, like a Sor

Juana, is placed in a site and time that is not of her choice. Cecilia likes to think, to inquire, and she is a hard worker. Her students constantly tell her to "do not think so much." But this is her primary task, a contemplative attitude that is not necessarily understood nor freely expressed because she cannot write "all what she thinks."

Today our critic continues her work. Last time I talked to her she was losing her voice, a recurrent problem that hits her whenever she overdoes it. I would like to present her struggle in Guayaquil and Ecuador as one full of pain and loneliness, but I am afraid that I discovered more contradictions than I expected. Contradictions that are born from a sexist, chaotic, and unruly society that, nevertheless, allows space for a public persona to develop more freely than anticipated.

I do believe, however, that Cecilia's situation is unique. She has managed to create out of luck, out of particular opportunities, out of sheer effort and discipline a space where her voice is awaited, where her opinions are listened to, where her suggestions are followed through. I would like to study briefly the public and private spheres in Cecilia's life as projects that shape her life, and as spaces that she has successfully created or not as the case should be.

I think that to write about women's cultural and artistic contributions in Latin America requires a double awareness: that of the social, political, and historical circumstances that make the public space that the artist inhabits, and that of the personal life of the woman, her dreams, relationships, and silences that are her private space. This double bind allows for a more profound reading, especially when there are admitted differences among women and "circumstances in which women's emancipation is bound up with the fate of the larger community" (Franco 1989, xi). This need to strike a balance is especially important, because the individual who concerns us is a woman and we must bear in mind that she has had a series of obstacles to overcome due to gender. On the other hand, class distinctions have opened to her opportunities that have shaped her strategies.

Privileges and difficulties will be discussed together, because they are complementary elements that have shaped Cecilia on her road to creating a space and acquiring a voice, key elements of power. If power is "the ability to take one's place in whatever discourse is essential to action and the right to have one's plot matter" (Heilbrun 1988, 18), we will have to see carefully what action and plot entitle.

One thing that strikes me is how strategies vary, how stereotypes are destroyed once we see concrete cases. Usually the need for women to go public has required that they embrace popular movements or political parties that ensure a new dimension in their lives, that is, increased participation in society. However, this is not the only road to action, as Cecilia's story shows.

Private and public take different meanings in Cecilia's life. A product of the period of democratization in the Ecuadorian universities (1967–73), Cecilia's active participation in culture has struck a balance between theory and praxis. Aggressiveness seems to be a leit motif in her life and temperament. The aggressivity of the city has tainted all her moves. The need to transgress becomes a creative reaction to the obstacles imposed by a system that still expect, of women, a submission that expresses itself as certain characteristics that define her: femininity, tenderness, gentleness, etc. These characteristics are opposite to Cecilia's concept of aggressivity. Cecilia says that she "is modifying" this concept, and she is, because this is a "vital attitude" to win a space that requires respect to a personality and a way of thinking that go against the current.

Only by expressing this discontent or disconformity in a public space does this energy have a meaning. Cecilia travels among the main cities in Ecuador (Quito, Guayaquil, and Cuenca) using the feminine mask of "teacher," although she divests it of its traditional maternal role by becoming a lecturer, a trend setter, a critic full of opinions that are eagerly awaited. Thus she has used her mission as a teacher to earn a public space. What is more subversive still is that she employs the key teaching instrument, the word, as a force that cannot be contained, slipping into private homes and public spaces, making her voice heard.

It is not a new strategy for women in Spanish America to move into public space through the symbolic and private image of motherhood, and by extension of the teacher. One has to remember the Chilean poet, teacher,[1] and Nobel Prize winner Gabriela Mistral. She was able to talk about the children in the Spanish civil war and about her continent, both as a poet and a teacher. Though childless and unmarried, she embodied the ideal of the teacher as mother. In a way this asexual woman through her public lectures and well-known poetry broke the space limits imposed by society.

Another example that comes to mind is the Argentinean Mothers of Plaza de Mayo, who took over the most public space in Buenos Aires, the Plaza de Mayo, and used many symbols (the white kerchiefs and blown-up snapshots of their "disappeared" children) to break with the traditional consecrated role of motherhood that the Argentinean nation had imposed on them.[2]

In this way the symbolic role that has been imposed on women to determine their value, space, and discourse in society is clearly subverted. Cecilia puts into practice this strategy with the same liberating results. To the surprise of an "outsider," society seems to accept this woman who is breaking free from mores and ties "to make her plot matter."

This is an all-encompassing strategy that turns the table topsy-turvy, without hiding anything. All takes place in the eyes of the beholder, who is not aware of the empowering action that is taking place. The mask is part of this strategy. To mask, to cover, to veil is so much a part of a woman's life that it can pass as just another trait of her sex. For many it confirms the deviousness of women. Although the upsetting of symbols is done in front of society's eyes, the woman must hide to organize her plot. It is here, at this moment, that the mask is necessary and most meaningful.

The mask tries to hide some ugly, unaccepted part of woman

(physical, social, psychological), covering it up with an illusion of perfection. If it is physical beauty we are seeking, makeup or plastic surgery are solutions. When it is ideas we are trying to cover up, we can only hide in apparent conformity, and oblige to the roles and values imposed on us. Although masks conceal, if put on by women with a clear purpose, they become a creative disguise that may gain some time for its user to figure out what to do next. In this way masks are of vital importance if one is to survive in a society that has little to offer. Masks have accompanied women for a long time. Like in Greek tragedy, a woman's life would not be able to go on without their aid. The mask is the expression of an alienated self, "duplication and difference" of a person (Carreño 1982, 9). Cecilia must employ different covers to make it in the social class to which she belongs but with which she has little in common.

But it would be misleading to think that masks lie in Cecilia's closet waiting to be put on for each occasion. It is not as mechanical as that. It is much more creative, and it goes together with a process of unmasking that takes place at home, with friends, and in her writing. To unmask can be painful and liberating at the same time. In Cecilia's case both processes are constantly taking place with success.

In this way through her teaching activities Cecilia's voice has expanded and formed a discourse that belongs to her. Many doors have opened, especially the journalistic one through what is called *periodismo de opinión*. In her column in *El Telégrafo*, Cecilia not only discusses education, culture, and literature but also expresses her opinion on diverse topics, forming what she calls a "humanistic militancy" in which women issues are openly presented. This is followed by radio and television interviews that confirm public recognition of Cecilia as an intellectual and critic. She enters this public space slowly but with a sure step, "armed" by experience.

Journalism in Ecuador, as in most Latin American countries, is not a profession that informs through the accumulation and presentation of facts. Journalism is much connected to essay writing and politics. More than a job, in many cases, it is a platform, a forum where your voice can be heard. It is not off-limits to women, because women are allowed to collaborate in any writing job that is not particularly well remunerated.

Cecilia's writings are unusually well written, they are concise, elegant, and clear. The first thing that strikes the reader is her careful and economic style, her control over the grammar and the syntax of the language, an art and discipline much forgotten today. There is no excess, and this is strange in a culture in which hyperbole and a florid style are the norm. However, she leaves space in her writing to express deep-rooted concerns. Cecilia is not afraid to express her feelings, her emotions, or opinions on themes that may require a less "subjective" expression. To write is to express a self that should not be imprisoned by any "prison of language":

> Creo en las obligaciones o deberes del crítico que enfatizo en un aspecto que podría soslayarse; te digo, el crítico debe escribir bien, y, es más, debe escribir de manera amena e interesante; un texto crítico no tiene porqué ser un texto de plomo, aburrido, que despierte interés sólo en los especialistas, . . . debe tener . . . un vuelo poético-literario que lo haga una pieza interesante.
>
> (I believe in the critics' duties, and I wish to emphasize an aspect that could be obliterated; I tell you, the critic must write well, and, even more, he/she must write in an entertaining and interesting manner; a text on criticism does not have to be a text of lead, boring, that is interesting only to the specialists, . . . it must have . . . a poetic-literary flight that makes it an interesting piece.)

Cecilia's honesty has earned her respect and admiration among her colleagues, students, and writers. In an interview in *Expreso,* a newspaper in Guayaquil, the journalist begins telling us that she is direct in her position and comments: "[Ella] nos refiere que para emprender el camino de nuestra identidad, es preciso conocer

nuestra literatura. Y ella se ha encargado de estimular esa reali-
dad" ([She] tells us to be able to begin the road to our identity, it is
necessary to know our literature. And she has taken care of stimulating this reality).

Another difference that sets her apart from many female and
male colleagues are the topics that interest her. She moves away
from the gossip scene, or the editorial pages that can be quite conservative, to dedicate most of her writing to cultural and women's
issues. In "Reclamos al crítico" (Demands to the critic), Cecilia responds and explains the so-called critics' silence and decreased
participation in the cultural and literary forum:

> Creo que en los *actuales* momentos, el mundo literario
> cuenta con numerosos participantes en el desarrollo del que-
> hacer crítico, tal vez más potenciales que actuantes, pues
> todos se encuentran cumpliendo compromisos primordiales
> de trabajo en razón de ganarse la vida . . .
>
> Entonces, los críticos escribimos artículos, concedemos
> entrevistas, presentamos libros, dictamos conferencias, aten-
> demos consultas, orientamos monografías . . . *Gratuita-
> mente.* Todavía nuestro país no acepta la idea de que opinar
> y escribir es un trabajo como cualquier otro, . . .
>
> (I think that today, the literary world has many members
> that participate in the development of criticism, maybe they are
> more potential than active critics, since they are all involved
> carrying out primordial tasks to be able to earn a living . . .
>
> Thus, we critics write articles, grant interviews, launch
> books, give conferences, are consultants, advice students
> with their thesis . . . *For Free.* In our country it is still not
> accepted the idea that to write and to do criticism is a job
> as any other, . . .)

In a way Cecilia has picked up an ongoing struggle among the
writers of the continent whose origins can be traced back to turn
of the century writers, such as Rubén Darío and Horacio Quiroga.

Wealthier and bigger countries like Argentina or Mexico have an intelligentsia that is recognized, but still there are few writers, critics, or intellectuals who can really live off their jobs.

Cecilia's commitment to women's issues means that her research and involvement in journalism and literary criticism as a feminist critic of culture centers on key problems of women's discourse. Cecilia not only detects the problem and diagnoses it but also demands that women act and propose change. At the moment she is studying Ecuadorian women essayists. Her demands, as usual, are clear: women essayists have to "renovate their discourse just as women narrators and poets have done." She believes that there is a need for these women to break with an academic and a rationalistic rhetoric to give way to a more flexible discourse, which would allow the free expression of the imaginative.

The shaping of a woman's discourse has meant hard work. In many ways self-taught, Cecilia reads enormously, writes prodigiously, and never seems to stop. To this, one must add the many hours "wasted" in convincing others, professors, editors, colleagues, that "what one says is worth it."

This summer I was a witness to this. Attending a conference in Quito, I could see the discomfort of some men, and in some cases, the aggressive responses of some professors and writers to two lectures applying a feminist critique. Then again, this is nothing new, because we have to deal with the same prejudices in North America. Somehow, though, in the North American academic or intellectual world there are commissions, departments, and centers that act as arbitrators or buffer zones where women can find some solace. In Ecuador, confrontations are frontal, personal. A woman defending her "plot" might find herself without any support. Some women prefer active silence, out of fear or boredom or simply from lack of interest. Women issues are not only gender-related but also associated with class.

Cecilia has been key to the creation and development of a women's group that is one of the most active, better known, and respected in Guayaquil. In 1984 the group Mujeres del Atico was born. Its name translates "Women of the Attic," the attic being a reclusive, imprisoning space (as in Jane Eyre) as well as a space for dreams. Cecilia says that the attic is a "complex and beautiful metaphor."

Among some of the group's goals: to promote and discuss systematically literary works, to learn and study the "specificity of women's discourse" and "the configuration of women as a social sign," "to create and strengthen a lucid understanding of women's conditions" in all spheres, and that the group's work reaches the public sphere. Originally, the Mujeres del Atico studied collectively in a private way; now they organize forums, hold a column in *El Telégrafo,* where they address women's issues and national problems, are invited to conferences, etc. In a way these women have been able to conquer a public space by organizing themselves and through much dedication and energy.

Even though Cecilia was one of the founders and first leaders of the Mujeres del Atico, the group has no president, only a coordinator. This position is not permanent and rotates among the members. The members are only women, and those who join must be introduced by a member. All decision making takes place at the meetings. In this way the group functions in a decentering fashion, power and responsibilities are shared by all. A clause in their *Rules* states very clearly that "no member can speak for the group, nor distribute the material that is produced, nor comment or talk about the personal experiences shared by the members in the group."

This exercise in "horizontality" encounters some problems. Among the women in the group there are some who take over the discussion, propose readings, that is, are active participants; others prefer the comfortable silence of those who are happy with their history being written by their women friends. This conformity stems largely from two factors: (1) the group has become a cozy space where some women feel safely surrounded by other women who can take care of them; and (2) Women still need some time to learn how to practice "horizontality," how to function on an assumption of equality. This takes much discipline and commitment. Furthermore, some of the members have engagements, family duties, some bourgeois values that impede them from becoming fully aware of a feminist perspective.

An important element that has allowed their continuous existence is their diversity. There is a plurality of thought, professions, and nationalities. I have attended many sessions and been able to notice their development, an increased hunger for knowing and understanding, a growing commitment to action and involvement in both cultural and public organizations. All this growth takes place in a friendly and tender environment where every woman feels secure, comfortable, and welcomed. At the same time this diversity and plurality has meant that "la preocupación por la situación de la mujer" (the preoccupation with the situation of women) does not express itself, necessarily, in a feminist way. Furthermore, the fact that the women in the group belong to the upper and middle classes suggests that most of them have had a "room of their own." The impossibility of some of them taking a contestatory stance in favor of abortion, of sexual workers, etc. is part and parcel of the group's ideology.

In this way the Mujeres del Atico cannot be a feminist group and must remain a women's expression to build a discourse based more on experience, stories and history, friendships and support than on theoretical concepts. I believe, though, that the group fulfills its premises because some of its members are feminists, and in a manner they are willing to give up their discourse. The dynamics of the group are very interesting, and an ongoing example of what respect can do for women.

Although publicly the Mujeres del Atico take a consistent approach to culture, they are not part of the feminist movement in the country.[3] Here is where, I believe, comes the paradoxical limitations of the groups and of some of Cecilia's work. Although these women have managed to break the silence through the group and their personal contacts, the public space they have gained is politically and ideologically private. It is still a space of privilege that excludes the wider *Woman*.

Cecilia is very aware of this situation. Even though it is with the Mujeres del Atico that she feels she has found solidarity and sisterhood, Cecilia confesses that even there "I feel alone." Her sisters think she is "inflexible," "obsessive," and "excessive" in her judgments and expectations. Cecilia says that she feels distanced from the "popular woman," and that by belonging and defending certain behavior of the dominant class, her "feminism is incomplete."

Living and working at this crossroads is not easy, and is the source of many contradictions. How to divest from some class values that permeate everything you are and do? Cecilia wonders: "How to enter in the world of the working class woman, to which I do not belong?" She continues: "I know that my class limitations impoverish me as a human being, I admit it, but I revise my personality and my life and I just cannot figure out from where the opportunity and the spirit to open myself to an experience contact and knowledge of the working class can come." Furthermore, although Marena Briones, one of the Mujeres del Atico, is a lawyer involved with sexual workers and working-class women, teaching them their rights, Cecilia does not know what role she could play in their associations. She is too much of an intellectual, maybe she does "think too much," as her students tell her.

Cecilia admits that she is accepted in the public space, and that she manages to earn more money thanks to her public high profile. It is interesting to see, however, that public persona and private life merge in an uncanny strategy. Once she has created an image, her colleagues, men, become generous, more broad-minded. Thus this image imposes itself. Her image is that of an "intelligent person," an austere critic who does not fall prey of friendships. In this way a male image is not necessarily more accepted or respected than hers solely because it is male.

Lately, though, since Cecilia has been exercising feminist literary criticism, she has noted skeptic smiles on many faces. She finds that the public faults her doubly: it is a woman's topic, treated by a woman. Thus this should not transcend the public space and remain as purely private or personal as "girls' talk." A feminist point of view is hardly known in Cecilia's environment. Cecilia now has to convince both the general and academic public that women who write or talk do it from a different historical position that has to be very clearly defined, so that these women's lives and work can be fully understood. Within the literary establishment she is a pioneer of feminism and recognizes that there is a lot left to do. Women practicing feminist criticism have to be willing to put up with the superficiality of the city. Gossip and rumor can ridicule and invalidate serious criticism. Solid theoretical approach can be swiftly destroyed with a stroke: "poor one, she is a conflictive woman!"

It would certainly seem that people are willing to accept the female critic as long as they can divest her of her gender and sexuality, as long as this person remains in a neutral limbo. The teacher is maternal, the cultural critic is an intelligent person, the idea of *Woman* has no place. Furthermore, Cecilia's image allows for the possibility that the reader will be taken over because it has broken with the "feminine" stereotypes expected in her culture. Her aggressivity, austerity, uncompromising attitude, and intellectual discipline are not "feminine." She is single, and together with her sister Rosi, the breadwinner of a household composed of a mother, another sister, and other elder relatives. In a word, a household lacking a male figure. But when the woman raises her voice and enacts the intention to express a theoretical body that is not neutral or male oriented, the same public space that once awaited her words now needs the defense of irony, of placid smiles that may turn into a much more violent expression any time.

Single life has been a clear choice for Cecilia. As she says, "I do not want to miss anything," and she certainly feels that her married friends and colleagues have too many family engagements. No one has ever seen her miss a play, a movie, a congress, a lecture, or a trip due to family obligations. To be single for her is a way of life and a statement of some of her beliefs. Cecilia finds that marriage and motherhood change women, and that in her society they might even discourage her from active participation. She says: "I believe that I am not part of those emblems of 'femininity.' I am not married. I have opted for a single life that is very independent. And I think that this helps my enormous capacity to work. My relationship with my family is very independent. I do not feel any obstacles in my life."

This public space that apparently has welcomed Cecilia so well is shaped by a class system determined by private schooling and the middle and upper classes. Thus this is a privately formed public world where only those who work, study, or belong to those classes have a key to it. Cecilia's discourse, therefore, goes through, many times, censorship and self-censorship. Among the examples she quotes are the fact that she teaches in a Catholic University, even though she is not a practicing Catholic; or the fact that she teaches in a private high school where her students still believe in a traditional family unit. Silence is necessary, not only because it might cause trouble, but primarily, in the case of young students, because Cecilia believes that it would be "unfair to impose on them the crisis and anguish of questioning their institutions, only because their teacher does not believe in them."

This does not necessarily mean that she caters to an elite. Cecilia travels to different cities and universities lecturing and exchanging ideas with many people and social groups. What it does mean is that her discourse stems from a particular social class that defines itself in privileged conditions. These privileged conditions ensure certain readings, the access to some materials and experiences that are not available to all. In this way, Cecilia's discourse is quite sophisticated and complex. This explains her failure at teaching in public schools, where absenteeism and the lack of discipline are the norm. She says: "I have always worked in private schools. I had an experience working in a public school which failed. My discourse, my teaching is too complex, and I could not simplify it to adapt it to less educated students, with a less developed intellectual level."

What the public does not seem to see is that Cecilia has clearly defined her feminist stance from the very beginning. The creation of a public persona that seems neither female nor male but neutral may have been an unconscious strategy to gain the necessary space to pronounce a female voice and agenda, that is, to gain power as action and as making one's plot matter.

Obviously, it is in her private life that Cecilia has never appeared to cover or "veil" with any secret or mysterious being what she has always been: a working woman and a feminist. That in the school and university halls her fame and reputation spread, together with the foggy allure of the single woman, not tied, by choice, to husband or children, seems inevitable in a society in which for women marriage and family still come before a career.

At the same time Cecilia likes to emphasize that she has good friends. She is solidly backed by numerous students, colleagues, and artists. As can be expected, her feminist position, and her rebellion against social and religious expectations, have won her some enemies and have made her lose some appointments. But this does not bother her.

Her private life is full of freedom. Her family understands and supports this independence, liberating her from any domestic duties that would take time from her research. In a way the public persona is fed by a private person who seems to have broken all the traditional links characteristic of Ecuadorian women. At the same time, Cecilia has experienced the growth of certain feelings that previously had remained foreign to her.

For Cecilia, children are a distraction, something that has to be given up for her intellectual pursuits. Motherhood has been an inexplicable inclination and an experience that happened to others. Much as Sor Juana, Cecilia chose the loneliness of her study and books. Through her contact with her high school students, nevertheless, Cecilia, to her own surprise, has developed warm relationships; she caught herself calling her students "my children," probably because she as the principal of the school is more interested in their private lives. She has to know about family matters to understand them more. At the same time she hints at a balance by keeping a distance and reminding them that she is their teacher and expects them to work hard. A ceremony Cecilia carries out with much pleasure as principal is the high school graduation. She does this with the loving care and hope of a teacher who has seen her students grow within her reach. It seems to me that Cecilia's relationship with her students and her reflections on being a mother are based on respect. A respect for their physical and intellectual well-being.

For instance, she treats her students as mature people who can make choices and decisions. She believes in discipline, not concessions. Cecilia developed in the Colegio Alemán guest lectures at which writers come and discuss their work with the students. Seldom are high school students given the opportunity to talk with the people who write the books they are reading. Rarely are they taken seriously and allowed to be heard. Cecilia gives them this opportunity and they love it.

Her thoughts are the same about bearing and raising children. Cecilia says that with children as with anybody, there is an attraction or a lack of it. At an irrational level she has not felt attracted to them. It is a tremendous responsibility to be the example, to have all the answers. And she expects to be this way because relationships with children must be based on equal expectations. She says that nobody receives an education to be a parent and, nevertheless, nearly everyone "embarks on this adventure." She goes on to say: "If I have not prepared myself either to be a mother, why should I fall so easily into the mistake I have criticized in others? Furthermore, how am I to know I would be a good mother?"

Cecilia has to be childless, in a society where motherhood is the usual choice and sometimes an imposition. What finally did trigger a crisis was the awareness of the tragedy of abandoned children in the country. For a while Cecilia thought of adopting a child, but fear of losing her hard-earned independence took over. Motherhood is not a clear choice for married women in Guayaquil. Married women have children, as part and parcel of a social contract that sees career and personal wishes as secondary. A woman without a family is lacking a key component of her feminine self.

Cecilia's life and actions reveal the complex reality of a feminist in a country like Ecuador. Her life is a mixture of advances and retreats, of courageous choices and concessions, of speaking out and keeping silent, of active self-criticism and some indulgences. In the long run, one is placed at the crux of the argument: Can the gains achieved by bourgeois feminists be relevant or useful to feminists at large (or to what Cecilia refers to as the "mujer popular")? I believe that as long as the bourgeois feminists are conscious of their limitations and of the need to develop theoretical and practical ties with their working-class sisters, as Cecilia is, there are real possibilities for the women's movement to grow. In the long run, there is more need to share than to keep away from each other.

Cecilia is an exceptional woman in many ways. Extremely intelligent, well read, and with a curious mind that never rests or conforms, an enigmatic persona that attracts young and old, gracious and elegant, she glides in different worlds. It is true that "nobody chooses the place one is born, but maybe the place one develops or lives in"; that is, one chooses the plot that must matter.

Cecilia, through the use of many strategies frequently employed by women (masks, silence, emblematic subversion), has made her voice and that of many women heard. That the road is lonely, who can even question that? What is most necessary is for her to keep being involved in gender-related issues. For Cecilia it has taken the shape of teaching others how to read women and men through a feminist perspective, and in the creation of a women's group. As long as she is not lured by theory she will find her space in the women's movement at large.

Cecilia's major contradiction stems from class divisions. Her public space is private in nature; her ideas on power and organization can be obliterated when reality demonstrates that there is a gap between theory and praxis, between the intellectual and the woman. However, Cecilia is neither seduced nor infatuated with men's concepts of power. We discussed the "Thatcher Syndrome": women enter into the world of "men's" politics and instead of changing the rules of the game, play ball with the boys.

Cecilia has occupied key positions in the Catholic University and the Colegio Alemán. She has been dean of the Faculty of Philosophy, the principal of her school, and vice dean of the Department of Literature. As she reflects on all this, she tells me of the opportunities, of the hard work involved. The power is sometimes limited and limiting. Suddenly you spend more time convincing others of your abilities than engaging in your agenda. You now must change; you are expected to be energetic, trustworthy, aggressive. Furthermore, from a feminist standpoint, it is a transitory situation because you cannot implement your beliefs of solidarity, horizontality, and communication without being categorized as weak. Power positions are important, but not necessarily the main objective for Cecilia right now.

Personal growth is key for her. And for this, she realizes she "would have to fill-in many silences. Say things that I keep to myself. I would have to multiply the creation of many Mujeres del Atico. I would have to begin work as a feminist activist right now." Also she would like to have a full year for her creative work, and maybe then we would get to read her poems.

Torn between all the "musts" and "have tos," Cecilia continues to teach and write. The silence of the women in the attic can be good and allow creation. Among Ecuadorian women it seems to be much valued. But once the women leave the attic, there is a need to tell. One hopes that Cecilia will find that much-needed time, those guineas and room of her own to revise her work and thoughts, to continue her growth, and to continue to talk so as to fill all her silences.

Marta Traba:

A LIFE OF IMAGES & WORDS

Gloria Bautista Gutiérrez

~ On November 27, 1983, a plane crash at Madrid airport prematurely ended the prolific and controversial life of one of Latin America's most talented art critics and writers—Marta Traba. This date goes down in history as one of the saddest days for Latin American arts and letters. Not since the plane crash that killed Carlos Gardel had the South American continent mourned such a tragic accident.

Marta Traba was the most respected art critic of contemporary times. Her short life, and her constant quest for a common denominator in Latin America, was surrounded by praise and turmoil. As both art critic and writer, she possessed a duality rarely found. She felt that to be a good art critic, one must also be a good writer, which she was. Her work serves as testimony to an artist's sensitivity and a writer's introspection. She published eight novels, twenty-three volumes of art criticism, and more than twelve hundred articles and reviews in newspapers and magazines in more than fifteen countries. From the beginning of her career, Marta recognized the essential solitude of a writer and her inescapable responsibility to society.

Marta Traba was born in Buenos Aires on January 25, 1930. Her parents were Spanish emigrants and her father a Bohemian journalist. She grew up surrounded by books and ideas. Her childhood was an ambulatory one; her family moved from apartment to apartment after being evicted each time for not paying the rent.

While she was growing up, artists and writers were making their contributions to the world and major events were taking place. Diego Rivera painted the frescos in the National Palace of Mexico City, André Breton published the *Second Surrealist Manifesto,* and Miguel Angel Asturias published *Leyendas de Guatemala.* Colombia and Peru, as well as Bolivia and Paraguay, were at war, and Spain declared the first and second republics and went through a three-year civil war. Guernica was bombed, an event immortalized by Pablo Picasso in his masterpiece. Sandino was executed in Nicaragua, and Somoza took over the country. Juan Vicente Gómez died in Venezuela, ending a twenty-seven-year dictatorship. Japan invaded China, and the United States implemented the Good Neighbor Policy toward Latin America.

At a young age, Marta devoured novels by Tolstoi, Dostoevski, Dickens, Victor Hugo, Virginia Woolf, and Gorky. Henry James introduced her to another world, and her passion for English literature developed. She also considered herself "a full time Proustist." After finishing high school in two years, Marta received a bachelor's degree in philosophy at the age of twenty. She applied for a summer grant to study in Chile, where Jorge Romero Brest, the best known Latin American critic of the time, remembers "her lucid intellect and obsession for literature." On her return from Chile, he invited her to contribute to the newly established magazine *Ver y Estimar.* There she published, in 1948, her first articles on art criticism, including the memorable "Leave and the Universe of Rodin and Rilke." It was only four pages long, but it revealed a sensitive spirit looking for a space to manifest itself.

In the meantime, the world was going through the Second World War, Francisco Franco became the dictator in Spain, and great thinkers such as Camus, Sartre, Brecht, Steinbeck, and Beauvoir soothed the human spirit with their writings. It was then that she traveled to Paris to study art history at La Sorbonne and visited Budapest and Rome. In Paris, she met the Colombian journalist Alberto Zalamea, whom she married in 1950. The young couple moved to Italy, where her son Gustavo was born, and in 1951 Marta published her first book of poems, entitled *Historia natural de la alegría* (The Natural History of Happiness).

In 1954, the Zalamea-Traba couple and young son moved to Bogotá. One can only imagine the transition for Marta, going from an exciting and vibrant European environment to the straightlaced and traditional Andean capital, where the stereotyped art in vogue was copied from the Mexican muralists. How could she believe that this was avant-garde art? To her discerning mind, it was nothing more than bourgeoisie art, attempted by painters of "good families with good consciences."

Marta soon found herself integrated in the younger elite's minority striving to liberate themselves from stagnant religious hypocrisy and officially declared intellectuals. Her relentless struggle started here. She founded the magazine *Prisma,* and although some people do not agree, art criticism, as a permanent activity, in Colombia started with Marta Traba. Her enlightened enthusiasm and convincing arguments gained her respect and admiration. To rediscover the value in Colombian art, she started from zero, and through Herculean efforts she developed a visual pedagogy to recognize and appreciate talent. This discovery path was one of great significance for Latin American art. Her newspaper articles did not go unnoticed by the old guard, and Marta found herself in constant controversy. Her thinking was considered sacrilegious by many for deviating from the accepted norms. She advocated the diversification of art in search of its own identity and expression away from the parochial.

In the next decade, Perón controlled Argentina, Batista ruled Cuba, Puerto Rico became a protectorate of the United States, Stalin died, and Nasser proclaimed Egypt as a republic. Meanwhile Cortázar, Arthur Miller, Hemingway, Rulfo, and Carpentier published landmark works. Marta Traba published her first art book, *El museo vacío* (The Empty Museum), in 1952.

In 1954, Traba began to teach art history at the University of America, and, later, she increased her teaching load and taught at the Andes University as well. Her articles began to appear in prestigious publications throughout Colombia. In these articles she intended to rediscover what was innately Latin American, as if she were on an interior conquest of her own land, relying on the clear intellect that characterized her life and writings. Her quest was to find the peculiar spirit of our continent, combating the folkloric conservatism and superficial realism to penetrate the spiritual system from where the essential culture emanates. In 1955, Marta gave art lectures on Colombia's newly established national television. Her persistence and hard work led to the founding of the Museum of Modern Art.

During the second half of the fifties, when Traba was in her twenties, Perón fell from power, Somoza was assassinated, and the Russians repressed a popular anti-Soviet uprising in Hungary. Vargas Llosa, Carlos Fuentes, Lukacs, Marcuse, and Fidel Castro began to receive notoriety. In 1957, because of censorship and political repression, Traba resigned from the national television. In 1958, after the fall of Rojas Pinilla's dictatorship, she returned to national television, and her "Hora del arte" got the highest rating of any television program.

1959 was a landmark year in Latin American history. Fidel Castro defeated the Batista dictatorship and entered triumphantly into Havana. Also, Traba's second son Fernando was born, and the Pan-American Union in Washington, D.C., published her book *Arte en Colombia*. In it, she attempted to define Colombian art by setting aside the overwhelming doubts and fears of a country full of guilt and fanaticism. Her merciless attacks on critics that favored "the untouchable mediocre" painters, rather than the best ones, kept Marta in a spot of controversy. She believed that honesty was the eminent moral condition of a critic, especially in Latin America, because the countries were so young; Marta believed that the initial effort would only triumph if the artists and critics relied on truth.

In 1960, Marta traveled to the United States as curator for the exposition *3,000 Years of Latin American Art,* and in 1961 she published *La pintura nueva en Latino América* (New Latin American painting). In the same year, John Kennedy was elected president, and relations between the giant of the north and Latin America improved.

The following year, 1962, the Museum of Modern Art in Bogotá was built and Traba was named director. The United States broke relations with Cuba and carried out the failed Bay of Pigs invasion, which precipitated the missile crisis. Russia placed the first cosmonaut, Gagarin, in orbit, and the United States vowed to put the first man on the moon before the end of the decade.

Another difficult year was 1963, with the assassination of President Kennedy. While the Beatles began to dominate the world's musical scene in 1964, Marta traveled to Buenos Aires, Santiago de Chile, Lima, and Caracas to establish art exchanges. Marta published *Seis artistas contemporáneos colombianos* (Six Contemporary Colombian Painters) and organized several art exhibitions and lectures on art.

In 1965, the United States invaded the Dominican Republic and stepped up the intervention in Vietnam. Norman Mailer and Octavio Paz became powerful voices in the literary world, and Marta published *Los cuatro monstruos cardinales* (The Four Capital Monsters) and *Conferencias sobre historia del arte* (Lectures on Art History).

The cultural revolution in China and Indira Gandhi's rise to power marked 1966. Marta Traba traveled through Central America, Mexico, and Cuba. She received the most prestigious literary award on the continent, Casa de las Americas, for her novel *Las ceremonias del verano* (Summer Ceremonies). The judges included Alejo Carpentier, Manuel Rojas, and Mario Benedetti. They extolled the novel for "its high literary quality, which encompasses the problems of expression and structure, the constancy of the poetic rhythm and the intelligence with which it balances the situations and achieves composition unity." This book, more than a novel, is a series of short stories nostalgically sweet, in which an adolescent in love revisits the different stages of her initiation. It recounts the bloody riots of April 9, 1948 in Bogotá and shows her delicate sensitivity, which transforms everyday events into a vital frenzy expressed in words that inflame and transport the spirit. She pays special attention to objects and landscapes, turning them into art and leaving the reader in awe of the world. In *Ceremonias de verano* the recurrent theme is love, the fleetingness of possession, the desire for communion, and the interior longing of the loss.

Marta wrote and published her second novel, *Los laberintos insolados* (The Insolate Labyrinths), in Spain and received great praise. In this work, she raises questions about the immaturity of men trapped in Oedipus complexes while society bleeds to death in pathological violence. With its modern transposition and odic cycles, this novel clearly exhibits the influence of Joyce. On a deeper level, the story deals with the meaning of the old yet mysterious history of culture and the journey of the human spirit. Marta metaphorically associates this quest with the tracks left by a bird in flight.

All along Traba defended the Cuban revolution in her articles and lectures. Her television program was suspended midway through when she protested the police's violent invasion of the National University. Her defense of the university's autonomy and her attacks on the Colombian intelligence agencies resulted in her being expelled from Colombia on June 23, 1967. Intellectuals and students protested, and President Lleras Restrepo reversed the suspension on July 6, under the condition that she would never teach in Colombia again. This mandate was immediately challenged by several universities and eventually revoked. This year was also one of the most volatile in Marta's life, not only politically but also personally—she divorced Alberto Zalamea, her husband of sixteen years.

Under all these pressures, Marta did not give up her research, and at the end of that year she published *El Arte Bizantino* (Byzantine Art). Through this work, Marta demonstrated to those who would deny her free speech that she would continue to teach, even if not from an academic podium.

In 1968, she received a Guggenheim grant to study contemporary Latin American art and published *Dos décadas vulnerables en las artes plásticas latinoamericanas, 1950–1970* (Two Vulnerable Decades of Latin American Art, 1950–1970). The same year, her book *Historia abierta del arte colombiano* (Open History of Colombian Art) came out. That year, Robert Kennedy and Martin Luther King were assassinated, unleashing unprecedented riots in the United States. Richard Nixon was elected president with the promise of ending the Vietnam War. Meanwhile, Marta traveled through Latin America and, in Montevideo, Angel Rama published her only book of short stories, *Pasó así* (It Happened Like This).

1969 was an elevating year for the world as well as for Traba. The United States placed the first man on the moon, Elena Poniatowska published *Hasta no verte, Jesús mío,* and Marta Traba married the Uruguayan literary critic Angel Rama and published her third novel, *La jugada del sexto día* (The Play of the Sixth Day). At the end of the year, she moved to Uruguay.

Salvador Allende was elected president of Chile in 1970 and Pablo Neruda won the Nobel Prize in literature. Marta went to teach in Puerto Rico, and in 1971 published two books, *La rebelión de los santos* (The Rebellion of the Saints) and *Propuesta polémica sobre el arte puertorriqueño* (Polemic Proposals on Puerto Rican Art). The same year, she discontinued her support of the Cuban revolution, when it became clear that Cuba was aligned with totalitarian Russia, where, in her opinion, the ideal socialist ideas were profoundly betrayed.

In 1972, Marta returned to Colombia at the same time that Juan Perón went back to Argentina after his ten years in exile. An earthquake destroyed Managua, and on the political scene, Richard Nixon made his historical trip to communist China.

The following year, Marta published *En el humbral del arte moderno* (On the Threshold of Modern Art), *Literatura y praxis en América Latina* (Literature and Praxis in Latin America), and *Dos décadas vulnerables en el arte moderno latinoamericano*. In this latest book, Marta conceived Latin American art as an expression of the whole continent by focusing on themes, conditions, and circumstances common to the entire area. It was the first time than an art critic articulated characteristics and tendencies as an expression of the Latin American culture that transcended political and geographic frontiers. She defined an artistic identity for Latin American art. This overview could only be perceived by Marta Traba because of her sharp observations, keen intuition, and constant travels.

1973 was shaken by the military overthrow of Salvador Allende in Chile and by his subsequent assassination. General Pinochet took control of the government and headed a dictatorship that lasted eighteen years and destroyed the country's democratic tradition. The same year, the artistic world mourned the deaths of Pablo Neruda, Pablo Picasso, and Pablo Casals.

1974 witnessed the resignation of President Nixon and the death of Juan Perón. Russia expelled Solzhenitsyn, Ernesto Sábato and Roa Bastos were spotlighted in the literary world, and Marta published *Mirar en Caracas* (Looking in Caracas). Disillusioned by the attacks against her because of her negative views of Venezuelan art expressed in this book, she thought of leaving art criticism and dedicating herself only to literature. This, fortunately, never came to pass.

Colombia was where Marta left her most luminous path. There, she shook the traditional consumerism of the nouveau rich who bought art for luxury but lacked introspection. She supported and encouraged great artists such as Botero, Grau, Obregon, Bursztyn, and Negret, among others. Her sharp wit and comments made her great friends and enemies. With the same pen, she would bless or excommunicate artists, tendencies, movements, or countries. She was a militant critic at a time when the Latin American upper classes ignored the subhuman conditions of a large number of its citizens. For Marta, art was the torch of her "revolution," and she never compromised her principles and critical judgments.

While Marta strove to awaken the public artistically in the Americas, Spain, after Franco's death, restored its monarchy with Juan Carlos I. Angola also gained independence, and the world seemed to move on a more peaceful course with the Helsinki treaty.

In 1975, Marta published *La zona del silencio* (The Silent Zone) and *Hombre americano a todo color* (American Man in Full Color). She also traveled to Austin, Texas, for a symposium, a landmark event for Latin American art. Marta stated that Latin American art was one of "resistance" against the greatest obstacles; she felt that the social, political, and economic conditions of the region kept their people "busy" with survival, leaving no time for art. This expression of the human spirit was a luxury afforded mainly to the rich and developed countries. Despite controversies, this symposium planted many seeds of aesthetic understanding in the international artistic soil. As a result, there have been many exhibitions of Latin American artists in the United States.

The bicentennial of the United States was marked by the election of Jimmy Carter, who with General Torrijos signed the Panama Canal Treaty, which will eventually give control of the canal to Panama. Marta went on to publish *Los signos de vida* (Signs of life) and *Mirar en Bogotá* (Looking in Bogotá). In 1977 and 1978, she taught in Venezuela, Nicaragua, Costa Rica, and Stanford, California. Her ability with words revealed her to be fascinating, and her international reputation grew.

The year 1979 was a tumultuous one. The Sandinistas overthrew Somoza, Russia invaded Afghanistan, and Ayatollah Khomeni overthrew the shah and proclaimed Iran an Islamic state, declaring the United States an enemy and taking their diplomats hostage. Marta, with her husband Angel Rama, lectured in Middlebury, Vermont, and at Harvard University, MIT, and the University of Maryland. At the end of the year, they lived in Washington, D.C., where she published what she considered her most important literary work, *Homérica latina* (Latin Homeric). This novel is about the abuse of power in repressive political systems and the struggle of some to aspire to freedom under tortuous circumstances. Marta also wrote another novel, *Casa sin fin* (Endless House), which was published posthumously. Both novels expose the deplorable political situation of Latin America and can be classified as "the literature of the oppressed," as Elena Poniatowska so profoundly called it.

The following year, Ronald Reagan was elected president and John Lennon was assassinated in the United States. The Museum of Modern Art in New York had the largest retrospective exhibition ever, with dedication of the whole museum to Pablo Picasso. Angel Rama received a grant by the Woodrow Wilson International Center for Scholars of the Smithsonian Institute and, accompanied by Marta Traba, went to teach at Princeton University.

In 1981, General Torrijos of Panama died in a mysterious plane crash. Marta Traba, who hated to fly but had no alternative with her busy schedule, traveled to Colombia, Brazil, Argentina, and France. In Mexico, she published the novel *Conversación al Sur* (Conversation to the South). In this book, a young woman, Dolores, whose miscarriage had been provoked by torturers, regains her voice and her past. Dolores has a long conversation with Irene, a forty-year-old actress who expresses her fears about her son caught in the overthrow of Allende in Chile. This long dialogue is a chilling exchange of emotions, fears, and anguish that unites these two women. They also talk about the Mothers of the Plaza de Mayo who parade daily, requesting the bodies of their sons, daughters, husbands. Dolores and Irene question what will happen to the executioners. The answer is that, like part of a well-oiled machine, they will remain free. For these women, the only way to survive is to imagine the worst crimes, the most unspeakable and aberrant horrors; then, and only then, one begins to prepare for reality. The women know that all they can do is not go insane. They experience a brief relief, and then there is a knock on the door, symbolizing the return of repression and the recycling of inescapable injustices.

Conversación al Sur—complexly plain, full of shame and ferocity—does not allow us to forget a tragedy of the dimensions and indifference that Argentina and Chile suffered during their recent military dictatorships. This novel exorcises the tragedies of thousands of silent lives and remains a testimonial to the horror and torture of man against man.

The most outstanding event of the following year, 1982, was the war between England and Argentina over the Falkland Islands. The swift defeat of Argentina brought Galtiere down, and General Bignone took over. The Mothers of the Plaza de Mayo continued to march and expose the crimes of the dictators. Marta, in the meantime, had an operation to remove a cancerous tumor in her breast. Soon after, she lectured at Smith College, Harvard University, and Marymount College in New York. She organized the art collection of the Organization of American States and wrote *A Guide to the Twentieth-Century Latin American Art*. She finished the novel *En cualquier lugar* (In Any Place), which was published posthumously. That year Marta and Angel Rama applied for residents' visas in the United States. Their application was denied by the State Department, presumably because of their past affiliation with socialists causes. Colombian president Belisario Betancourt offered them Colombian citizenship while intervening on their behalf with president Reagan. It was to no avail.

Argentina regained democracy, and Alfonsín was elected president in 1983. The United States invaded the island of Grenada. In the literary scene, Umberto Eco published *The Name of the Rose* and Marta Traba received grants from both the National Endowment for the Arts and the National Endowment for the Humanities. She finished another book and moved to Paris. Angel Rama and she were flying to Bogotá on November 27, 1883, as guests of honor of president Betancourt, and boarded the fateful flight that crashed in Madrid. This was such a sudden and tragic ending for Latin America's greatest woman art critic.

Marta's central preoccupation was Latin America. She identified deeply with egalitarian socialist ideas and detested the prepotent abuses of power by the fascists. Her erudition oscillated between the Greek temples and abstract art. She wrote more than seven hundred articles, always trying to spread the joy of learning and the exaltation of the spirit. With her vast knowledge and sharp sense of humor, she was a restless critic of provincial bourgeois and corrupted governments.

Marta transformed the vision of a museum as a pantheon into a dynamic cultural center in service of the individual. She did not see artists as exceptional human beings but rather as citizens with a clear sensibility to perceive and describe the world that surrounds them in images. Abstract art strives to express ideas and feelings without relying on figuration; the abstract painter, in his zeal to give content to forms, achieves his own personal style. For poor countries, like Colombia, where every hour a child dies of malnutrition and where a large number of the population is illiterate, it is normal that art is ignored by the majority. The more fortunate classes scorn art and knowledge in an effort to ignore their role in a corrupted society that perpetuates injustice. Only a small intellectual elite was able to appreciate Marta's heroic labor to show the truth in art and to enlighten the public.

The reactionary individuals prefer "realistic" art that does not stir up their conscience and threaten their "tradition." The role of an art critic, according to Marta, was not only to explain a piece but to bring the viewer closer to it by pointing out how aesthetics enriches and reveals spiritual qualities that a layman may not be trained or sensitized to see. The art critic is the intermediary between the work and the public. Art is a discipline and a vehicle to knowledge. Therefore, Marta saw her role as a didactic and elucidating one. At the same time, in the narrow Latin American environment, abstract painters and seekers like Traba had a difficult job because they had little to work with, mainly good will and selflessness.

For Marta, art for the Latin American masses was failure, only reflecting demagogic attitudes and a deep lack of respect for them. These people were too hungry and could barely read and write. All they could do was laugh at the inexplicable and absurd paintings, thus turning the situation into the mocking of the mocker. Because of these ideas and those of other stern critics, she was called "the castigating woman." Nevertheless, she remained immune to her critics, understanding that every exposition was a battleground where she must challenge the lethargic critic and artist. For her, art has no recipe, and its approaches need to be renovated constantly for art to remain alive and dynamic. The artist must unify the objective and the magical worlds to arrive at the physical perception of a mental representation. Art must also be accurate and prophetic and expressed in the balance of color, rhythm, and composition. She hated mediocrity and conformity, because they paralyze art and bottle the spirit.

People who knew Marta described her as "timid but with great courage." She was tender and felt deep solidarity toward the oppressed. She detested the bourgeoisie class to which she belonged and perceived them as traitors, selfish and mindless. Most of these bourgeois women seemed frivolous as they wasted their lives on trivial activities such as playing cards and gossiping. Obviously, Marta's frankness and fortitude caused many people to feel threatened by her.

In Colombia, a small number of women who escape the societal numbness run the cultural aspects of the country museums, theaters, cultural sections in institutions, newspapers, and television. Marta had many realms of opportunity in which she could excel.

She prided herself as being a political and romantic feminist before the term made turbid compromises.

Marta was critical of the Mexican muralists because their message stayed at a political or didactic level. To her, this was demagoguery, because their art was compromised by ideology and therefore not truthful. She felt that Latin American artists live surrounded by traps. They can not work peacefully because if they copy the European tendencies, they are labeled traitors, and if they copy the American landscape, they are labeled provincial. So they must sketch an original discourse: their spirit must eviscerate unexplored mysteries and depths to create universal art. At the same time, with Latin America being so diversified, artists have a fertile environment to create their own universe by confronting, opposing, or juxtaposing realities. They can resurrect primitive spirits, mythical memories, and innocent visions of an evolving continent. The artists must throw themselves in a volcanic America to uncover its essence. Art must shake and convince at the same time. Artists live what is around them, but they can only see what they dream.[1]

Art for Marta was like a mirror in which one could reflect oneself to arrive at the bottom of the unfathomable well, to the soul. It is ridiculous to pretend to express the unreachable depth in a conventional or agreeable form. As Dali said, "Art is not necessarily concerned with beauty but with truth." However, art is man's creation and it reclaims its image; so it is necessary to give it form, but it must be immolated and open, torn or deformed, without a dependence on physical reality. A good painter must incorporate misery in his creation to invoke a supraphysical world pushing the limits of reality and dream.[2]

Revolutionary spirits are the ones that move humanity forward, not conformists. Marta was a revolutionary of ideas. How could she not have been, in Latin America, where horror happens everyday? Marta questioned and challenged conventions and restructured the artistic vision. She disemboweled mysteries to penetrate the hermetic symbolism of great art.

The vision of Marta Traba that is engraved in the minds of many Latin Americans is one of youth, dynamism, joy. Her enthusiasm for life made her look adolescent. Her untamed spirit, brilliant polemics, and overwhelming force mobilized the stagnant Latin American art world. She believed that art would not be perfected until it was expurgated.

Marta Traba has been called the "Latin American Joan of Arc." Her life and writings propel us to live and to think deeply and clearly, to question the established order, to be critical, to create and to remember, to remember women, who, like her, carved paths in the human consciousness.

Carmen Naranjo:
FROM POET TO MINISTER

PATRICIA RUBIO

⌐ CARMEN NARANJO'S CONTRIBUTIONS to Costa Rica in particular, and to Central America in general, have been manifold. Not only is she an influential and prolific writer, but she also had occupied important government positions and is one of the most original cultural critics in Central America. In 1953, Carmen Naranjo (1931) completed a degree in philosophy and letters at the Universidad de Costa Rica, but instead of pursuing a teaching career, the common venue for such a degree, she joined the Welfare Department in 1954, at a time when Costa Rica was rapidly expanding its social service sector. Her successful civil service career allowed her to stake new ground for women, as she became the first female undersecretary of the Social Security System in 1961, and its first woman first administrative officer ten years later. In 1972 she was appointed ambassador to Israel, an important diplomatic assignment given the intellectual and economic influence of the Costa Rican Jewish community. In 1974 she was recalled to become the sole female member of the cabinet of president Oduber, as minister of culture, youth and sport.

Naranjo was an extraordinary minister of culture, not only because she was the first woman in her country to occupy such an important public office but also because she placed cultural policy at the center of the government's social and economic agendas. In *Cultura: La acción cultural en Latinoamérica. Estudio sobre la planificación cultural* (1978), Naranjo discusses the conceptual framework of the cultural policy she attempted to establish during her ministry. The book, written after her resignation in 1976, presents a blueprint for cultural development in the context of social and economic growth applicable not only to Costa Rica but also to most Latin American countries.

The centerpiece of her plan is that cultural development is essential for and the key to economic growth and social improvement, with the understanding that such growth responds to the needs of the population at large, and not primarily to the interests of privileged groups. In Costa Rica, just as in most of Latin America, the capital is the largest city and the hub of economic and political power. The inclusion of the margins, both social and geographic, is central to an agenda of democratization, and for the attainment of economic development responsive to the rights and needs of all groups. "Cultural development," she states, "must accompany commercial integration, the creation of new markets, and the economic restructuring of the regions."

At the heart of her thinking lies a concern with securing the cultural identity of the country, which she sees threatened by economic development, for the most part propelled by foreign interests ignorant or impervious to its internal consequences, and implemented by national interest groups. Although her propositions were novel in the context of Costa Rican official cultural policy, they connect with a long-standing Spanish American intellectual tradition that, since the nineteenth century, began to voice its criticism of the expansionist undertakings of first, Great Britain and later, the United States. Intellectuals like Darío (Nicaragua) and Rodó (Uruguay), for example, stressed the cultural differences separating both Americas, and denounced the dire consequences of U.S. expansionism for the cultures of Spanish America. The time and the context have obviously changed. Naranjo is, nevertheless, reacting to a similar threat: the imposition of foreign cultural models on her country, whose own cultural identity has historically been threatened first by colonialism, next by neocolonialism, and now by a local bourgeoisie eager to collaborate with transnational interests when its economic and political future stand to benefit.

Naranjo's cultural policies seek to subvert the traditional Latin American view whereby culture is seen as a luxury that exists for the pleasure of a refined elite. She understands artistic creation as work combining special intellectual and manual potentials. More important, however, she believes that only inclusive, widespread non-elitist cultural development will enable the population at large to withstand the pernicious effects of the foreign-based market, manifested in numbing advertising, empty slogans, and indiscriminate consumerism. To this end she created the National Theater Company and the Costa Rican Symphony. In addition, and more in keeping with her plan to bring high level culture and information to the people, she founded the Costa Rican Film Institute, knowing that cinematic and television images were important instruments for the realization of her goals. She advocates the development of a strong Latin American film industry—an objective that Cuba and Mexico had already realized, and that Brazil, Argentina, and lately Colombia have also accomplished—and the production of videos destined for television as an alternative to the foreign, mainly U.S., films and television series controlling Costa Rican screens, large and small.

Her progressive cultural policies, however, soon became the target of attacks by the conservative political opposition, which firmly opposed her objectives of cultural democratization. The trigger of her resignation in 1976, apart from the frustration of not being able to fully implement her policies, were a series of documentaries made for television by the Costa Rican Film Institute. The documentaries exposed the indiscriminate exploitation of the country's rain forests by both local and foreign interests, the effects of widespread malnutrition among Costa Rican children, the recourse to prostitution by poor women as a means of survival, and the existence of rampant alcoholism in the country at large. The conservative right accused her of fomenting subversion. Naranjo responded by defending the honesty and sincerity of the films, stressing the need to call the country's attention to its economic and social ills in need of immediate action. In her resignation speech she accused her critics, the immediate beneficiaries of widespread consumerism, for their self-serving positions. She linked the rise of crime and violence in Costa Rica to the increasing appetite of the poor sectors of the population for material goods. Turning the tables on her critics, she pointed out that "subversion is propitiated by those who relinquish the independence of our culture to benefit a foreign culture which only conceives of us as a market."

Naranjo's successful and influential administrative career is paralleled by an equally relevant and groundbreaking literary career. Her first book of poems, *América* (1961), was followed by six other collections, the most noted of which are *Misa a oscuras* (1967), *Idioma de invierno* (1972), and *Mi guerrilla* (1974). She is better known, however, for her fiction, which renovated Costa Rican narrative by breaking with the *costumbrista* tradition prevalent in Central American literature until the early sixties, and by experimenting with fragmentary structures *(Los perros no ladraron, Responso por el niño Juan Manuel, Diario de una multitud, Sobrepunto)*. In her work she explores themes that reveal her concern regarding the social and individual cost of Costa Rica's economic development. Most of her works portray individual alienation in a materialistic and routine-driven society; human frustration, isolation, abandonment, and loneliness in a society that stresses egocentrism over the interests and rights of the community.

Both her novels and collections of short stories have been awarded Costa Rica's and Central America's most prestigious literary prizes. Her first novel, *Los perros no ladraron,* received the 1966 Aquileo Echeverría award; *Camino al mediodía* and *Responso por el niño Juan Manuel* won the Central American Floral Games in 1967 and 1968, respectively; and *Diario de una multitud,* which critics have hailed as a "fundamental work in the context of Costa Rican literature," received the Premio EDUCA in 1974. Her collection of short stories, *Hoy es un largo día,* was awarded the Editorial Costa Rica Prize in 1973, and *Ondina,* the EDUCA prize in 1982.

Naranjo's extensive knowledge of the inner workings of bureaucracy, both at the national and international levels, clearly influenced her writing. In 1982 she worked for UNICEF in Guatemala in the planning and implementation of child-care centers for Central America. Before then, while she was still working on social security issues, she served as technical assistant for social security planning at the Organization of American States, in Washington, D.C. She was also a consultant to the Salvadoran and Dominican governments. Back in Costa Rica she directed the Museum of Costa Rican Art, and EDUCA, the largest Central American publishing house.

Her characterization of the bureaucracy, especially in *Los perros no ladraron* and in several fragments of *Diario de una multitud,* is extremely critical, not only for reasons of inefficiency, which she stresses, but primarily for the effects the system has on those who serve in it. As Naranjo sees it, bureaucratic work destroys the individual's creativity by limiting him or her to restricted, boring, and repetitive tasks. The important decisions are made at the highest levels, and everyone else is "just a name, which no one remembers and which is exchangeable by any other name." Limited opportunities for advancement thoroughly poison the workplace; low- and middle-level employees spend much of their time plotting against their fellow workers: "How much hatred lies behind a desk! I have learned to identify the symptoms. At first, it's a trickle of guile, then a torrent of stinking excrement, seeking to soil even the most noble expressions of humanness." Worst of all, however, is the sense of entrapment and helplessness of the petty bureaucrat. S/he is a victim of directors who, as political appointees, use their subordinates in order to advance their own interests. Despite the constant job insecurity, low remuneration, and demeaning work conditions, most are wedded to their jobs for life, lacking any credentials: "The worst is to remain silent, to deny my right to being someone, to corner myself, so that no one can touch me . . . not my dignity, but my job . . . that horrible job."

The bureaucratic dystopia of *Los perros* finds its opposite in the utopia of Olo (*Nunca hubo alguna vez*, 1984), the town that has found a society guided by mutual respect and consideration for the individual and the community. One day an amusing visitor arrives who is abhorred by the absence of an established decision-making body. He attempts to establish a city government with laws, statutes, and rules, but the Olanos kindly escort him out of town after they "patiently listened to the main laws and saw the charts which resembled the encroachments they detested. By mutual and silent dialog, the straight line and all the angles and vertices had been abolished by Olo. They only used the circle."

In her "Los quijotes modernos," title of her acceptance speech to the Costa Rican Academy of Letters, Naranjo highlights the value of imagination and idealism, which she believes modern societies have suppressed: "blind in matters of values, the reason why we do not dare to see." Today's idealists have felt their entrapment in "a world of decals . . . of successful sentences, and fixed smiles." Her theme, of course, is once again the negative influence of consumerism and the inability of the country as a whole to find alternatives to its blind and culturally devastating material development. "Our people do not dream," and as a result, "the individual has become a number and his/her living space a huge market." The issue is so critical for Naranjo that she returns to it in three novels, *Camino al mediodía, Diario de una multitud*, and *Sobrepunto* (1985), and in her book of essays, *Cinco temas en busca de un pensador* (1977).

The civil war of 1948 marks the ascendance to power of the urban middle class and the beginning of the Costa Rican state as we know it today. Naranjo is the first writer to reflect these social and political changes. All her novels and many of her short stories take place in San José; her characters belong to various bourgeois segments, although she often focuses on the powerful Costa Rican urban elite, criticizing its life-style in general and its administration of the country in particular.

The relationship between the individual and its society, and the circumstances determining the integration to Costa Rican society of certain sectors to the exclusion of others, are recurrent concerns in her work. "We were both foreigners, although we were both born in this same land," expresses one of the main characters in *Sobrepunto*. At the core of her work lies the notion that despite the essential equality of all human beings, an individual's life potential is often curtailed, and even aborted, by the economic, social, and personal circumstances in which s/he develops: "The tragedy of life is to be in a specific time and space, but imbued with an energy which is meant for achieving deeper dimensions of being."

Naranjo identifies the city as that inhospitable place where the forces confabulate against individuals, forcing them to lead alien-ated lives and depleting them of their humanness. "The best defi-nition for the city," she writes, "is that of a hole, with little light, without air." While she frequently depicts the city as a polluted and polluting environment, she also stresses the fakeness of San José, which aspires to be a modern city but does not succeed in shaking its rural identity. In order to be worldly in the "city sur-rounded by coffee plantations, orange trees, with vegetable gar-dens in every yard . . . one only needs to join the caravan of tourists en route to Europe . . . to spend one night in Paris at the Folies Bergères." She places the blame for such social degradation largely with the ruling elite, although she is equally critical of the passiv-ity of those who are economically and politically disenfranchised. She indicts the governing powers, which have successfully sold to the world a positive image of the country as the Switzerland of Central America, as an exemplary democracy with a high standard of living, neglecting, and finally forgetting in the mirage of its own image, the problems affecting the country, and the legitimate rights and aspirations of all Costa Ricans.

Her criticism of the elite, however, goes further; she identifies its pervasive narcissism as the force determining its behavior and determining much of the national decision-making processes. Her cultural philosophy, as we have discussed it, stresses the importance of nurturing a weak national identity while pursuing economic development. Narcissism, however, stresses the identity of the self, drowning the individual's sense of pertinence to a community, and his or her loyalty and responsibility toward it. As Christopher Lash and other post-Freudian cultural critics and psychologists have defined it, narcissism is both a psychological and a cultural condition. It is the consequence of changes in the society and the culture produced by the exacerbated individualism of the middle class, the cult of consumption fostered by the market, the proliferation of media images, and variations in the socialization patterns, including the family structure: "Everyone, absolutely everyone is in the system, a hybrid system which . . . always favors the privileged, the gentlemen of opportunity waiting for the deal, the easy money" *(Diario)*.

In a narcissistic society, social intercourse is characterized by the absence of moral principles. Interpersonal relationships are degraded to the extent that other individuals are only valuable as providers of the validation each individual requires in order to feed his or her self-esteem. The goals in life are material success and immediate gratification. The narcissist prefers envy to respect, celebrity to fame, and the recognition of his or her image to achievement. Both the protagonists of *Camino al mediodía* and *Sobrepunto* are accurate representations of the narcissist. In the first, the protagonist is a corrupt executive who knows no boundaries in the manipulation of everyone around him to maintain his social position and to prop his self-image: a mannequin-like wife who brought much-needed cash and convenient family ties to the marriage, business, and political connections that protect him from embarrassing exposures of unethical business deals, and numerous lovers he buys in order to kill his boredom. For both him and Olga, the protagonist in *Sobrepunto,* "life was precisely that, the enjoyment of the moment, the ability to take advantage of the situation . . . You would so easily fall for the brilliance of the moment . . . that you would lose yourself in the voice of your own mirror."

In *Sobrepunto,* Naranjo's only novel with a female protagonist (which contains her most severe indictment of the upper middle class in general and of the bourgeois woman in particular), the author identifies the breakdown of the family as both a product and agent of narcissism. This theme, which recurs in other works (*Memorias de un hombre palabra, Responso por el niño Juan Manuel,* "Los dos santos medioevales de mi abuela bizantina," and "El de las cuatro"), stresses the notion that a strong family structure is fundamental for healthy individual and social development. The sense of community, experienced first in the family setting, is central to the child's development of a strong self, and of his or her sense of loyalty and responsibility for the group. It is in this social microcosm that the individual learns that beyond the I, there are "other pronouns with equally legitimate rights."

Olga is one of Naranjo's most tragic characters. She is driven to her fate by a set of circumstances she cannot change, and against which she is incapable, first, and then unwilling to rebel. She is the offspring of a marriage that her wealthy parental grandparents do not approve of, due to the social differences between their son and his wife. Her father dies during Olga's early childhood, and her grandparents refuse to support the child if she stays with her mother. Too poor to raise her, her mother accepts money to relinquish custody. In her grandparent's house, Olga replaces the lost son, growing up in a bountiful but morally bankrupt world, where she is treated as an adornment, "as a . . . doll to play . . . house with" rather than an individual. She is left alone to define her place in a family setting devoid of affection, responsibility, and purpose. Her existence is acknowledged by the immediate satisfaction of her desires, culminating in the selection of a husband who is worthy of the family's wealth. In a house full of mirrors that, like the pool in Ovid's story, only reflect the appearance, an image devoid of any depth, Olga focuses on hedonistic pursuits. She formulates a "sport philosophy," which stresses indifference and the pursuit of pleasure. Its main principle is "to play the game of life correctly; there are no means, only ends; morality is like a dress to be worn according to the circumstances." Olga's narcissism is more terrifying than Eduardo's, the main character of *Camino al mediodía,* because her life has no purpose and she is incapable of accepting any commitments. Her marriage deteriorates after the novelty of the roles of housewife and mother wears off. She seeks to relieve her boredom in fleeting love affairs, which eventually lead to the collapse of her marriage. After her husband takes custody of the children, as a result of her self-destructive behavior under the influence of drugs, Olga is unable to confront her own failure and loneliness, and she commits suicide.

As the narcissist concentrates on the immediate satisfaction of his/her pleasures, s/he lives in an eternal present, erasing the relevance of both the individual and the collective past. At the social level, such denial of the past results in the immediate weakening and eventual loss of indigenous values and traditional ways of life. The ensuing impoverishment of national culture, as Naranjo sees it, leads to further acceptance of imported values at the expense of national virtues, and the ultimate sacrifice of indigenous distinctiveness. The opportunity to achieve a strong national identity is thus lost, and with it the country's ability (and the ability of Spanish American culture) to determine its own destiny.

Although Naranjo identifies narcissistic behavior largely with Costa Rica's upper middle class, her portrayal of Costa Rica's lower middle class is, albeit for other reasons, also very critical.

The "Don Nadie" (Mr. Nobody) figure features prominently in her work. The main characters of *Memorias de un hombre palabra, Los perros no ladraron,* and of most fragments of *Diario de una multitud,* are anonymous individuals situated in the lower half, or at the bottom, of the social pyramid. One of her books of poetry, *Homenaje a Don Nadie* (Homage to Mr. Nobody), offers a scathing and at the same time empathic portrait of everyday individuals and the world they inhabit. She comes back to the same topic in her book of essays, *Cinco temas en busca de un pensador* (Five themes in search of a thinker), where she focuses on particularly negative characteristics of the Costa Rican character. This time she approaches the topic from a linguistic venue: With characteristic originality, she isolates five commonly used phrases ("ahí vamos," "qué le vamos a hacer," "a mí qué me importa," "de por sí," and "idiay"), which connote important idiosyncrasies of the Costa Rican people.

Returning to a topic she already had explored in her novels dealing with the bureaucratic establishment *(Los perros no ladraron* and *Memorias de un hombre palabra),* she highlights once again the individual's endurance of the numbing routine of life, "the circle which entraps, the infinitely identical day, the repetition of customs, the cinematographic image of everyday life, of the same, devoid of surprise." She connects such acquiescence with the teachings of traditional Catholicism (as opposed to those of liberation theology), which stress an unquestioning acceptance of fate. Naranjo is critical, of course, of the institutions fostering such behavior, but she also holds Costa Ricans accountable for their easy, almost indifferent and irresponsible, acceptance of such a state of affairs.

The expression "qué le vamos a hacer" (there is nothing we can do), "the most common and telling expression of our language," is particularly revealing of the individual's acquiescence to fatalism. The expression both supports and calls for accommodation. As Naranjo points out in both "ahí vamos" (this is where we are) and "qué le vamos a hacer," such accommodation is not only individual but also collective, as the plural form of the verbs indicate. The individual, instead of fighting adversity or engaging in acts of rebellion, seeks refuge in the plight of others, in the recognition that his bad luck is not just his, but a collective state of affairs. In the collective "we," the individual finds refuge from his own truth, evades his own definition, and avoids the recognition of his own passiveness. Naranjo accurately points out that the singular form of the expression "qué le voy a hacer" or its formulation as a question, "¿qué le vamos a hacer?" stress a need for action, or at the very least a conscious decision for inaction.

Lack of ambition is in her analysis a trait shared by a majority of Costa Ricans: "Our people dream little, or hardly dream at all." She proceeds to describe her nationals as "a mass without ideals, without goals in the culmination of a quiet day, hoping for an identical tomorrow." Such lack of drive and vision preclude the nourishment of indigenous virtues and values; everyone becomes easy prey for the empty rhetoric of the politicians, the professional men of vision, or the empty images and material objects coming from outside. Anything to fill the vacuum and boredom of their lives. Above all, she contends, Costa Ricans age prematurely, because age shields them from the recognition of immobility and failure, from the "deep fear of facing reality without pretexts."

Despite such a pessimistic assessment of Costa Rican society, Naranjo does not relent on the vision that guided her tenure as minister of culture, that is, to develop a society and a culture with a strong identity, one responsive to the needs of the people. Surely much of her writing would lead us to believe that such a vision is a pipe dream at best. Naranjo always comes back, however, to her confidence in the human potential, and in the force of both the individual and collective yearning for a society that has respect, dignity, sincerity, fraternity, and freedom at the center of its existence. As negative as she is about her society, she believes in the power of those she calls "the modern quijotes," and in their ability to lead, despite the fact that most of her visionary characters ultimately fail.

Rigoberta Menchú:
THE ART OF REBELLION

MARY JANE TREACY

I'd like to stress that it's not only my life, it's also the testimony of my people. The important thing is that what has happened to me has happened to many other people too: My story is the story of all poor Guatemalans. My personal experience is the reality of a whole people.
—RIGOBERTA MENCHÚ, *I, RIGOBERTA MENCHÚ: AN INDIAN WOMAN IN GUATEMALA.*

Rigoberta Menchú might not approve of this effort to put together a brief biography for this volume. It is not that the winner of the 1992 Nobel Peace Prize does not have an important or compelling life story to tell. To the contrary, this young woman from the highlands of Guatemala has organized for Indian rights and social justice throughout the turbulent 1970s and 1980s and has seen her own family members die, one by one, as victims of the poverty and repression that characterize the recent history of her country. In part because she is a Quiché Indian and her people value community over individuality, and perhaps also due to the terrible tragedies that she has witnessed and described in *I, Rigoberta Menchú: An Indian Woman in Guatemala* (1984), Rigoberta chooses to present herself as a person whose life story is important because it encapsulates the experiences of her people.

Because she does not care to focus on her own life as unique, Rigoberta does not provide the same kind of biographical information that we have come to expect in conventional autobiography. We learn that she was born in 1959, in a hamlet near San Miguel de Uspantán in the northwest, primarily Indian, province of El Quiché. She had five older siblings and three younger. As a young girl, she was immersed in the Mayan culture of her ancestors through the Quiché language and teachings of village elders, who urged her to respect mother earth, to cultivate the land, and to care for its animals. Like the women before her, Rigoberta was trained to grind corn and make the dough for tortillas, to grow the beans that are the staple diet of her people, and to weave the clothing that mark her identity as a member of one of twenty-two Indian groups in Guatemala today.

It is unlikely that the child Rigoberta paid much attention to the nation whose citizenship she bears. She did not speak or understand Spanish, did not go to school, and therefore did not learn to read or write in any language, and she did not socialize with any non-Indian children in her racially segregated society. But she did learn how difficult it was for Indians to survive in a country where a mestizo minority (called Ladinos in Guatemala) control all national institutions and create their wealth from Indian labor. She and her family spent approximately four months of every year in their highland home growing subsistence crops of corn and beans, and the rest of the year—together or apart—working in coastal coffee, cotton, and sugar plantations. Rigoberta worked beside her mother in the fields from a very early age, either gathering crops or tending to her younger siblings, and she got her first paying job picking coffee when she was only eight years old. Plantation life was extremely hard for young and old alike: Indians were transported there in covered trucks, stacked up in barracks with few sanitary conditions, forced to work long hours for very little pay, and treated with contempt by their Ladino overseers and landowners.

It was on the plantations that Rigoberta came into contact with Indians from other groups and realized that they suffered the same exploitation. It was there, too, that one older brother died of pesticide poisoning, and she watched as another brother died of malnutrition. And it was there that the plantation owner's henchmen exacted work under threat of violence. As a teenager, Rigoberta began to see that she was destined to the same bestial work, poverty, and suffering as her mother, and, although lacking a clear direction, she began to get angry and look for ways to escape what seemed like an ominous fate. A short and humiliating period as a maid in Guatemala City convinced Rigoberta that Ladino women exploited Indians in the home just as Ladino men did in the fields. The girl was living out the cruel statistics of her country: 85 percent of the population survive in poverty, some 60 percent in utter misery; 63 percent are illiterate, and female Indians have a life expectancy of only forty-seven years, compared to forty-nine for their male counterparts.

Yet there were avenues to possible social change. During Rigoberta's childhood, a national religious movement, Acción Católica, was sending catechists to work with the Indians. Originally a conservative group whose goal was to assure doctrinal orthodoxy and social assimilation of the Indian, Acción Católica sent many clergy and lay workers who genuinely sympathized with the economic plight of the Indians and initiated religious study among them that had potential for raising consciousness about social conditions. By bringing people together for prayer, Acción Católica established a means of organizing. Its Bible study, perhaps intended to lull Indian participants into resignation to the status quo, in fact allowed the faithful to relate religious teachings—not surprisingly, David and Goliath was a favorite—to their Guatemalan reality.[1] Rigoberta's mother and father became catechists. This gave them an opportunity to travel to other villages in the region, not only bringing prayer but also the conversations necessary to fight for a modern-day exodus of their people.

Rigoberta tells us that she too was a catechist since she was "a girl," and that her current political activities are those of a revolutionary Christian. She tells us that Indians are profoundly religious, seeing the sacred in all aspects of life. Accordingly, she does not make a distinction between the religious aspect of her activism and the political nature of her faith:

> Well, my work is just like being a catechist, except that I'm one who walks on the Earth, not one who thinks that the Kingdom of God only comes after death. Through all my experiences, through everything I'd seen, through so much pain and suffering, I learned what the role of a Christian in the struggle is, and what the role of a Christian on this Earth is. We all came to important conclusions by studying the Bible. All our *compañeros* did. We discovered that the Bible has been used as a way of making us accept our situation, and not to bring enlightenment to the poor. The work of revolutionary Christians is above all to condemn and denounce the injustices committed against the people.[2]

Unfortunately, Rigoberta and her *compañeros* found much to denounce. Since the Spanish conquest, Guatemala has been a country of profound social inequalities supported and maintained by weak and often corrupt governments. In the twentieth century the power of the United Fruit Company as the country's largest landowner, the development of a national oligarchy whose wealth was based on export crops, and the use of the military to support such a social system has only aggravated existing injustices. When 1960s and 1970s saw a rise in guerrilla insurgency, the state unleashed the terror of counterinsurgency campaigns—informal death squads, militarization of the countryside, massacres of entire towns, and scorched earth policies—that made mere survival a central concern for most grass roots organizers and their sympathizers. It is said that Guatemala gave Spanish America the infamous and frightening verb "to be disappeared," coined after so many were taken away from their home, never to be seen again. Stories of Guatemala's repression, tortures, and cruelty abound, and the Indians, feared to be and to harbor guerrilla fighters, received the brunt of this violence. Rigoberta's brother was disappeared, tortured, and then burned alive with other unfortunates in front of the townsfolk who were forced to watch the army's display of power. Later, her father was killed during a protest in the Spanish embassy in Guatemala City. Later still, her mother was raped, tortured, left to die, and refused burial as an example to others who aspired to social change.

Indians had few options during these dangerous decades. Some became informers, others guerrilla fighters, and still others joined political organizations. As did her father before his death, Rigoberta started to work with the Committee for Peasant Unity (Comité de Unidad Campesina, or CUC), founded in 1978 to protect peasants from the appropriation of their land and exploitation of their labor. Still strong today, the CUC fights for just wages, decent working conditions, and fair prices for crops. It also demands the right to organize peasants, to keep Indian lands, and to maintain cultural identity and dignity for Indian peoples as well as the right to live and be free from repression.

Even Rigoberta's nonviolent work for peasant and Indian rights made her a target for disappearance and political assassination. One day soldiers spotted her in the street, and she had a narrow escape by hiding in a local church. Realizing that she was in danger and that her presence also would endanger others, she managed to find temporary quarters working, yet again as a servant, in a convent until her *compañeros* could get her on a plane to Mexico. She left in 1981. Rigoberta now lives in exile and has become well known worldwide for her activist work on behalf of Indian people and all of Guatemala's poor. She has been able, after winning the

Nobel Peace Prize, to return to Guatemala on short visits, and her writings are now available in her country. But Guatemala's passion is not over, and she still cannot go home.

U.S. readers first heard of Rigoberta Menchú when her life story was translated and published in English by the London-based Verso Press in 1984. By this time, Latin Americanists and literary scholars had become interested in what seemed to be a new genre of literature, the *testimonio*, or witnessing act, which gave voice to the silenced majority of people in Central and South America. Like several other politicized women in the region, Menchú recounted her experiences to an intellectual, the Venezuelan anthropologist Elizabeth Burgos-Debray, who in turn structured the oral material and fashioned it into what appears to be a first-person account.[3] Critics have been examining just how the intellectual, who does not speak in the testimonial text itself, really stands behind the scene asking the questions, ordering the narration, and giving the tone or political direction that best suits her or his interests. Indeed, there is an irony that the very act of "giving voice" (that is, providing a vehicle for the disenfranchised to reach a public forum) to the marginalized may also involve appropriation of their lives. For instance, the first editions of *I, Rigoberta Menchú*, which were published simultaneously in Spanish and French in 1983, present Elizabeth Burgos as the author and view Rigoberta as the object of her study. Examples such as this ask First World readers, and perhaps Third World elites as well, to consider how we look at the marginalized whose stories we read and how we represent these "others" in our thinking, literature, and art.

We are perhaps most comfortable viewing the experiences of Third World peoples as exotic and quite different from ourselves. We tend to see through an idealized "tourist" lens that provides a Rigoberta colorfully dressed in Indian garb, a vision that appears on the cover of every edition of her work and is described in almost all the newspaper and magazine articles written about her. We also focus on her suffering, which permits us to feel compassion while entertaining a certain frisson of horror at the violence detailed in this testimonial story. Responses such as these do not point only to the individual reader's appropriation of the life story for our own interests but also to the existence of hegemonic modes of seeing or reading that, unchecked, reinscribe colonialism and the social dominance inherent in it. The Third World comes to our awareness for our pleasure or need. Thus, even as we read *about* Rigoberta Menchú, we may very well be seeing only what is important to us. Rigoberta, the twenty-three-year-old Quiché woman, becomes a mirror reflecting our own dreams or nightmares.

Some North Americans look to Rigoberta's story as means to transform the way we understand the world around us. They claim that we usually do not hear the opinions of those who hold little or no social power. We tend to exclude all but a few exceptional women, poor, racial, and ethnic minorities and other outcasts from our thinking; if they can write, they are not published, if they are published, they are not widely read. As a result, we see only the views and debates of those with some claim to power. Although seemingly self-evident, this notion has far-reaching implications: it suggests that what we have come to think of as knowledge is not truth but rather an interpretation constructed in the context of hierarchical social relations and passed on as objective fact. And if we begin to interrogate knowledge, we come to ask how it was developed over time, who participated in its development and who was excluded from this process, and what these silent observers might have added or questioned.

Rigoberta, who is triply marginalized as a Central American, an Indian, and a woman, not only has different opinions than do most Ladinos or North Americans on such pertinent issues as the place of the Indian in modern society, but also reveals a distinct framework for understanding the world that challenges our own. Her concepts of what it means to be an individual, a woman, or what social justice entails do not fit easily into the paradigms we generally hold. Thus, she is in a position to reorient and to enrich our ways of thinking, or at least this is the hope of those who support the current multicultural movement to introduce ethnic, racial, and international perspectives in our U.S.-European world view.

Of course, new paradigms are also disturbing and not everyone supports opening up traditional Western thought to include the perspectives of the non-elite. Indeed, when Dinesh D'Souza singled out Rigoberta Menchú as the epitome of all that is wrong in contemporary American education, the Quiché woman—most probably unbeknown to her—became a rallying cry of both the Right and the Left in the "culture wars" of the 1980s and early 1990s. Whereas research on Rigoberta and her text now proliferates on our campuses, D'Souza sees the inclusion of *I, Rigoberta Menchú* into university curricula as the symbol of a multiculturalism that not only removes any notion of hierarchy in cultural values but also legitimizes radical feminist and Marxist views as it establishes a sort of victim studies to appease minority interests. His third chapter, "Travels with Rigoberta: Multiculturalism at Stanford," rails at academics' idealization of the Third World and use of what he would consider to be second-rate materials to sustain a simplistic critique of Western culture:

> Rigoberta's victim status may be unfortunate for her personal happiness, but is indispensable for her academic reputation. Rigoberta is a modern Saint Sebastian, pierced by the arrows of North American white male cruelty; thus her life story becomes an explicit indictment of the historical role of the West and Western institutions.[4]

D'Souza and other conservative thinkers are correct to suspect that inclusion of Rigoberta and other Third World voices into the curricula can do more than just give equal time to "others." If culture is a site where power relations are maintained or enhanced, then a policy of decentering a Western world view reduces the importance of traditional works and perhaps calls the values they embody into question. Latin American testimonial literature, narrated as it is by the disenfranchised, often calls for profound social change if not outright revolution. Rigoberta's testimony can be used, and maybe even is intended to be used, to encourage political action against the Guatemalan government, to gain support for progressive parties and organizations, and to bring to light the plight of the Indian in a discriminatory society. It is undoubtedly a political text. Moreover, its focus on social injustice and organization of mass resistance may well spill over to advance a left-wing or progressive agenda in other countries as well.

For this reason, some view Rigoberta Menchú as a political threat. Certainly the Guatemalan military saw her as a "subversive," intent upon undermining the authority of the state. Her critics in the United States also perceive Rigoberta as a revolutionary and an ally of the guerrillas. Both groups are partially correct, for those who wish to see Rigoberta only as a symbol of a harmonious multiculturalism fail to acknowledge that she is calling for social revolution, often but not exclusively in Marxist terms. Her CUC analyzes Guatemala's situation in terms of economic exploitation by foreign capital and native elites and has as its primary agenda the development of a popular revolutionary war. Rigoberta considers the masses to be the only group capable of social change and therefore has dedicated her life to the politicization of the people. Indeed, her testimony is not the autobiography that the English title might suggest but rather a story of her own ideological transformation, which is stated explicitly in the Spanish title of her book: *My name is Rigoberta Menchú and This is How My Consciousness Was Born.*[5] Its purpose is to inform as well as guide our interpretation of contemporary Guatemalan social conditions.

Rigoberta's Christianity leads her to value sacrifice, even of one's own life, for the benefit of others and the eventual triumph of her political ideals. But she does not speak only of martyrdom. Bible study has also led Rigoberta to espouse the possibility of a just war against an oppressor and violence against the state is one of the strategies to be used in this war. Even as a girl Rigoberta took part in her village's defenses against possible army intrusion. She learned to lay traps for and to ambush soldiers; to throw lime, chili, salt, and hot water into their faces; and to throw stones with deadly intent. Later, as an adult, Rigoberta does not make a clear distinction between herself and other members of a nonmilitary organization like the CUC and the guerrillas: all are the friends/ comrades who are referred to as *compañeros*. The only difference seems to be geographical: the guerrillas are the *compañeros* in the mountains, the others work elsewhere. She mentions that her mother had contact with the guerrilla and that two of her sisters took up arms. A conversation with one of her guerrilla sisters that Rigoberta reports shows how both women employ the language of love and sacrifice to articulate their political commitments. The sister tells Rigoberta: "I'm happy. Don't worry about me. Even if I suffer hunger, pain and long marches in the mountains. I'm doing it with love and I'm doing it for you."[6] The two then hear mass and take communion. Catholicism, Indian values, and guerrilla warfare are inextricably blended together to form one multifaceted movement for social justice. Thus Rigoberta shows no signs of horror at the existence of a guerrilla movement or its left-wing philosophies; she has merely decided to work elsewhere toward the same goals.

If news and magazine accounts are any indication, North American supporters of Rigoberta are rather squeamish about her links to guerrillas and try to distance her from them by emphasizing her work for human rights. Although her personal suffering during the repression as well as her public condemnation of atrocities helped focus world outrage at Guatemala's genocidal practices, attempts to ignore or downplay her revolutionary social agenda only serve to make Rigoberta more palatable to North American liberal audiences. They also force her into a U.S. political framework that divides reform from revolution and politicians from insurgents. Indeed, this is one area where Rigoberta may ask us to rethink our paradigms and to imagine what work for social justice and human rights in a Guatemalan context may actually entail. She may remind us that Guatemala during the repression of the 1970s and 1980s was a world "so evil, so bloodthirsty that the only road open is our struggle, the just war."[7]

If reading Rigoberta asks us to examine our cultural values and political assumptions, it also poses questions about how one can live in multicultural societies. Guatemala has a Ladino minority with power and a majority Indian population, divided into twenty-two groups that are separated by geography, language, and history. Rigoberta tells us some of the customs and traditions of her village that pass on a Quiché ethnicity to a younger generation. After the birth of a child, for instance, parents make a public commitment to teach their newborn to honor the ancestors, to maintain a traditional way of life, and to keep the secrets of the Indian people. Children learn that the Spaniards dishonored their ancestors and that Ladinos are not to be trusted. Rigoberta's grandfather used to tell her that "the caxlans [Ladinos] are thieves. Have nothing to do with them. You keep all our ancestors' things,"[8] and her father refused to send her to school in order to keep her from Ladino influences. What Rigoberta does not tell us, however, is that traditional Indian societies were breaking down during the time of her childhood. Conscription of Indian men into the army, public schools, as well as modern media such as the radio brought more contact with Ladino society, while proselytizing evangelicals and the Acción Católica directly undercut the authority of village elders and institutions. As victims of racist oppression and genocidal attacks, many Indians sought to counter a possible ethnic eradication with the development of a pan-Mayan identity.[9] The descriptions of Quiché customs that Rigoberta gives in her testimony are, therefore, more than an offering of ethnographic curios surrounding the primary tale of ideological development. They are one half of a dialogue with the dominant Ladino culture which asserts resistance to it, either showing how the Quiché hold on to ancient rites as a mark of identity or create new "traditions" to develop a Mayan sense of self worth for the present day.

It appears that Rigoberta grew up in an ethnically "pure" environment. She learned the traditions and wore the Indian clothing of her region, refusing makeup and other coquetries characteristic of the Ladino girl. But as soon as she left her highland village to work on the plantations, she came into contact with other Indians and soon recognized that the cultural isolation of each group actually fragmented and disempowered them all. She therefore set out to learn several Indian languages as well as the language of power in Guatemala, the one language that consistently had been used against the Indian, Spanish. Now Rigoberta turned the "master's" language against him; with it she could communicate with others within Guatemala and also bring her country's plight to world public opinion. Moreover, while working, presumably in Spanish, with the Committee for Peasant Unity, Rigoberta began to realize that there were poor Ladinos as well as rich ones and that these poor were as exploited as the Indians. She began to see how unanalyzed racism divided and weakened them all: poor Ladinos still found dignity in their contempt for the Indian, Indians rejected other Indians who lost their traditions or who interacted with Ladinos, even Rigoberta recognized the "thorn in her own heart" that led her to dismiss all Ladinos as unable to understand or work with her. Rigoberta decided to keep her commitment to the CUC and to continue contact with Ladino peasants and sympathetic intellectuals. In so doing, she broke with the isolationist tradition of her people as well as the more recent Mayan separatism.

Rigoberta Menchú did not lose her Indian heritage, nor did she become, as some say, a mouthpiece for left-wing class analysis. She remains as fervent in her support of Mayan identity and Indian rights as in her hope for a Christian social revolution. But she is a skilled organizer who knows that progressive Guatemalans need to work in coalitions to build a new society and a savvy politician who uses foreign intellectuals and presses to help this cause. So although her interlocutor and editor Elizabeth Burgos could fall into reveries of a Venezuelan childhood as she watched Rigoberta make tortillas in her Paris home, we can bet that Rigoberta knew exactly why she was in France telling her life story to a woman with excellent international connections.

Academics and intellectuals have often demanded that Rigoberta represent something: either an idealized indigenist past or absolute resistance to the West (she points to anthropologists and sociologists as the most common offenders). But she rejects these interpretations of her role as much as she dismisses the notion that Indians cannot and should not participate in Western culture. To the contrary, in her latest work Rigoberta asserts:

> This separatist agenda is not very intelligent and does very little to help indigenous peoples. I, for instance, use the fax quite a bit, I like the fax. Do they expect us to protest by mule? The Mayans discovered the concept of zero, so we have the right to advance in the sciences, to understand the world in all its complexity, to have opinions on things besides our own ethnic problem.[10]

Thus, she sees no contradiction between maintenance of an Indian identity and modernization of Indian life. Rigoberta envisions a Guatemala that is committed to human development as well as to human rights, where Ladinos and Indians can work together, and where Indians can maintain their heritages as they become involved with world affairs. She will wear her Quiché clothing and send her fax.

On October 16, 1992, the Norwegian Noble Committee recognized Rigoberta's work for social justice and ethnic reconciliation by awarding her that year's Peace Prize. In her acceptance speech, Rigoberta urged her public to "fight for a better world, without poverty, without racism, with peace."[11] At the beginning of a new decade and five hundred years after the European conquest of America, it was fitting to honor an Indian woman who wishes to stand for the existence and well-being of the indigenous peoples who lost their lands and autonomy to European settlers and who urges us all to transcend our differences in order to work together toward a common goal of social justice and peace. What her activism, her testimony with the collaboration of Elizabeth Burgos, and the positive and negative reception to her work throughout the world reveal is just how difficult it is to go beyond one's world view and to hear what another is saying. This is perhaps Rigoberta's greatest challenge to us all.

The Mayans have a saying that "every mind is a world," that is, that any one person is as rich in complexity and change as the universe. So even if Rigoberta did not tell us explicitly that she was not going to reveal all her Quiché secrets, we would still understand that we can never grasp this woman in her entirety. Rigoberta escapes our desire to know her and even hints that our attempts to gain this knowledge is a desire for possession. Even though she gives us only what she wants us to know about Rigoberta the public figure, she tells us enough about her values and dreams to confound attempts to reduce her to a mere symbol to fulfill someone's need for a left-wing menace, the downfall of Western culture, the salvation of a multicultural America, or the essence of the eternal Mayan. Rigoberta's life story represents her vision of a better Guatemala: she embodies her Quiché heritage yet is open to the world beyond it, she makes public the extremely painful deaths of family members to speak out for human rights, and she maintains an ideal of social justice after many years of struggle and sacrifice. Rigoberta Menchú is a woman of courage who still has much to teach us.

Julia de Burgos:
WOMAN, POET, LEGEND

CARMEN ESTEVES

⌐ SINCE HER DEATH IN 1953, when she was found unconscious at the corner of Fifth Avenue and 105th Street in New York City, the name Julia de Burgos has kindled a variety of images and emotions in her readers and has become an integral part of the Puerto Rican psyche. Poet, worker, teacher, political activist, devoted daughter and sister, passionate lover, immigrant, exile, alcoholic: Julia de Burgos, a women ahead of her time. Her life and poetry mirror our aspirations, our ideals, our fears, our passions.

The great popularity and admiration she has achieved among poetry lovers and critics and in nonliterary circles is a response to the quality of her poetry, the poetic universe she created, and a fascination with her persona, which to this day remains shrouded in mystery and contradictions.

In terms of quantity, her literary production is limited: three books of poetry, and essays, reviews, and other poems scattered in newspapers, especially in *Pueblos hispanos*. Still, given the difficulties she faced in her short life, the fact that she was able to complete three books of poetry speak of the power of her creativity and her strength and will to carry on.

Julia de Burgos was born in 1914 in the neighborhood of Santa Cruz in the town of Carolina, in the countryside, surrounded by hills, flowers, and fruit trees. From her house she could hear the wind that dwells in the mountains and, above all, the whisper of her river, the Río Grande de Loíza. Wind, river, whispers, elements that nurtured her poetry. As a young child she would accompany her mother and sisters to the river, where her mother would narrate stories about the water spirit who lived in a palace surrounded by angels and children at the bottom of the river. Julia's love and devotion for her mother reached poetic form in "Mi madre y el río" in which mother and river, two axes of her emotional and poetic world are united. Her imagination was also nourished by her father, an avid reader who would recount stories—real and fictional—to his children and would take them horseback riding at night. Many times these outings would end with the family sleeping outdoors in open fields surrounded by the sounds of the night.[1]

The beauty and poetry of the countryside she loved, and which would sing in her poems, was far from a perfect world. Her childhood and adolescence were marked by extreme poverty, burdens, and difficulties. She was the oldest of thirteen children, only seven of whom survived hunger and disease. Her father was an alcoholic, a path she eventually followed. Although her drinking problem has always been attributed to the constant tribulations that followed her life—especially her love life—it is now recognized that the children of alcoholics often succumb to the same addiction. This is an important fact and one that, to some degree, should dispel the notion that Julia de Burgos drowned in alcohol solely to forget her lover.

From 1920 to 1926 she completed six years of elementary school in her neighborhood and then transferred to a school in Carolina, where she completed the seventh and eighth grades, graduating with honors. After her graduation in 1928, her family moved to Río

Piedras in order to provide her with a better education, although this move represented an even harsher economic reality for them. In the countryside they had a small plot of land that provided vegetables to feed them or which they sold to buy other goods. She completed high school in three years, graduating in 1931 from the High School of the University of Puerto Rico. Burgos went on to the University of Puerto Rico, where she enrolled in a Department of Education program that prepared elementary school teachers in two years. She was able to attend her second year through a scholarship she received due to her extreme poverty. Julia always admired the teaching profession, and years later, when her sister Consuelo wrote to her expressing interest in a teaching career, Julia had inspiring words of encouragement for her. At the university she learned about the nationalist movement and its leader, Pedro Albizu Campos, and from then on she became an ardent advocate of independence for Puerto Rico and fighter against all forms of colonialism.

The 1930s were years of worldwide economic depression, and in Puerto Rico the median family income fell by two-thirds. After she graduated in May 1933, Burgos found work distributing breakfasts to needy children under the Puerto Rico Economic Rehabilitation Agency (PRERA), part of Roosevelt's New Deal. When this program ended in 1935, Julia went to work as an elementary school teacher in the countryside, in the mountain town of Naranjito, where she wrote "Río Grande de Loíza," one of her best and well-known poems. Her mother was diagnosed with cancer of the leg in 1935, and after several operations, her leg was amputated and she died in 1939. In order to provide financial support for her mother's medical expenses, Julia traveled throughout the island trying to sell her first published book of poetry, *Poema en veinte surcos*. Her mother's death left a profound sorrow in Julia's spirit.

After teaching in Naranjito for one school year, she moved to Old San Juan and took two courses at the University of Puerto Rico. She always wanted to complete her bachelors degree but her financial circumstances never permitted it. Still, she was an avid reader and borrowed books from the Carnegie Library and from the library at the Central High School, where her sister Consuelo was studying. A few years later in Cuba she would also enroll in courses at the University of Havana.

During the school year of 1936–37, she worked as a writer for the School of the Air, a program sponsored by the Department of Education of the government of Puerto Rico that was modeled on the educational programs of the Columbia Broadcasting System (CBS). Some of its goals were to fight illiteracy and to offer information about social, agricultural, and economic problems, especially to farmers and farm workers. It is possible that Burgos came to know about this project through friends of her first husband, the journalist Rubén Rodríguez Beauchamp, whom she married in 1934 and divorced in 1937. Only four of the texts she wrote as part of this program have been preserved: two written for children, "Llamita quiere ser mariposa" and "Un paisaje marino," and two used as teaching aids in other social programs addressed to rural areas, "La parranda del sábado" and "Coplas jíbaras para ser cantadas."[2] "Un paisaje marino" is an early example of Julia's ever-present fascination with the sea as she projects her feelings into a child-poet's reaction when he first sees the sea.

Burgos's struggle for equality and women' rights is well known. In "La parranda del sábado," subtitled "Diálogo," Joaquina, a peasant, answers back to her boyfriend when he accuses her of fearing everything, and she asserts simply and categorically that she does not fear him. It is not certain why Burgos stopped working at the School of the Air. Some biographers believe it was for political reasons given the climate of repression that existed at the time and her known political militancy, but this has never been established.

Burgos's first political poems appeared at the same time as the political activities of the Nationalist Party, presided over by Pedro Albizu Campos, began to unfold. In 1934 Pedro Albizu Campos participated directly in a strike by sugarcane workers. This action precipitated the beginning of the repression of the *nacionalistas*. On October 24, 1935, three people were killed and forty wounded in an attack by the police on a nationalist activity, which has become known as the Río Piedras Massacre. Pedro Albizu Campos and other nationalists were accused and sent to jail for the murder of Francis Riggs, the chief of police. These attacks culminated on Palm Sunday in March 1937, in the Ponce Massacre, where by order of the governor, Blanton Winship, an attack on a rally left twenty-one people dead and two hundred wounded. Pedro Albizu Campos, who was in prison at the La Princesa penitentiary, in Old San Juan, was then transferred to Atlanta, Georgia, where he would remain for ten years. Juan Antonio Corretjer, her good friend, was also jailed in Atlanta. That same month Julia published the poem "Domingo de Pascua," inspired by the massacre.

It was during this turbulent year that she organized what is considered her first collection of poems, *Poemas exactos a mí misma*. Only references to this collection now exist.[3] In November of that same year she published "Cortando distancias" in the journal *Renovación,* and in December, in the daily *El Imparcial,* she published several poems: "Interrogaciones," "Paisaje interior," "Ronda nocturna," "Ya no es canción," "Pentacromía," and "Ven."

While she lived in Old San Juan in 1938 she met and developed friendships with the poet Luis Lloréns Torres and other members of his literary circle at El Chévere, a coffee house restaurant in Santurce frequented by artists and intellectuals, among them the poets Evaristo Ribera Chevremont and Luis Palés Matos. In December, her collection *Poema en veinte surcos* was published.

1939 was a highly significant year in the emotional life of Julia de Burgos. In the first half of that year she met the man she loved most deeply, and who most deeply hurt her, Juan Isidro Jimenes Grullón, a medical doctor and political leader from the Dominican Republic. And in October of the same year her mother died despite all the sacrifices Julia had made to provide her medical care. Two days after her mother's death, a poetry reading in Burgos's honor was given at the Ateneo Puertorriqueño. On that occasion she read an elegiac poem in honor of her mother, "Mi madre y el río." In December her second book of poetry, *Canción de la verdad sencilla,* was published, and it received an award from the Instituto de Literatura Puertorriqueña.

Grullón's departure for New York City, in November of 1939, marked the path Julia would follow—a path of no return to her homeland. In January 1940 she arrived in New York City to live with Jimenes Grullón. During her first stay in New York she was the subject of several interviews, reviews of her work appeared in the newspaper *La Prensa,* and a recital of her poetry took place at the Master Theater. Shortly afterward, Grullón departed for Cuba, but financial problems prevented her from following him. She tried to sell her books to survive but was unsuccessful. She worked for two weeks in April for the U.S. Census Bureau and in June left for Cuba. In July she wrote to her sister from Havana about the possibility of a return visit to Puerto Rico but conceded in the letter that such a trip would be emotionally impossible for her. This letter, dated July 17, 1940, is significant in trying to understand her self-imposed exile, as well as the pleasure and satisfaction she derived from writing poetry.[4] The letter speaks of her surprise and extreme happiness over an award given in Puerto Rico to her book *Canción de la verdad sencilla.* What so surprised her about the award was that she did not expect justice or recognition for her poetry from people on the island, where she always claimed to have left behind many undeserved enemies. Who were they? Probably members of a patriarchal society that condemned her for being a divorced woman, and of a society that castigated her for her outspoken political ideas of freedom for Puerto Rico and for her militancy in the party of Albizu Campos. There are many references in letters to her sister Consuelo to the rejection she felt from Puerto Rican society. When Consuelo wrote to Julia about her wish to become a teacher, Julia replied with encouragement, adding that she hoped that Consuelo would not suffer discrimination because of being unfairly identified with her. Burgos concluded that she had received the literary award because the power of her poetry had overcome the resistance to her views.

The rejection Burgos experienced in Puerto Rico had another dimension in New York. She had left her island and her family to follow the man she loved, but the family of Jimenes Grullón always rejected her. When his family left New York and established their residence in Cuba, the son followed and Julia soon joined him. Burgos stayed in Cuba for two years, from June 1940 to June 1942. These were years of love, isolation, pain, humiliation, study, and intense creativity. She wrote most of her third book of poetry, *El mar y tú,* between September and October 1940, and in January 1941, sent the almost completed manuscript to Puerto Rico with the poet Carmen Alicia Cadilla. She also published poems and articles in newspapers and magazines in Havana and Santiago, and she was the subject of an article in the magazine *Vanidades.* Her departure from Cuba followed the rupture of her relationship with Grullón after the conflicts with his family reached a crisis. He chose his family and its social standing over her.

On June 19, 1942, Julia returned to New York City. In the city that became her second home she held a variety of jobs, lived in different places, and went from one emotional crisis to another, that led to her drinking and eventual death from cirrhosis of the liver.

Between 1943 and 1944 she worked for the weekly *Pueblos hispanos* as a reporter and interviewer.[5] From June 8, 1944, to August 26, 1944, she served as the director of its cultural section, which focused on providing information to residents of the city as well as the travelers who had an interest in Latin America. As director she attended concerts, art exhibits, recitals, and conferences given by prominent members of the Latin American community who resided in New York or were passing through. Both these positions enabled her to participate in an intense cultural life and to attempt to rebuild her life by focusing her efforts on the "pains of the world in order not to feel her own so deeply."[6] Once again her political ideology was brought to the foreground as she discovered her interest in disseminating the culture of the Americas as a way to foster the pan-American ideals of her teachers Juan Albizu, José María de Hostos, José Martí, and Gabriela Mistral. In *Pueblos hispanos* she published eight poems, seven essays, six reviews, seven interviews, and one story. All the poems were of a political nature.

This was also the period of the massive exodus from the Puerto Rican countryside to New York City, in the 1940s and 1950s, after the decline in Puerto Rican agriculture left thousands unemployed and the government failed to recognize this as a problem. Burgos's story "En la cantina de la juventud" deals with this migration on a personal level. As Julia did so many times, the main character of the story evokes her earlier life in the Puerto Rican countryside. The washerwomen, Comai Sica, recalls the clear water of the stream where she was able to earn a living washing neighbors' clothes, the loss of her customers, the letter written to a son in New York asking for help, and the ticket he sent making it possible for her to flee the island to join him in New York. This pattern, followed to this day by the poor of Puerto Rico, is captured early on by Julia's sensibility, perhaps because she always saw herself as an outsider in New York. Here is one more dimension of Julia that contributes so much to her enduring appeal: like so many other members of the Puerto Rican community she chose exile for personal, political, economic, and cultural reasons, although her love for her country and the integrity of her vision of a free motherland always remained intact.

While she worked for *Pueblos hispanos* she married Armando Marín, a musician and public accountant. Julia lived in Washington, D.C., for a year, where he worked. However, this city, "the city of silence" as she called it in a letter to her sister, only deepened her nostalgia for Puerto Rico and made her long for a return to New York City, where its large Hispanic population made her feel closer to her true home. In Washington she felt as if she were living in a vacuum. It is in this letter that she called New York, the city of steel, her second home.[7]

Julia returned to New York in August 1945. That year she published the essay "Ser o no ser es la divisa" in the weekly, *Semanario hispánico,* and for it she received an award for journalism from the Instituto de Literatura Puertorriqueña in 1946. This award prompted several New York activities and readings in her honor. In this essay Burgos outlined her social and moral ideology: Humankind has two choices, to be on the side of freedom or to be on the side of reactionary forces; in concrete terms, to unite our voices and efforts to destroy the regimes of Somoza, Trujillo, and Carías or through indifference or sympathy to support their criminal governments; to side with the Spanish Republic or support the traitor Franco.[8]

After 1946 her alcoholism became more dramatic; she developed cirrhosis of the liver, and her emotional state further deteriorated. Her pilgrimage through New York City hospitals began in 1947. Even so, she continued to work on *El mar y tú* but was extremely disappointed because her sister Consuelo was unable to publish it in Puerto Rico. But her spirit was never completely broken. Until the end Julia de Burgos was faithful to her art and her creative spirit. In 1951 she participated in a radio program dedicated to Luis Lloréns Torres and she read her "Homenaje al cantor de Collores," as Lloréns was known. A few weeks later she suffered a violent crisis that brought her close to death, and in the midst of it she wrote "Poema con un solo después." The original has a notation at the end: "Después de mi muerte vencida. En mitad del 25 de julio de mi vida amenazada" (After I overcame death. In the middle of July 25th when my life was threatened). She also worked as director of the Album Literario Puertorriqueño between 1950 and 1951.

While she was hospitalized in Goldwater Memorial Hospital, between January and May 1953, she wrote two poems in English, "Farewell in Welfare Island" and "The Sun in Welfare Island." She also wrote many letters to Consuelo, letters that testify to her anguish, her depression, her desperate financial situation, and her attempts, despite all this hardship and illness, to maintain her dignity. Finally, after escaping from the home of friends several times, she was found unconscious on July 5, 1953, on the corner of Fifth Avenue and 105th Street and taken to Harlem Hospital, where she died minutes after her arrival. Because no identification papers were found on her, she was buried in a common grave at Potter's Field. It was not until a month later that her body was identified, exhumed, and taken to Puerto Rico for burial in Carolina—her first true place of rest—near her river, immortalized in her poem "Río Grande de Loíza."

Since her death many people have paid tribute to Julia de Burgos. Writers, painters, critics, intellectuals, political activists, journalists, people from all walks of life have been drawn to her persona. For Julia the greatest homage would have been to know of the publication, in 1954, of her third book of poetry, *El mar y tú,* and the knowledge that her poetry remains read, vibrantly alive, and a source of inspiration and courage for today's artists.

The reader who opens *Poema en veinte surcos,* her first book, encounters in this collection of twenty-one poems an open challenge to the social conventions that attempt to set limits and boundaries on women; a poet who reaches for her poetic voice to fight against the silence and submissiveness society imposes on women. Hers is a cry for social justice, for independence for her island. These are the poems in which the poverty that surrounded her childhood became poetry. As José Emilio González, one of her most dedicated critics said, "If Julia de Burgos had only written just this one book she would still be considered one of Puerto Rico's most important poets."[9] Her metaphoric skills, her imagery, her conflict-filled relationships, her poetic diction, are already present in her first collection of poetry.

Three of her most famous poems are included in *Poema en veinte surcos:* "A Julia de Burgos," which opens the collection "Río Grande de Loíza," and "Yo misma fui mi ruta," the poem that closes the collection. In "A Julia de Burgos" we see for the first time one of Burgos's most important themes and her mature poetic style: the poet-subject dichotomy, the confrontation of opposites. The poetic voice opposes her authentic "I"—the poet, the essence— to the false "you"—the conventional woman molded by society— establishing a radical difference between them:

> *La que se alza en mis versos no es tu voz es mi voz;*
> *porque tú eres ropaje y la esencia soy yo;*
> *y el más profundo abismo se tiende entre las dos.*
> *Tú eres fría muñeca de mentira social,*
> *y yo viril destello de la humana verdad.*[10]

The presentation is dramatic and lyric, two constants in her writing, and the poem, with its perfectly structured and balanced theme of ambivalence, attains a dialogic relation with itself. Verse by verse the poet establishes the contrasts that separate the subject from the poetic voice. It is significant that the opening poem in her first collection takes us in depth to one of her recurrent themes: the plurality of the "I."

In the poem "Intima," the poetic voice objectifies herself again through the image of a path, a voyage, once again favorite images in her poems:

> *Peregrina en mí misma, me anduve un largo instante*
> *Me prolongué en el rumbo de aquel camino errante*
> *que se abría en mi interior*
> *y me llegué hasta mí, íntima.*
> *Conmigo cabalgando seguí por la sombra del tiempo*
> *y me hice paisaje lejos de mi visión.*
>
> (p. 11)

It also points to her preference for movement and change, which implies growth, over what is static and lacking fluidity. This existential position is reflected in the motion she creates in her verses, and in water, her favorite element.

To the Río Grande de Loíza, the river of her childhood, Burgos dedicated what is probably the best-known and most-quoted of her poems. It is a poem that combines lyrical eroticism, the man-river, with the deepest patriotic feeling for "mi esclavo pueblo." The poem is built around a time that has past—remembered fondly—and a cruel present with the image of the river and its rich tones of red, white, black, and blue holding together the temporal distances. Burgos's symbolic world finds its roots in nature, especially in things related to water: streams, rivers, the sea, rain, tears, brooks, droplets. It is important to understand that water serves as a symbol of both the subjective or collective unconscious, a representation of intuition and artistic imagination. Seen through this perspective, many of her poems can be read as artistic explorations of the creative spirit, and of the process of writing itself.

Luz María Umpierre has examined how the sea serves as a metapoetic code in Burgos's collection *El mar y tú.* [11] This code is already present in *Poema en veinte surcos* and offers another interpretation to "Río Grande de Loíza." The verbal pattern of the third stanza is an apostrophe to the river in the imperative form that can be read as a recreation of the creative process, with the poem "the rose" as the final product: "confúndete en el vuelo de mi fantasía / y déjame una rosa de agua en mis ensueños" (p. 13). In the poem that serves as closure to *El mar y tú,* "Poema para mi muerte," her poetry is symbolized by a flower, in this case a carnation. In "Río Grande de Loíza," as in "Yo misma fui mi ruta," the poetic voice speaks of "abrir nuevos surcos," "alcanzar senderos nuevos," and of separating herself from the "horizontes aprendidos," self-referential phrases to her poetry and her departure from previous poetic traditions. One of the characteristics of the semantic and symbolic world of a poet is the possibility of offering in a single poem several levels of meaning, several readings. This is why "Yo misma fui mi ruta" can be read as a search for definition and authenticity, as a feminist manifesto, and at the same time as an exploration of the creative process and of the writer as she confronts a poetic tradition. Each interpretation points to several layers of meaning and each enriches our understanding of her poetry.

The journey the poetic voice delineates in *Poema en veinte surcos* is that of a female voice who refuses to accept imposed societal roles, who identifies with the independence of Puerto Rico, with the proletariat, the underprivileged, as well as with the victims of the Spanish Civil War, and who finds in her poetry the path to address her creative self.

In 1939, a year after the publication of *Poema en veinte surcos,* Burgos published her second book of poems, *Canción de la verdad sencilla.* This book, written after the poet met Jimenes Grullón, was dedicated by the author to "la verdad sencilla de amarte en ti y en todo."[12] The reader does not encounter in these poems the sociopolitical concerns reflected in *Poema en veinte surcos. Canción de la verdad sencilla* has been seen as a celebration of euphoric passion and love. Love is presented as the force that saves the poetic voice. But this love extracts a price. In poems such as "Alba de mi silencio," "Te seguiré callada," "Transmutación," and "Yo fui la más callada," the poetic voice speaks of the silence the experience of love brings with it: the silence imposed on women by convention, a silence the poetic voice seems willing to accept in order to enjoy the ecstasies of love. Ivette López Jiménez has pointed out that these love poems are not constructed around the lover as the central theme but rather around love as part of human experience and as integrated with the cosmos.[13]

Although their erotic dimension is undeniable, there are other aspects consonant with her concern for the artistic imagination present in *Poema en veinte surcos.* The poem "Noche de amor en tres cantos" begins with the lines "¡Cómo suena en mi alma la idea / de una noche completa en tus brazos" (p. 22), the poetic voice seems to announce the genesis of a poem; she has the idea, the seed that will germinate a poem. We witness a creative process, a process of love that ends at dawn, the night is gone, the process is over, and the poetic voice is left with "y hay un niño de amor en mi mano."[14]

The image of the child will reappear in one of Burgos best and well-known poems, "Poema para mi muerte," in which the poetic voice confronting the moment of death reaffirms what defines her: "me llamarán poeta." The images of both the child and the carnation symbolize her poetry. In "Poema perdido en pocos versos" we find another reference to her writing as she describes her poems as "Sencillo espejo donde recojo el mundo. / Donde enternezco soledades con mi mano feliz" (p. 21). *Canción de la verdad sencilla* is a hymn of love: love of Eros, and love of the Muses, a celebration of artistic intuition and imagination.

A year after her death, and fourteen years after she wrote its first two parts, *El mar y tú* was published in Puerto Rico. This book comprises the poems she wrote in Cuba between 1940 and 1942 and most of the poems she wrote in New York after her return from Cuba in June 1942. This group of poems appears under the heading *Otros poemas*. The poems belonging to her Cuban cycle are divided into two parts: "Velas sobre el pecho del mar" and "Poemas para un naufragio." As the title and the subheadings indicate, the imagery of the sea permeates these poems. The poems in this collection have been analyzed as a return to the opposites she presented in *Poema en veinte surcos,* her first book of poetry, and also as the destruction of the harmony, of the conciliation of those opposites through union with the loved one described in her second book. The voice of the poet perceives the contradiction between love and personal integrity. It is a confrontation with solitude, anguish, and death.

In *El mar y tú,* the poetic voice shows two different states of mind. The first eighteen poems still present hope in love and in the positive forces of the creative spirit. The sea represents a moment of plenitude, sea and lover, sea and poetry unfold as an entity. In their analysis of the first two poems of this collection, "Poema de la cita eterna" and "El mar y tú," Eliana Rivero and Luz María Umpierre have shown how the "tú" is a component to the poetic "I," and the sea is another component of the "I," "who writes and

unfolds as 'you' in order to be able to perceive the interaction between the sea and the I/Poet who writes."[15] The imaginative powers of the spirit can still nourish and carry on the poetic voice. As
in "Río Grande de Loíza," the sea is witness to the existence of the
poetic voice and merges with it.

But this moment of plenitude begins to crumble. The poem
"Canción amarga" already in its title points toward the uneasiness
the poetic voice feels, and in the poem, death appears as her companion. In this poem we encounter the images that abound in the
second part, sadness, shadows, agony; she intuits the torment that
lies ahead of her. It is her singing, her poetry, her creativity what
keeps her alive and makes sense of her life. The sea is absent, and
when it reappears it is equated with the death, not only of her physical and moral self, but also of her creative instinct. When the
reader reaches the second part of this book, "Poemas para un
naufragio," the title already announces a descent toward death.
The first poem, "Poema de la íntima agonía," describes the mag-
nitude of her fall: "Creyéndome gaviota, verme partido el vuelo, /
dándome a las estrellas, encontrarme en los charcos."[16]

However, as María Solá has pointed out, this descent is not always constant in its movement.[17] In poems such as "Poema de la
estrella reintegrada" and "Entre mi voz y el tiempo" from the second part from *El mar y tú* and "Poema con un solo después" and
"Poema para mi muerte" from the third section, there are moments of hope and strength. "Poema para mi muerte" reaffirms
her faith in herself and in her art. The tone is serene and solemn.
This poem, believed to have been written in Cuba but included in
El mar y tú under "Otros poemas," is a reflection about death, and
the desire to transform that inescapable reality into poetry. The
last hemistich—"me llamarán poeta" (p. 92)—reverberates like the
sound of a bell in the mind of all her readers.

In "Farewell in Welfare Island," written in English four months
before her death, when she was hospitalized on welfare island,
Burgos's poetic voice still stood firm:

It has to be from here,
forgotten but unshaken,
among comrades of silence
deep into Welfare island
my farewell to the world.[18]

Elena Poniatowska:
SEARCH FOR THE VOICELESS

KAY S. GARCÍA

⌒ I WRITE IN ORDER TO BELONG. Elena Poniatowska belongs to Mexico, to women, to the poor, to the oppressed, to the people of the world.[1] She belongs to the cooks, the seamstresses, the students, the servants: people she immortalized in her books on the massacre of student demonstrators in 1968 and the earthquake that hit Mexico City in 1985.

I absorbed Mexico through the maids, following them around as they made the beds and mopped the floors, listening to their chatter as they prepared the hot tortillas. Elena's mother was the daughter of a Mexican landowner who lost his hacienda in the Mexican Revolution. Her mother's family traveled throughout Europe, never seeming to belong anywhere. Her father was a descendant of the last king of Poland, who was exiled to France after the partitioning of his country. Sometime during their travels, her parents met and settled briefly in France, where Elena was born in 1933. During World War II, when Elena was nine years old, she moved to Mexico with her mother and sister; her father, who was fighting at the front, joined them after the war. Elena wanted desperately to belong to this vast, rugged country, and she quickly began to create roots for herself.

One way of belonging was to listen, to see faces, to take them into oneself, to observe laps, hands. Elena learned Spanish and much about Mexican life from the maids, watching all they did and asking endless questions. Her questioning became a way of life. *I believe I will die like this, still searching, with a question mark engraved on my eyelids.*

Mexico adopted Elena. Her own parents were elusive and secretive. *My mother, the most beautiful of all women, is the one who most inspires my love, because I have never been able to reach her.* Elena's mother was always rushing off somewhere, leaving Elena behind with the sound of the slamming doors echoing in her ears. *Suddenly I look at her and she's not there. I look at her again, she's defined by her absence. She has gone to join something that gives her strength and I don't know what it is. I can't follow her, I don't understand the invisible space where she has gone.*

Although Elena's father was a war hero, she never heard stories of the war. *My father was my son, just as today my son Mane is my father . . . He never knew how to ask anything of anyone. In Mexico his heroism was his secret. He never formed part of any chorus. One had to grasp him intuitively. It was on the piano that he expressed himself best, but at age 70 he stopped believing even in musical notes. When he died I knew that he was inside me, that I would become him, as all my dead are in me.*

Into that parental void have tumbled all the people of Mexico. Elena has an uncanny ability to connect to people immediately, and to have them tell her their innermost secrets within minutes of meeting her. She uses her writing as a way to delve into other people's reality, to hear their accounts of abuse, torture, natural disasters, and despair. *Writing is also a way to relate to others and to love them. What I cannot say out loud because I am too timid, I write.*

The first time I went to Elena's house to interview her, she took me up her winding staircase to a tiny, womblike study, and we sat facing each other, almost touching knees. There were no preambles, no small talk. She mentioned a novel she plans to write about a North American woman who has a romance with a Mexican man, and immediately asked me about my former marriage to a man from Guanajuato. My list of questions fell to the floor as the stories tumbled out and the pain, joy, and confusion flowed out of me and were absorbed by Elena's soft eyes, two whirlpools of compassion that pulled my experiences out of me and transformed them into literary grist. Thus I entered her writing as she has entered mine: two lives, two works intertwining. *Dearest Kay, Thank you for the articles you sent me. I'm working on the novel about the scientist, with lots of daily interruptions, my children and grandchildren, presentations of books, prologues, interviews, articles, and trips. In March I'm going to Italy, in April to Tucson, Arizona, in May to the Canary Islands. I work a lot and I'm happy but I would prefer to shut myself up in a home in the country and just write, sleep, read, eat, and write. Wouldn't you like that? Of course that's an impossible dream, but it's worthwhile dreaming it. I think your book is going to be very useful and informative and I'm very honored to be included in it. I'll write you more later. Your friend who loves you, Elena. P.S. : Don't forget you have to tell me more about your Mexican love, for my next novel.*

Elena is a beautiful woman, in the deepest and truest meaning, with a sense of sturdiness in spite of her slight stature. Her thick blond hair is laden with gray, and her eyes are heavily underlined by her own suffering and that of others. Her courage to publish criticism of the government is remarkable considering the fate of so many journalists in Mexico: 60 Mexican journalists were killed at work between 1970 and 1990, and during those same years another 366 reporters were attacked while on the job. *Well, they've never given me an important position; I will never be a millionaire, never anything, but they have never put me in jail. They allow me to write and to publish, and they have never done anything to me, so I am not afraid. It's no use being afraid.*

For Elena there have been consequences for chronicling Mexico's tragedies, however. The catastrophes weigh her down, they accumulate. *As you can see I can't stand it; for example, with [my book on the earthquake] I got sick and it took me a long time to recuperate. If there is a third tragedy here in Mexico, I won't be able to chronicle anything, it will have to be someone younger. I won't be able to get involved at all because I know that would be the end of me; no, it is too much already. Even if I recuperate and try to forget, and even though time is a marvelous healer, when something happens it opens the old wound that was still very tender, very rotten, or fragile, and then I can't go on.*

Elena attended French and English schools in Mexico, and the Sacred Heart Convent in Philadelphia, where her formal schooling ended. After returning to Mexico, she started writing newspaper articles and interviews for the cultural supplement of the Mexico City newspaper *Novedades,* and she was so successful that soon she was publishing an interview a day, including conversations with celebrities such as Diego Rivera, Luis Buñuel, Jorge Luis Borges, and Gabriel García Márquez. She also directed cultural programs for radio and television, and published poems, short stories, essays, chronicles, and novels. She traveled to Cuba, Brazil, Venezuela, the United States, Europe, Czechoslovakia, and Vietnam. All this she managed to do while being married to the astronomer Guillermo Haro, and having three children, although it was not easy.

Alcohol has a strange effect on me because the red wine is throbbing in my temples, it surges through my veins, it stirs me up and then at night I curl up on the bed waiting for sleep and staring at the emptiness. I look for (my husband) Guillermo's valiums; I can't find them so I roll myself up into a ball again; it's useless, all I can do is wait for it to be six-thirty in the morning when I have to get ready to take the children to school. All of my Polish atavisms are circulating in my blood.

Elena's books have been translated into English, French, German,

Italian, Polish, and Czechoslovakian. She was awarded the National Journalism Prize in 1978, and the Mazatlán Literary Prize for her novel *Hasta no verte, Jesús mío* (Here's to you, Jesus). She rejected the prestigious Villaurrutia Prize, which was awarded to her for *La noche de Tlatelolco* (translated as *Massacre in Mexico*), asking President Luis Echeverría in an open letter if someone was going to give a prize to all those killed in 1968. She was also named the Mexican Woman of the Year and given a prize called the Coatlicue by the magazine *Debate Feminista* in 1990, in honor of her work in support of women writers.

Unlike many Mexican writers who claim to be feminists, Elena is open about her affiliations. *It would be absurd to say that I am not a feminist. I am completely on the side of women, I want women to progress.* She is also quite clear about her attitude toward traditional Mexican men. *The Mexican macho is always ready not only to dominate a woman, but also to squash her if he can; when he has squashed her and rubbed her into the floor, then he says, "Now you need me." Then he picks up that human garbage, that mop on the floor, and then she is his woman who will wait on him, bring him coffee, take care of him and more or less take care of his children, because he has taken all of her blood, all of her will and desire to do something in life other than serve him and be his property. That happens to any woman in Mexico who wants to do more than be a self-sacrificing wife, because Mexican husbands in any field will not tolerate a woman who does more than that.*

Elena has written prologues for women's works, she presents their books, and she has given workshops for and about women writers, both at the University of California-Davis and at the National Autonomous University of Mexico. She has been a mentor to many women writers, and many of her characters are strong, independent women. Elena sees a connection between her writing and that of women from all over the world. *There is a new language throbbing in the writing that for good or for bad has been called women's literature, that which we all weave together, forming an interdepen-*

*dence that could put an end to patriarchal domination, intertwin-
ing our words and our lives, in Colombia and Nicaragua, in Peru
and Cuba, in El Salvador and Paraguay, in Puerto Rico and Brazil,
in Chile and Argentina, in the United States and Canada, in Pales-
tine and Venezuela, in Uruguay and in France and in Spain, spin-
ning our intuitive, visceral threads that unite us all and that should
be taut and fierce, just as taut, fierce and intense as is our hope.*

Elena refers to her characteristic manner of narrating as "testimonial literature," which combines methods of oral testimony
with elements of history, fiction writing, and new journalism. She
grapples with doubts about her writing, and with a pervasive sense
of guilt that underlies much of her reporting. She is very aware of
the contrast between her own comfortable existence and that of
the people she interviews.

In the summer of 1968 Elena followed the student demonstra-
tions with trepidation, unable to attend because she was expecting
a baby. On October 3, three women came to her home and told her
that the army and police had massacred many men, women, and
children in the plaza of Tlatelolco, in Mexico City. *I believe that
the plaza of Tlatelolco is just like any other public square in the
world, don't you think so?* Elena thought the women were hyster-
ical, so the next day she went to the plaza to see for herself. There
she saw all the bullet holes on the walls, the blood still not washed
away, the army still there; many people had abandoned their homes
around the plaza, and personal items were scattered on the ground.
She started listening to the stories of those who wanted to talk, and
the result was her book *Massacre in Mexico*, which is now in its
forty-ninth printing.

*They come down [the streets of Mexico City], laughing, students
walking arm in arm in the demonstration, in as festive a mood as
if they were going to a street fair; carefree boys and girls who do
not know that tomorrow, and the day after, their dead bodies will
be lying swollen in the rain, after a fair where the guns in the shooting gallery are aimed at them . . .*

In *Massacre in Mexico* Elena juxtaposes declarations from speeches by President Gustavo Díaz Ordaz *(Peace and calm must be declared in our country. A hand has been extended: it is up to the Mexican citizens to decide whether to grasp this outstretched hand)* and his successor Luis Echeverría *(Mexico is endeavoring to maintain a rule of freedom that is almost without parallel in any other country)* with hundreds of eyewitness accounts of the government's actions *(We were looking down from the speakers' platform at the chaos in the plaza, the waves of people that tried to escape and couldn't, the mobs running back and forth, the walls of bayonets)*. Elena also uses newspaper articles, picket signs, banners *(Soldiers, don't shoot, you are the people, too)*, slogans from buttons, chants *(Freedoms for political prisoners! Freedom, freedom!)*, and shouts captured on a tape recorder *(Down with the mummies!)*. Fragments of songs, poems *(Worms are crawling through the streets and the squares / and the walls are spattered with brains . . . With these deeds / we have lost the Mexican people)*, and stories from modern Mexico and from different times and places are woven into the intricate tapestry of the text to establish parallels between the present oppression of Mexican citizens and that of our people throughout history. *(Bye bye love / bye bye happiness / Hello loneliness / I think I'm gonna cry.)*

Having provided these heterogeneous means of communication with a historical, social, and political context, Elena has managed to create a collage of voices that describes events from the victims' point of view and makes a mockery of the pompous, hollow words of the official discourse.

Young targets, just children, children who marvel at everything, children who see every day as a holiday, until the owner of the shooting booth told them to line up one beside the other like a row of little silver ducks that moves along, click, click, click, click and is right at eye level. Aim, fire!, and they fall back brushing against the curtain of red satin.

In the final pages of *Massacre in Mexico*, Elena provides a brief chronology of the events described throughout her text. Skirmishes between the police and students began in the summer of 1968 and increased in intensity with the approach of the Olympic Games, scheduled to begin on October 12 in Mexico City. Government officials did not want the games marred by the student protests, and they were particularly fearful of bad publicity as foreign correspondents began to arrive in the country. Students fanned out across Mexico City to hand out flyers that stated their six demands: freedom for all political prisoners, revocation of the law against "social dissolution," disbandment of the corps of riot police, dismissal of the chief and deputy chief of police, indemnities for the families of those killed and injured since the beginning of the conflict, and determination of the responsibility of individual government officials implicated in the bloodshed. Underlying this specific agenda was a deep desire for change that connected the Mexicans to the youth protest movements of the sixties in the United States, France, and many other parts of the world.

The owner of the shooting gallery gave the rifles to the soldiers and ordered them to shoot at the target, and there were the little silver dolls with astonished eyes and open mouths, facing the barrels of the rifles. Fire! The green lightning of a flare. Fire! They fell down but they didn't spring up again so they could be shot at once more; the mechanics of the fair were different; the springs were made of blood, not wire; a slow, thick blood that formed pools, young blood trampled in this destruction of life all over the Plaza of Three Cultures.

On October 1 a group of students announced a demonstration the next day in the plaza of Tlatelolco, in defiance of a government-ordered "truce" to precede the Olympic Games. The October 2 demonstration began peacefully but was interrupted by a green flare launched from a helicopter, a signal to the soldiers stationed around the square to begin shooting. People panicked and ran from one side of the square to another, trying to escape, but they encountered police blockades and gunfire from all sides.

More than four hundred people were killed; thousands were wounded or arrested.

Here come the youngsters, they're coming toward me, there are a lot of them, no one has his hands up, nobody has his pants down to be frisked, there are no surprise knife wounds or blows with a stick, no humiliation, no vomit from being tortured, no piles of shoes. They breathe deeply, they walk confidently, with determined steps. They come towards me with picket signs in their childlike hands, because death makes hands more infantile; they are pale and a little blurry, but happy. There are no more walls of bayonets, no more violence; I see them through a curtain of rain, or perhaps it is tears, and I hear their voices, I hear their steps, step, step, step, steeeeeep, steeeeep . . .

The Mexican newspapers reported the deaths of twenty to thirty people, blaming everybody but the government. Due to a massive cover-up, most of the Mexican people outside the capital were unaware of the massacre until they talked to an eyewitness, or read Elena's book. It was not until ten years later, in a chapter on the student movement included in her book *Fuerte es el silencio* (Strong is the silence), that Elena could speak of some positive consequences of the violent repression. The student movement was the detonator that broke the traditional Mexican mutism and allowed the resentment handed down from generation to generation to be expressed. According to Elena, this explosion destroyed the official image of Mexico as a country above the rest of Latin America and thus incapable of the brutal repression that has plagued this continent for centuries. The massacre provoked the formation of new leftist organizations in Mexico, and served as a catalyst for the radicalization of many intellectuals. The student movement provided leadership and consciousness-raising opportunities for women, and pressured President Echeverría to include young people in both state and federal government unprecedented numbers.

Like the lives of many individuals, Mexican history was divided by the massacre: before and after October 2, 1968. The lessons learned, however bitter, have not been forgotten. The dialogue established by Elena's book continues, as new articles appear (see the October 3, 1988, issue of *Proceso*) and new movies are made about the student movement and the massacre of 1968 (such as *Rojo amanecer*, produced by Cinematográfico Sol). Many recent books have references to Tlatelolco, which indicates that the tragedy still lives in the collective consciousness of the Mexican people. One such book is Elena's *Nada, nadie: Las voces del temblor* (Nothing, nobody: Voices from the earthquake).

On September 19, 1985, an earthquake hit Mexico City, and Elena served once again as the voice of the people. First she participated in the rescue work, carrying buckets of debris from the ruins and helping at the shelters, but then she received a message from the journalist Carlos Monsiváis: "What is the best chronicler of Mexico doing sitting in her home? Start writing." Elena published articles in the newspapers for fifty days, first in *Novedades* and then in *La Jornada,* until she was told that they were too depressing to publish. *Outside, "operation ant" (digging with picks and shovels) does not cease, each minute that passes is precious; covered with dust, the rescuers stop to drink water; here under the umbrella (the roof of the building where the National Reconstruction Committee is meeting), time is the same as before the earthquake, political time: slow, rhetorical, anachronistic, devious, personalist and usurious. The speakers string together phrases that don't mean anything and nobody says what we hope to hear.*

Suspecting that the government had pressured the newspapers to stop publishing her articles, she began gathering them into a book. Students enrolled in her literary workshop helped with the rescue effort also, and then contributed articles and testimony to Elena's book. She spoke with everybody that she could, without taping the stories, but rather writing them down at night by memory. She couldn't just write, however—she would go find her interviewees a wheelchair, some food, or medicine—she just couldn't isolate herself from the problems she was recording. *And I also die even though I might pass a comb through my hair or even take out lip-stick to form another mouth on mine, a mouth which now moves in front of me, the eyes that now cloud over in front of my eyes, the thin skin which reddens, the grimace of crying, the nervous hands that try to stem the crying and those trembling, salty lips that rain salt and are distorted and they are mine and they are Gloria Guer-rero's. Gloria Guerrero, Gloria Guerrero, whose 5-and-a-half-year-old daughter Alondra died.*

The people told her stories of government ineptitude, lack of preparation for disaster, a blatant corruption. They asserted that the federal soldiers sent to facilitate rescue missions actually im-peded the rescue in many cases. ("Attention survivors in section D as in dog, please knock ten times.") The soldiers were equipped with rifles rather than shovels, and many abandoned their posts to carry off loot from the rubble. ("Survivors, we know you are there; don't despair, we are working and we are going to get you out.") The government did not provide maps of the disaster areas, and there were no floor plans of the destroyed buildings to guide the rescuers. Volunteers did not know where they were needed, and once they arrived at a crumbled building, there was nobody in charge to organize their efforts. ("'No, I'm going back in for my television.' We tried to stop him but he dove down into the tunnel where we had dug him out. The walls collapsed and he died.") Some of the volunteers were arrested or beaten up, just for trying to help. This chaos prevailed for days after the catastrophe, and many victims who could have been saved died due to lack of an or-ganized emergency plan utilizing the help of local volunteers and foreign experts, who at first were not even allowed to enter the country. ("The government showed that it was more prepared to repress the people than to rescue them from disaster.")

Violations to the building code had been routinely ignored by the government, resulting in the collapse of many building that should have been condemned, including the Nuevo León building in the plaza of Tlatelolco. *(First there was the massacre in Tlatelolco, now it is the Nuevo León building: corruption is also a crime.)* Elena connects the two disasters by mentioning that many of the volunteers in 1985 had been student demonstrators in 1968. *(The plaza of Tlatelolco was covered with shoes, like trampled flowers, as it had been on October 2, 1968.)* In *Nada, nadie,* Elena quotes an Aztec poem about the conquest, the center of which is reproduced in *Massacre in Mexico* also *(Worms are crawling through the streets and the squares . . .),* juxtaposing the disasters of 1521, 1968, and 1985. The unifying elements are greed, violence, and the desire for control, and the implication is that in all three instances the people were victims of those in power.

When she was so exhausted that she couldn't work on the manuscript any longer, she turned it over to her publisher, and *Nada, nadie: Las voces del temblor* was born. It is a tribute to the Mexican people and an expression of Elena's profound love for her adopted country. *Nevertheless one can find something positive in all this. We ought to question the old feeling of inferiority that we Mexicans have. We Mexicans are not inadequate, the system is. We saw that if we work together we can do it well.*

In addition to the works already mentioned, Elena has published the following collections of her interviews: *Palabras cruzadas* (Crossword); *Domingo 7* (Sunday the seventh), in which she interviews the presidential candidates; and *Todo Mexico* (All of Mexico). Her essays are profoundly personal, getting to the center of the human being that she is interviewing, as well as revealing her own developing identity. A visit to the architect Luis Barragán becomes a study in contrasts between his concrete reality and her dream world. *For years I have doubted everything, I walk with the weight of many voices, sounds tangled up in my head; I want to trap this contagious city. The rest exercise their fascinating power while I sleepwalk, hypnotized; I live in such confusion that the orange glow around Luis seems like a halo, and I've always been attracted to light. Luis is contemplative. His interior and exterior are one. He is his houses, his sense of time and space are his mystic re-*

ality. He operates within a solid notion of reality. For me, since I live on illusions, on possible alternatives, on dreams within dreams, being in his presence is a profound surprise.

Elena has also published a collection of literary essays, *¡Ay vida!, no me mereces* (Oh life, you don't deserve me), a labor of love and gratitude to Juan Rulfo, Gabriel García Márquez, Rosario Castellanos, and other authors that have nourished her work. The story of a woman with cerebral palsy who manages to educate herself and to adopt a child is told by *Gaby Brimmer*. In more tributes to her adopted homeland, she published *El último guajolote* (The last turkey), about disappearing Mexican traditions; *Todo empezó en domingo* (Everything started on Sunday), about the celebrations of the poor; and *La casa en la tierra* (The house on the earth), about the homes of poor people in the country.

She also has published two collections of short stories: *Lilus Kikus* (the name of a girl) and *De noche vienes* (You come by night), many of which have been translated into English and published in anthologies and literary journals. The first is noteworthy for its extraordinary expression of a young girl's view of life. The second collection brings to Mexican literature some of its first female characters that don't pay homage to La Malinche or the Virgin of Guadalupe, such as Manuela in "Ruptura," who collects a lover as she would a fine piece of china, or Esmeralda, the nurse in the title story who is happily married to five men. *(Mondays were for Pedro, Tuesdays for Carlos and so forth through the week, and Saturdays and Sundays she washed and ironed clothes and cooked something special for Pedro, the pickiest of them all. They all accepted the situation, just so they could see her, and the only condition she insisted on was not giving up her career as a nurse.)*

Elena has received the most recognition from literary critics for her novel *Hasta no verte, Jesús mío*, which is a long monologue by the protagonist, an impoverished woman who had an active role in the Mexican Revolution. *Jesusa Palancares was a soldier in the Mexican Revolution who doesn't have the so-called feminine char-*

acteristics; *she is not self-sacrificing nor submissive, she's not even a mother. On the contrary, when she gets hit it's because she has already struck twice.*

Another work of hers that has received a lot of attention is *Querido Diego, te abraza Quiela* (Dear Diego, affectionately, Quiela), which may be published in English with the title "Dear Diego." This is an epistolary novel, a collection of fictional letters that the Russian painter Angelina Beloff wrote to Diego Rivera after living with him in Paris for ten years and having his son. When Diego returned to his native country, he promised to send money to Angelina so that she could join him. He never did send any money, and when she finally traveled to Mexico and spoke to Diego on the street, he passed by without recognizing her. Angelina did not ray to contact him after that humiliation. This anecdote inspired Elena to write the novel, to illustrate the contrasting public and private images of a famous man.

One of Elena's most autobiographical works is the novel *La "Flor de Lis,"* which tells of her childhood in France and Mexico, and the complex relationship that she had with an inspirational Catholic priest.

Her latest work is the enormous novel *Tinísima* (Very, very Tina), based on the life of the Italian photographer Tina Modotti, who spent part of her life in Mexico. *Dearest Kay, Here is my Tinísima, which has had such good luck. It is taking giant steps all by itself; it has won the Mazatlán Literary Prize and it is first on the list of sales, so I am very pleased. A big affectionate hug for you and your family, Elena.*

Besides Elena's obvious success in literary and journalistic circles, she has had a profound effect on the people of Mexico, who know their government and their country better because of her work. Her courage and her honesty are inspirational, and she is deeply revered by even those who have not read (or could not read) her books. The taxi driver who took me to her house warned me that I might be followed as I left the premises, but he said so with respect, even awe.

The essence of Elena is her love of all human beings, and her love of life. She feels a deep connection to all parts of the universe. *I have always walked. I think as I stroll along: How much of me there is in these faces that don't know me and that I don't know, how much of me in the subway, in the steps that pile up, how much of me in the rain that forms puddles on the pavement, how much of me in the Colonia del Valle-Coyoacán buses that rush along until they crash and form part of the cosmos.* Our connection is interrupted by loud knocking and a confident voice at the door. "I'm here to pick up my wife." He doesn't say former wife. I haven't seen him for nine years, and he's here to pick up his wife. Elena looks at him, takes him in, and as he stands there with the rain dripping off his jet-black hair and that impatient gleam in his eye, he is transformed into one of her characters. She sees the dark little room at the back of my heart where he will always reside, and she smiles. She knows.

And as I walk out onto the streets of Mexico City, I remember Elena's last wish at the end of one of her books. *All that I ask I that I be allowed to accompany the last wild turkey, that I may walk with him through God's streets, the streets of my city, until my knees go numb and my eyes blur and I keel over like Sergeant Pedraza in an improbable olympics, with my early full of the street vendors' calls and chants, and Mexico, Mexico, rah, rah, rah. (Ah, and my belly full of shredded-beef tacos!)*

Then turning to my companion, I walk out of Elena's story and into my own, a drama that Elena will some day immortalize. Elena, Elenita, with your angel's wings and halo as they draw you in the newspapers; Elena, with your confusions and insights and intuitive connections, your courage and fortitude and never-ending sorrow, you have touched us all, and we have touched you.

Delmira Agustini:
PORTRAITS & REFLECTIONS

RENÉE SCOTT
TRANSLATED BY NANCY ABRAHAM HALL

⌒ THROUGHOUT LATIN AMERICAN LITERARY HISTORY there have been women writers whose lives and work are so difficult to explain that some critics consider them "pathological cases." Perhaps the most notorious of these women is the Mexican nun Sor Juana Inés de la Cruz (1651–95), who, at the age of nineteen, voluntarily left the viceroy's court to enter a Carmelite convent. Why did she choose a religious life? Was it because of unrequited love? Did she believe that her illegitimate birth impaired her socially? Did she want more time to devote to intellectual and artistic pursuits? These are some of the questions that continue to interest critics. As in the cases of other extraordinary women, the life of the Tenth Muse was tragically cut short when, in 1695, she succumbed to the plague epidemic that ravaged Mexico.

Another very different, but no less fascinating, case is that of the Argentinean poet Alfonsina Storni (1882–1938). At the age of twenty, Storni took her illegitimate infant son, left her mother's home in Rosario, and headed for Buenos Aires in order to be closer to the center of the literary world of her time. Alfonsina Storni's life also ended prematurely and tragically, when, in 1938, knowing that she suffered from an incurable disease, she drowned herself in the ocean. She left her rebellious and contradictory poetry in which she expresses resentment against men as inferior beings who try to dominate women yet maintains that women need men.

Uruguay also has its "strange woman," and she is Delmira Agustini, one of the most outstanding poets and, at the same time, fascinating literary figures of the American continent. "Of all the women who today write poetry, none has moved me more than Delmira Agustini," wrote Rubén Darío, the great modernist poet, in 1912.[1] Nevertheless, more than eighty years after her tragic and premature death at the age of twenty-eight, the life and work of this poet are still shrouded in mystery. How could a young woman with little formal education write such accomplished poems? How can one explain the fact that a woman who led a very protected life in the bosom of a traditional, middle-class family, who was even called "Baby" by her loved ones, dared to write the most erotic feminine poems of her time? And finally, there is her death in 1914, shot twice in the right temple by her former husband, who then took his own life.

As in the other cases of outstanding women writers, critics have seen Agustini as a pathological case. The question underlying most research is whether Delmira Agustini suffered from a split personality. Was she really a slightly less than ingenious girl when among family members, but a mature woman when she put pen to paper? Or did she intentionally assume these roles?

Agustini's contemporaries saw a case of split personality. In everyday life she was the innocent daughter of a domineering woman and had very little experience outside her home. Artistically, however, she was a burning pythoness who wrote sheet after sheet of red-hot verses full of unexpected eroticism that had no basis whatsoever in her daily life (Silva 1968). Carrying this notion further, Agustini's erotic poetry has been interpreted not as a desire for carnal knowledge, but rather as evidence of her metaphysical concerns (Zum Felde 1967).

Nevertheless, most recent studies suggest that Agustini was in reality fully conscious of her erotic impulses—some of which she even fulfilled—and that her childlike behavior was merely a deliberate pose created to avert social conflict (Rodríguez Monegal 1969), by design a form of "protection and solution of convenience" (Molloy 1985).[2] Yet a third "personality" has been postulated. Apparent in some of her poems, this non-erotic personality reflects her most profound existential preoccupations (Visca 1978). These diverse interpretations serve to underscore how bewildering her case is, and at the same time, how impossible it is to know the true nature of the poet's private life. In this chapter I will present Agustini in terms of her own world. I am interested in showing that the poet not only lacked a pathologically split personality, but that she tried to satisfy her intimate desires and achieved self-fulfillment. Like other women who deviated from accepted behavioral norms of their time, Agustini led a tormented life and paid for her transgressions.

Delmira Agustini was born in Montevideo in 1886, during a period of profound historical, social, and cultural change known in Uruguay as the Nineties. Historians José Barrán and Benjamín Nahum describe it as follows:

> . . . in a little more than twenty years, the country went from
> the mental structure and demographic behaviors associated
> with the European Ancien Regime to the world of moder-
> nity. A silent revolution took place in demographic terms.
> The new model, while decreasing population pressure on
> the political and economic structures, ended up consolidat-
> ing and strengthening them. By 1920 a new and different
> Uruguayan civilization had replaced the traditional one.[3]

In Uruguayan history the Nineties mark the end of the civil war and the beginning of more cooperation between the two political parties, the White or Nationalist Party, and the Red or Colorado Party. The Colorado president, José Batlle y Ordóñez (1903–7, 1911–15), developed social legislation and promoted the nationalization of businesses, which brought about a profound restructuring of the country. For example, his government undertook a campaign of laicism, which resulted in the removal of crucifixes from hospitals. Batlle and his followers were also allies of feminism. In 1907, Parliament sanctioned and enacted the first divorce law. The author of the bill, Oneto y Viana, served as Delmira Agustini's lawyer when, in 1913, she sued for divorce under the provisions of this law.

Toward the turn of the century, Montevideo's intellectual life also showed great vigor. The energy that had been contained prior to 1886 during military rule now burst forth in a display of feverish activity. Intellectual life in the Nineties was characterized by the coexistence of diverse positions and currents. Positivism in philosophy and realism, naturalism, and modernism in literature first share the stage with, but then overtake, the romantic idealism that had, up to that point, been dominant. During this period, and thanks to the rise of newspapers and magazines, professional writers emerge, individuals who were able to dedicate themselves full time to their craft, and earn a living doing so: essayist José Enrique Rodó, short story writers Javier de Viana and Horacio Quiroga, and poets Julio Herrera y Reissig and Delmira Agustini, among others. This was one of the most important generations of writers in the history of Uruguayan letters. The general openness was also evidenced by where intellectuals chose to gather. If the Ateneo, the country's most important cultural center, had served the needs of previous generations, the writers of the Nineties preferred the democratic café, open to all, in the new spirit of the age. In Montevideo the Polo-Bamba became truly important, much as Los Inmortales was in Buenos Aires.

Nevertheless, turn-of-the-century modernity did not necessarily mean more sexual freedom for women. Despite the fact that women were joining the work force in increasing numbers, their lives continued to be governed by a series of social rules that assured their virginity until they married and insisted that social behavior never compromise morality. As Barrán and Nahum point out, the new social system suggested a new image for women by replacing the nineteenth-century cult of fecundity with that of virginity. One of the obvious ways to control the birth rate was to delay the age of marriage, which gave rise to a pathological sensibility in young women. During the Nineties, and as a direct result of sexual repression, psychological disorders among women became fashionable. Bromide pastes were used by specialists to treat hysteria, migraine headaches, and insomnia.[4]

Delmira's family belonged to the upper middle class. Her grandparents had come to Argentina and Uruguay from Europe in the mid-nineteenth century, following the path taken by so many other Europeans who, at the end of the century, made up almost half the population along both shores of the River Plate. Her paternal grandfather, Domingo Agustini, was a French privateer who had fought alongside Napoleon in the Battle of Trafalgar. Her maternal grandfather, Luis Murtfeldt, was a wealthy gentleman descended from German nobility, a lover of music, and an exquisite violinist. The Agustini-Murtfeldt household was established in 1882, when Santiago Agustini, a Uruguayan banker, married Maria Murtfeldt, an Argentinean. The Agustinis were somewhat ahead of their time. They married late—she was twenty-one and he twenty-six—and had already established themselves financially. In addition, they limited their family to two children. Parental support for Delmira's literary career can be explained, then, by their modern values, as well as the obvious adoration they felt for their daughter.

Like other young women of her social class, Delmira spent a very safe and comfortable childhood and adolescence within the protected environment of her father's home.

Agustini's daily life was described as follows by Andrés Giot de Badet, her friend and contemporary who later became a Uruguayan-French writer:

She spends the winters in Montevideo, a city that has preserved all the old, Iberian customs. She rarely leaves the
house, and when she does, she is always accompanied by her
mother, who adores her. Their outings have only one purpose: to give alms to the poor, candy to any children they
may meet, and crumbs to the poor sparrows who cry out
with hunger during the months that the pampa winds blow
all seeds away.

Spring returns her to the country house [the family villa in
Sayago] and it is there that we are neighbors every year. An
ombú—that tree whose trunk is as enormous as it is hollow—extends its great branches for us, as if they were comfortable chairs upholstered in a slightly wrinkled fabric. And
as we are the same age—she is as much a child as I—we
have the best time sitting in the tree, imagining projects that
will be admired by the entire world once they are brought to
fruition. And within seconds we invent thousands of plays
that, in light of our enthusiasm, can be nothing less than
masterpieces.[5]

In addition to the limits imposed on women during her lifetime,
Agustini had to contend with an overbearing and domineering
mother. Doña Murtfeld made the poet the center of her life and all
her efforts. Delmira had a brother—Antonio Luciano—who was
four years her senior. However, his birth did not fulfill their
mother, who "dreamed of combing the golden locks of a little girl."
The dream came true only with the arrival of Delmira in 1886.

There are numerous testimonies regarding the mother's exaggerated behavior. In the archives of the Biblioteca Nacional (National Library) there is an embalmed bird in a small wicker coffin
along with the following note: "Pedrito, Delmira Agustini's dear
little bird, murdered in 1896 by María Campos, a servant. His
death brought enormous pain to our home, and Papa had him embalmed in the Museo Nacional."

Also in the National Library one finds the doll that so resembled

Delmira. Blonde, blue-eyed, and dressed in blue silk, the doll sat for years in the corner of the family living room preferred by the poet. Other accounts of the mother-daughter relationship abound: "Her mother was very religious and strict, and exercised a great deal of control over the daughter," declared her French teacher, don Willems. Doña Saseve de Roldós, her piano teacher, recalled that Delmira "was very obedient, and held down by her mother. The mother had a great deal of influence over her."[6] This would explain why, until the day she died, Agustini accepted the role of "Baby" for her parents and fiancé, an identity diametrically opposed to her public persona of intellectual woman and poet.

The mother's controlling nature also determined how the poet was educated. Despite the well-known and important efforts of teacher José Pedro Varela to establish primary education throughout the country at that time, Agustini remained at home until she turned twelve. Like other upper-class children, she did not attend school. The only children's books that have been found among her belongings are Defoe's *Robinson Crusoe*, Charles Perrault's *Little Red Riding Hood*, and Hans Christian Andersen's *Soup Makers* and *The Bell*. As a teenager, Delmira was given painting, piano, and French lessons.

Delmira's poetic vocation was apparent quite early. On September 27, 1902, when she was ten, her first poem, "Poesía," appeared in the magazine *Rojo y blanco* at the request of its editor, Samuel Blixen. In 1903, an article in the magazine *La Alborada* praised the young poet and announced that she would be a contributor. That same year, a series of Delmira's articles about intellectual women and artists of the day appeared in the magazine under the pseudonym Joujou.

From the beginning, Delmira's parents supported her vocation with enthusiasm. They took pains to ensure the respectful silence that their daughter required when, shut up in her room and within herself, she would produce her poems, late at night, in miniscule handwriting. If Delmira even sensed the presence of another person nearby, she could not work. Once she emerged from her "trance," her father and brother would copy her barely legible words for her. The fact that her parents showed no particular reaction to a body of work that became increasingly daring is a mystery that can only be explained by their blind adoration of the poet.

Agustini wrote the following books of poetry: *El libro blanco* (The White Book, 1907), *Cantos de la mañana* (Morning Songs, 1910), *Los cálices vacíos* (The Empty Chalices, 1910), and *El rosario de Eros* (Eros's Rosary) and *Los astros del abismo* (The Stars of the Abyss), both published posthumously in 1924.

The White Book, Agustini's first collection, contains twenty-eight poems and was published in 1907. The book's editor, Orsini M. Bartini, worked with the most prominent writers of the Nineties. The following verses are from the long poem titled "Intima" (Intimate):

> *I will tell you my life's dreams*
> *In the still of the blue night . . .*
> *My naked soul will tremble in your hands,*
> *My cross will weigh on your shoulders.*

> *Life's peaks are so lonely,*
> *So lonely and cold! I buried*
> *My longings within, and complete*
> *As an ivory tower, I lifted myself up.*

> *Imagine the love I must have dreamed*
> *within the icy tomb of my silence!*
> *Larger than life, more than dreams,*
> *Beneath the endless azure it felt trapped.*

> *Imagine my love, love which seeks*
> *an impossible life, a superhuman life,*
> *You who knows if it matters, if the soul*
> *And dreams of Olympus are consumed in human flesh.*

Ah! You will know my love, but we must go, far
Across the flowering night;
Here what is human frightens, here life
Is endlessly heard, seen, felt.

Let us go further into the night, let us go
Where not even an echo rebounds within me,
Like a nocturnal flower over there in the shadows
I will sweetly open for you.[7]

As in most of Agustini's poems, the subject of "Intima" is love. The poet addresses an ideal lover who will liberate her from a world in which she feels imprisoned. The tone of the poem is pessimistic: the poet feels alone, not understood, and she yearns to satisfy her spiritual and carnal desires, something she herself realizes is impossible. Moreover, the following lines contain such erotically charged images that they were uncommon at the time they were written: "My naked soul will tremble in your hands" and, especially, "I will sweetly open for you," with which the poem closes.

The spirit is romantic, although firsthand knowledge of the modernists (Rubén Darío, Julio Herrera y Reissig, Leopoldo Lugones) can be detected, for example, in the image of the ivory tower. The language is representative, and there is an evident search for a musical form in which to express ideas and states of mind. Also present are two constant themes of her poetry: tragic destiny and erotic desire.

With this poem, a woman writer expresses, for the first time, and without modesty, her desire for total union with man. Whether she intended to or not, Agustini forged the path that would be followed by Alfonsina Storni of Argentina, Gabriela Mistral of Chile, Juana de Ibarbourou of Uruguay, and others who would later create written sexual imagery to express their most intimate desires as women.

Within the intellectual community of Montevideo, *The White Book* was met with admiration and astonishment. Instead of recognizing the unusual eroticism in Agustini's work, the male writers of her day referred to her as the "child prodigy," despite the fact that, at the age of twenty, she was hardly a little girl. The venerable philosopher Carlos Vaz Ferreira wrote: "In comparison to others, and considering your age, your book must be considered nothing short of a miracle . . . How you were able to know, to feel what you have put on certain pages, completely defies explanation."

Instead of openly challenging this image, Agustini opted for the more socially acceptable position of "prodigy," and thus initiated what could be called her double life: while she recorded her most intimate yearnings in ever more sensual poetic language, she continued to lead a very conventional daily life. As we shall see, however, this did not mean that she did not give in to her passionate nature on more than one occasion. As Zum Felde has pointed out, if Agustini had been born in Paris, her biography would be quite different. The poet herself echoed this feeling when she told her friend Giot: "If I were in Europe, I'd have the right to sit alone on the terrace of a café, without half the city yelling: 'Scandal!'"[8]

In 1906 Agustini became engaged to Amancio D. Solliers, a journalist and literary dandy from the state of Minas. The relationship lasted only one year, and in 1908 she announced her formal engagement to Enrique Job Reyes, her future husband and, tragically, her assassin. Reyes was twenty-three years old, one year her senior, and worked as a cattle auctioneer. He was a handsome man, as can be seen in a wedding photograph, and certainly this must have pleased Delmira. Unfortunately, the couple had very little in common on a spiritual level. While she was anxious and temperamental, he was a traditional man. Their lack of compatibility is evident in a painful letter Reyes wrote to his wife after she left him. In the letter, Reyes accuses Delmira's mother of encouraging her to practice birth control, and he adds: "I remind you of two instances in which I behaved as a gentleman and in a proper manner towards you: first, the night you wished to be mine and I refused, saying I would never do that until we were married in the eyes of the law and of God. On many occasions you recalled that night, saying that I had behaved nobly, and been a gentleman."[9]

At the very least, Agustini felt deep affection for her fiancé. As critics have noted, "the poet" had little in common with him, but "Baby," that infantilized persona she assumed at home to satisfy her mother, and that on a certain level, made her feel more protected, was able to share his life on a mundane level. While Agustini visited her mother's family in Buenos Aires, she wrote several notes to her fiancé. Most are written in a conventional style, but a few have intrigued scholars and contributed to the myth of her two (or three) personalities.

These are the notes written in an artificially childlike manner, displaying the tone, grammatical errors, and spelling mistakes typical of a young child's work. One of these notes states:

> Enrique: Baby is much better, thank God. I received Dear's little letter good and early. It won't be long til we see each other, G. willing . . . Ah, I feels the 25th will never get here. I think the days have gotten longer. There's still today, tomorrow, and . . . then comes . . .
>
> Baby felt so much better yesterday 'cause she finded out that D. was coming, and so she was able to go out for a bit of sunshine, and at night she ate a little din-din. For four days she had nothing but milk in her tummy. Tell me everything tomorrow, G. willing, goodie, goodie, goodie . . . I still think I dreaming. I say this so you'll have to guess, and today I'm mailing it in your letter, because you'll receive it the day you sail.
>
> 'Nighty night, my tweet love. Best wishes and kissies from Me.[10]

These letters are truly fascinating, and seem to justify the theories attributing a split personality to the poet. However, the following point has been made by Arturo Sergio Visca, a scholar who has studied Agustini's letters in great depth:

In a way, the letters are written in code. But there is more. Because in the margins of many of the postcards, in handwriting so miniscule as to be difficult to decipher even with a magnifying glass, there are statements which clearly reveal the true situation . . . The conclusion to be drawn from these letters is very clear: Delmira Agustini deceived her mother regarding the life she led. She wore the mask of the fictitious "Baby," as she was always called at home. But that "Baby,"—innocent, ingenious, owner of the famous doll—had another life of which her mother was unaware, and which she never even suspected.

In addition, as Visca has shown, there are love letters that are evidently not secret, in which the poet abandons the childish tone altogether.[11]

As a young man, Zum Felde used to visit Delmira at home, and he also noticed that as soon as her mother left the room, the poet would drop all pretense of shyness and childishness. This, too, would indicate that the poet's split personality was not real but a pose assumed to keep her parents and fiancé happy.

In 1912, Agustini met the great modernist poet Rubén Darío when he stopped over in Montevideo during his travels as the editor of the Paris-based journal *Mundial*. Darío's books, *Azul* (1888) and *Prosas profanas* (1896), marked by a passion for form and enthusiasm for precious subject matter, and later *Cantos de vida y esperanza* (1905), in which spiritual preoccupations predominated, had transformed both poetry and prose in the Spanish language. The Nicaraguan poet awakened a new artistic consciousness among the poets of Agustini's generation, who, until then, had adhered to the sentimental and exalted canons of romanticism. When Darío arrived in Montevideo he was only forty-five years old, but he had aged considerably thanks to a Bohemian life-style, and his most creative period was behind him. However, he was internationally famous as the renovator of Hispanic American poetry. For Delmira, a woman of sensitive and fiery temperament, having contact with the Nicaraguan poet was glorious.

Agustini went to welcome Darío at the docks in Montevideo, and later she made note of the exact hour and minute of their memorable meeting. During his stay, the poet visited Agustini at her home, and wrote a page that would appear one year later in the first edition of *The Empty Chalices*. In Darío's honor, a literary soirée was held at the Urquiza Theater. Agustini was sick and could not attend, but one of her poems was read during the evening. Clearly, Agustini was an up-and-coming figure within literary circles. The gulf between her private and professional lives, between "Baby" and "The Poet," was widening.

After their meeting, Agustini and Darío briefly corresponded. Evidently Agustini felt a spiritual affinity with the great Nicaraguan poet, and the two letters she sent him shed light on her deplorable state of mind at the time. In one of the letters we read:

> Forgive me for bothering you once more. Today I have
> achieved a moment's calm within my eternal and painful ex-
> halation. These are my saddest hours, as I gain conscious of
> my unconscious. I don't know whether your neurasthenia
> has become as acute as mine. I don't know if you have stared
> insanity in the face and wrestled with it in the anguished si-
> lence of a hermetic spirit . . . By mid-October I intend to
> check my neurosis into a sanitarium from where, for better
> or worse, I will emerge in December to marry. I have re-
> solved to hurl myself into the horrifying abyss of marriage.[12]

Following Darío's reply, in which he counseled tranquillity, Agustini wrote him again, this time in a more resigned vein:

> How right you are to advise tranquillity! To show you what
> my state of mind is like these days, let the following suffice:
> since I was planning to marry soon, I had told my fiancé that
> I intended to write to you, the most genial and profound of
> spiritual guides. Yesterday he asked me, casually, if I had
> written to you, and whether you had replied. I became so

upset, and stalled so much, that he began to imagine the impossible. Today I ask myself: Why? You see, I am a different woman, at least I want to be. I will be easygoing, soft for you. Sculpt me smiling.[13]

The letters are radically different in tone. The first is a sincere cry for help, basic to understanding Agustini's inner conflicts. The second is more literary, and reveals a subtle flirtatiousness that sheds interesting light on this aspect of the poet's personality.

In 1913, one year before her death, Agustini published her masterpiece, *The Empty Chalices*. Rodríguez Monegal asserts:

[The poems] are the first deep cry of feminine sexual poetics in Hispanic America. With this book (in large part, new, and also an anthology of her past work) Delmira places herself in the lyrical vanguard of the continent; she forges the path that will later be followed by Gabriela Mistral of Chile, Alfonsina Storni of Argentina, and Juana de Ibarbourou of Uruguay.[14]

One of the poems of *The Empty Chalices* is "Another Family Tree":

> *Eros, I want to guide you, Blind father . . .*
> *I ask for your all-powerful hands,*
> *His sublime body overflowing on fire*
> *Upon my body laying faint among roses!*
>
> *The electric corola that I unfurl today*
> *Offers the nectar of a garden of Wives;*
> *To his vultures on my flesh I surrender*
> *An entire swarm of pink doves.*
>
> *Give to the two cruel serpents of his embrace*
> *My great febrile stalk . . . Absinthe, honeys,*
> *Pour me from his veins, from his mouth . . .*

Stretched out so, I am a burning furrow
Where the seed of another sublimely insane
Family Tree can be nourished.[15]

The poet no longer addresses a flesh-and-blood lover, but rather Eros, god of Love, to whom she offers the book as if to recognize that only a supreme force would be able to satisfy her most intimate, womanly yearnings, and be worthy of her surrender. The language and the images surge naturally throughout the poem to express an intense and pathetic eroticism. *The Empty Chalices* contains twelve poems, but each one, by virtue of images charged with mystery and beauty, is a small literary gem. If in *The White Book* one could still see the influence of the romantics and the modernists, in this collection we find poems that are at once unique and of high aesthetic value, the manifestations of a gifted woman whose extraordinary voluptuousness is sublimated in poetry.

Although it is impossible to know whether Agustini's poems were inspired by a real or an imagined lover, her biography does allow us to suggest that they might have been born of the passionate love she felt for the Argentinean writer Manuel Ugarte. Certainly Agustini's passion for Ugarte further intensified her already tormented inner life.

The poet's relationship with Ugarte began in 1910 on a strictly literary basis. At the time, Ugarte edited the magazine *La lectura* in Madrid, and Agustini sent him copies of *The White Book* and *Morning Songs*. In 1912, when Ugarte was in Montevideo, he visited Agustini often. These visits, always carried out under her parents watchful eyes, appeared to be those of a courteous writer who, like many others, enjoyed dropping in on the poet. Agustini, however, fell madly in love with Ugarte, then thirty years old, single, elegant, and dark. Despite her engagement, she and Ugarte exchanged suggestive and passionate letters, although there is no indication that they were ever physically intimate. Ugarte, apparently, was quite pleased to correspond with an ardent and famous admirer, but unfortunately, he had no interest in a commitment. On her wedding day, and already dressed in her white gown, Agustini was still having second thoughts. She asked Ugarte and the Uruguayan poet Manuel Zorrilla de San Martín, who were to serve as witnesses at the ceremony, whether she should go through with it. They both said yes, and the wedding took place. In a photograph taken that day, Ugarte's head appears between that of the bride and groom, a presage of the tragedy to come. Agustini even wrote an intensely erotic poem for Ugarte titled "Serpentina," which appeared in the Buenos Aires magazine *Fray Mocho* in 1914.

The following excerpt from a letter written by Agustini to Ugarte leaves very little doubt as to her feelings:

> . . . I should tell you that you provided the anguish for my wedding night and my absurd honeymoon . . . What could have been a long, funny novel became a tragedy. I will never be able to express how much I suffered that night. The room was a sepulcher which I entered only in hopes of seeing you. As they dressed me, I asked again and again whether you had arrived. I could tell you about all my movements that night . . . The only conscious look I recall, the only untimely greeting I offered was to you. I was struck by a lightning bolt of happiness. It seemed that you were looking at me, and that you understood me.[16]

On August 14, 1913, Agustini married Reyes, but less than two months later she left her husband and returned to her parents. The letter Agustini wrote to her husband explaining her action has been lost, but according to his sister, the letter made it clear that her decision was irrevocable. Reyes, in turn, penned a response full of bitter accusations against his wife and her mother. The immediate cause of this break, so unusual for the time, will never be known. Had the newlyweds fought about Agustini's mother, with whom Reyes, apparently, did not get along? Did Agustini realize that she would never be happy as the traditional wife her husband yearned for? In a letter to Ugarte, the poet wrote that she returned to her mother's house to seek refuge from vulgarity. She also mentioned that the only item she had taken with her was a novel by Ugarte, and that she longed to see him again, making it clear that she wished the relationship to continue.

On June 5, and under the new divorce laws, the Reyes-Agustini marriage was permanently dissolved. Incredible as it may seem, Agustini, obviously a very unusual woman for her time, continued to see Reyes during the proceedings in a room he had rented downtown. As Reyes's sister later observed, she seemed to "want to take her husband as a lover." There was more. While she was meeting clandestinely with her husband, and still writing romantic letters to Ugarte, she was also carrying on a rather erotic correspondence with N. Manino, one of her admirers. All this led to what her father termed, in his diary, "Baby's fatal day." On July 6, 1914, in the very room where they carried out their secret meetings, Reyes shot her twice in the head, and then took his own life.

The headlines about the murder-suicide were not even eclipsed by subsequent news of World War I. The details about a couple who, while divorcing, continued to see each other in secret, and the photograph of Agustini's partially clad body, were widely disseminated in the popular press. One paper, *La Tribuna Popular of Montevideo,* attributed the murder to women's growing independence.

In conclusion, this chapter attempts to analyze Delmira Agustini's life and work in terms of the historical period and circumstances in which she found herself. In light of the documentation examined, it is apparent that although the poet did not openly defy the restrictions placed on women during her lifetime, she did try, in a more discreet way, to fulfill her intimate desires through behavior that, by early-twentieth-century standards, was extremely bold. But for a passionate woman like Agustini, these actions did not suffice, and it was only through her magnificent poetry that she was able to express the totality of her spiritual needs.

Clarice Lispector:
DREAMS OF LANGUAGE

Giovanni Pontiero

⌒ CLARICE LISPECTOR WAS BORN IN THE UKRAINE IN 1920. Her
parents emigrated to Brazil in 1926 and settled first in Alagoas, and
then in 1929 they moved to Recife in northeastern Brazil, before
finally settling in Rio in 1937. As a child she read compulsively and
began writing short stories while still in her teens. She studied law
while working as a journalist, a profession that brought her into
contact with other young writers who would soon achieve recognition. Lispector married a future diplomat in 1943, graduated in
1944, and published her first novel, *Perto do coraçao selvagem* (Near
to the Wild Heart), that same year. The novel attracted the attention of influential critics and was awarded the much-coveted Graça
Aranha Prize.

As a diplomat's wife she was to spend the next fifteen years away
from Brazil. The couple spent some months in Belém do Pará before being posted abroad: first Naples, then Berne, six months at
Torquay in 1951, then Washington, D.C., in 1953. During this period Lispector also became the mother of two sons: Pedro, born in

Berne (1949) and Paulo, born in Washington (1953). In 1959, she parted amicably from her husband and returned to Rio with her children. She had never stopped writing throughout these years, but her first major success came in 1960 with the publication of a remarkable collection of short stories, *Laços de Família* (Family Ties). This book established Lispector's reputation in literary circles. Throughout the sixties and seventies she produced some of her best work, and before she succumbed to terminal cancer on the eve of her fifty-eighth birthday, she had produced nine novels, eight collections of short stories, four books for children, and a Portuguese translation of Oscar Wilde's *Picture of Dorian Gray,* in addition to a vast output of articles and chronicles for newspapers and journals.

In 1976, the year before her death, she was awarded first prize in the Tenth National Literary Competition for her outstanding contribution to Brazilian literature. In recent years her books have been translated into French, German, Spanish, Italian, Dutch, Japanese, and Ukrainian.

The upsurge of interest in women writers has helped in recent years to enhance Clarice Lispector's reputation worldwide. Translations of her novels, chronicles, and short stories into all the major European languages have brought her a degree of recognition few women writers from Latin America can ever hope to enjoy. In feminist circles she is revered as an intensely feminine writer who articulates the needs and concerns of every woman in pursuit of self-awareness. Critics worldwide have made much of her introspective writings, both fiction and nonfiction, and the way in which they probe the delicate terrain of human relationships as experienced by women. With an unsparing eye she takes us through the solemn rituals as women develop physically and emotionally from infancy to old age. Hence the general perception of a serious woman writer interested in the more opaque side of existence.

Yet there is much more to this remarkable human being who rarely thought of herself as a professional writer and claimed to write as one lives. Out to please no one and indifferent to praise, she shunned literary circles and insisted on pursuing *her own thing*. And while boosting her reputation, certain feminist interpretations of her work have somehow missed out on her warmth, vitality, and devastating wit. Lispector should not simply be seen as a recluse or creature of anguish and despair in a male-dominated society. Philosophical musings couched in poetic language are only one aspect of this chameleon-like writer whose feet were firmly on the ground when it came to coping with life's mundane realities. Writing fiction was not seen by Lispector as a means of *unburdening oneself* or *scrutinizing one's soul*. And this explains why she towered over other women writers of her generation. Lispector believed sentences were born rather than made, and worked on the written word until she unlocked its mysteries; each phrase constructed to evoke her vision of the world. Her experiments with language are in constant pursuit of that perfect equilibrium between epiphany and its verbal expression.

In Brazil, Lispector was to inspire and influence a whole generation of women writers, but the critics were mainly interested in her unusual concept of narrative form and the startling originality of her language.

Even as a little girl with a precocious talent for writing Lispector instinctively felt that there was something different about her kind of storytelling. The pieces she submitted for publication in the children's page of her local newspaper were invariably rejected. None of them began with the inevitable *Once upon a time . . .* , for as Lispector explained, she had no facts of episodes to relate, only sensations and intuitions. She confessed: "I thought a book was like a tree, like an animal, something that is born. I had no idea there was an author behind all this."[1]

A compulsive reader of Brazilian and foreign fiction throughout her teens, she went on writing in secret, too embarrassed to confide even in her own family. Eventually, persistence paid off. An intrepid coward in her own words, she badgered editors until her stories were finally accepted for publication in several magazines and the satisfaction of seeing her work in print more than compensated for not being paid.

When Lispector published her first novel, *Perto de Coraçao Selvagem,* in 1944, she was in her early twenties and completing her law studies while working as a reporter for a Rio newspaper. The novel also coincided with her marriage to a fellow law student, Mauri Gurgel Valente. Several influential critics hailed *Near to the Wild Heart* as "Brazil's first truly introspective novel," and they described the narrative style as a new experience, different from the psychological novel or the experimental prose of the modernists.

Here was the first of Lispector's tales of self-discovery and, as with so many of her narratives, one senses a deep affinity between the author and her female protagonist. The fears voiced by Joana about the constraints of marriage are unmistakably those of Lispector herself: "Secretly she rebelled . . . She feared the days, one after another, without any surprises, days of total devotion to one man."[2] Lispector's characters tend on the whole to mistrust emotional ties likely to stifle their inner freedom: "My God!—never to be yourself, never, never. And to be a married woman, in other words, someone with their destiny mapped out . . . Even boredom with life has a certain beauty . . . when you suffer it alone in quiet despair."[3] Deceived by her husband and caught up in a love triangle, Joana recognizes that as human beings we have "a greater capacity for life than knowledge of life."[4] Marriage exacerbates the conflict between what society expects of women and their private needs and inclinations. Joana's troubled thoughts as she tries to come to terms with who and what she is, echo those of Virginia in *O Lustre* (The Chandelier, 1946) and Lucrécia in *A Cidade Sitiada* (The Besieged City, 1949), who are also plagued by the *doce mal* (sweet evil) inherent in their nature. These early novels register the deep frustrations of women who try to rebel against the restrictions imposed on them by fate and circumstance. Chilling monologues bare the souls of these restless spirits.

From the outset, Lispector's approach to fiction was largely intuitive. She dismissed the idea that her narratives should have any predetermined form. Moments of insight and their repercussions were allowed to surface and flower as if by an act of nature. Fascinated by what others might consider worthless, incomplete, or simply awkward, Lispector drew inspiration from fleeting sensations, from some word overheard by chance, some trifle without substance or form. Her aim was to touch life rather than become entangled in mere description, and she could scarcely be more lucid in stating her preferences:

> The greatest drawback about writing is that one has to use words. It is a problem. For I should prefer a more direct form of communication, that tacit understanding one often finds between people. If I could write by carving on wood or by stroking a child's head or strolling in the countryside, I would never resort to using words.[5]

Words, as she uses them, become as vivid as gestures, and the dialogues she forges with her readers miraculously preserve that "tacit understanding" and sense of tactile communication with nature and life.

The rare perceptions and unorthodox style of the early novels ruled out any immediate popularity or commercial success. Wider recognition came only with the stories she began writing in the forties. Six of them were published in 1952 under the title *Alguns Contos* (Some Stories) and subsequently reprinted with seven others as *Laços de Família* in 1960. These stories show how effectively Lispector's intense lyricism works in shorter narrative forms. Varied in theme and style, they are nevertheless linked on the one hand by the central theme of relationships as experienced by women in different roles—wife, mother, daughter, mistress, matriarch—and on the other hand by the even more enigmatic relationships between humans and the animal and natural order. Two outstanding narratives in the book embody all the qualities that characterize

Lispector's writing. In "Amor" (Love), the grotesque sight of a blind man chewing gum at a bus stop drives the protagonist, Anna, into a maelstrom of self-discovery. Taking refuge in Rio's botanical garden, Anna contemplates a world that has become alien:

> The trees were laden, and the world was so rich that it was rotting. When Anna reflected that there were children and grown men suffering hunger, the nausea reached her throat as if she were pregnant and abandoned. The moral of the garden was something different. Now that the blind man had guided her to it, she trembled on the threshold of a dark, fascinating world where monstrous waterlilies floated. The small flowers scattered on the grass did not appear to be yellow or pink, but the colour of inferior gold and scarlet. Their decay was profound, perfumed. But all these oppressive things she watched, her head surrounded by a swarm of insects, sent by some more refined life within the world. The breeze penetrated between the flowers. Anna imagined rather than felt its sweetened scent. The garden was so beautiful that she feared hell.[6]

Laura's inner thoughts in "A Imitaçao da Rosa" (The Imitation of the Rose) trace out a woman's perilous journey back to so-called normality after a nervous breakdown. A prey to order and perfection, Laura retreats into a world of scruples that threatens to engulf her. A bunch of roses bought on impulse to send to a friend proves to be her undoing. Rarely has the battle with self been expressed with such delicacy and pathos:

> Laura became a little frightened: because things were never hers.
> But these roses were. Rosy, small, and perfect: they were hers. She looked at them, incredulous: they were beautiful and they were hers. If she could think further ahead, she would think: hers, as nothing before now had ever been.
> And she could even keep them because that initial uneasi-

ness had passed which had caused her vaguely to avoid looking at the roses too much.

"Why give them away then? They are so lovely and you
are giving them away? So when you find something nice, you
just go and give it away? Well, if they were hers," she insinu-
ated persuasively to herself, without finding any other argument beyond the previous one which, when repeated, seemed
to her to be ever more convincing and straightforward.

"They would not last long—why give them away then, so
long as they were alive?"

. . . "They would not last long; why give them away
then?" The fact that they would not last long seemed to free
her from the guilt of keeping them, with the obscure logic of
the woman who sins.[7]

Both stories illustrate her uncanny penetration of the human
psyche and the delicate balance between tranquillity and trauma,
between hope and despair. Lispector later confided that she identified closely with both Ana and Laura and, when questioned some
ten years later about the style of "The Imitation of the Rose," the
author clarified another notable trait in her writing: " 'The Imitation of the Rose' gave me an opportunity to use a monochromatic
tone which I find most pleasing: repetition always gratifies me, for
the deliberate use of repetition denotes a gradual process of penetration, an insistent cantilena which has something to express."[8]

The stories guide us through the different stages of womanhood
from self-conscious puberty to cynical old age. A sense of nervous
anxiety and embarrassment prevails in "Preciosidade" (Preciousness), in which a teenage schoolgirl can no longer count on her
anonymity in order to feel protected. Her world has suddenly become inhabited by potential monsters. Men are no longer mere
boys. As her sixteenth birthday approaches, the girl finds herself
"obliged to be venerated . . . and she, too, venerated herself, she,
the custodian of a rhythm!"[9] The same mysterious rites are enacted in "Mistério em Sao Cristóvao" (Mystery in Sao Cristóvao).

Three masqueraders invade the privacy of a garden on an autumn evening, and a broken hyacinth signals the altered condition of the nineteen-year-old girl watching from her bedroom window. With this symbolic gesture "the laborious structure of her years dissolves."[10] Her passage to womanhood even transforms the garden: "now seeming to expand, now to fade away: butterflies hovering like sleepwalkers."[11] There is less lyricism and much more grit in the rebellious musings of the female narrator in "Devaneio e Embriaguez duma Rapariga" (The Daydreams of an Inebriated Woman) and in the sly thoughts of Catarina in the title story of *Family Ties*. Both women momentarily break free from their stereotyped roles in order to explore the roles they might have played in other circumstances. Their hidden resentments and unfulfilled desires arouse conflicting emotions: "horrid ecstasy, atrocious delight, voluptuous impotence, and sweet evil." How much simpler the primordial existence of plants and animals where one detects greater integrity and harmony. The child in "Uma Galinha" has no difficulty in recognizing the inner tranquillity of a chicken "warming her offspring . . . neither gentle nor cross, neither happy nor sad; she was nothing, simply a hen."[12] And the same could be said of the dog abandoned by its master in "O Crime do Professor de Matemática" (The Crime of the Math Teacher), a dog condemned to "the anguish of existing in such a perfect way that its happiness became unbearable."[13] Lispector found animals more congenial than human beings and somehow closer to God, "living each moment to the full rather than taking it in easy stages."[14] For Lispector, mankind somehow lacks the reassuring integrity of animals. Human beings are much more flawed and complicated, our loyalties more suspect. This led her to the conclusion that we must use our frailty in order to achieve salvation: "Sometimes our very vices can save our soul."[15]

Lispector's women characters, young, middle-aged, and senile, exploit their own *being* as a form of knowing. They are moved to pity and, at the same time, revulsion, by the reflection of their own image. Yet despite all the doubts and uncertainties, she sees life as a God-given mandate and deplored Virginia Woolf's suicide, which she considered an unacceptable act of abdication. Aware that so many human lives smack of melodrama, she steered her characters toward a sense of purpose. Solitude and inner silence were simply the preconditions for self-appraisal before confronting reality. The stark quality of her first novels is tempered in these shorter pieces by her superb ironies, sometimes playful, often savage. Like some *voyeur*, she catches these women off their guard. Fleeting, furtive glances are enough to tell us what life's ups and downs have done to them. The moments which have left their mark are somehow more revealing than a whole lifetime of experience.

Her fourth novel, *A Maça no Escuro* (The Apple in the Dark), took Lispector rather longer to write. She began working from notes in the early fifties but did not publish the book until 1961. Critics saw the novel as a decisive landmark in Lispector's development. Narrated in the first person, this time by a male protagonist, *The Apple in the Dark* is a moving soliloquy about love and death. After attempting to murder his wife, Martim tries to rehabilitate himself in society and forge a new identity. Courage fails him at the eleventh hour. A sense of guilt and expiation runs through most of Lispector's narratives. Like most serious writers she is preoccupied with human error and insistently poses the question: How does one retract from failure and rebuild one's life? Life, like art, consists of tentative gestures, "that unsteady manner of plucking an apple in the dark without letting it drop."[16]

When invited to address the eleventh congress of Iberoamerican Literature held at Austin, Texas, in 1963, Lispector made one of her rare appearances as a lecturer. She read what is probably her most hermetic narrative of all, "O Ovo e a Galinha" (The Egg and the Chicken), a story she herself claimed *not to understand* but what better illustration of what she meant when she argued that all art is essentially experimental in nature.

The same labored subtleties of thought and expression characterize *A Paixao Segundo G. H.* (The Passion According to G. H.), published in 1969, generally considered to be her most penetrating novel. Intensely poetic and philosophical, the novel evoked comparisons with works by Kafka and the French Existentialists. The title echoes the Passion of Christ and universal concepts of human suffering while emphasizing the Judaic strain in Lispector's writings, her obsessive quest for God, and the deeply personal faith she shares with so many of her characters. The protagonist of this powerful novel is a sculptress, identified simply by the initials G. H. embossed on a traveling bag. Having dismissed her maid, G. H. decides to clean out the maid's room and accidentally crushes a cockroach to death in a wardrobe door. The sight of that tiny corpse has a mesmeric effect on G. H., who is drawn into an anguished questioning of self in relation to the world around her. She devours the dead cockroach and this bizarre gesture unleashes all that is good and corrupt in her nature. By devouring the cockroach she touches the depths of revulsion in order to be spiritually cleansed. In willful contamination she purges her soul. *The Passion According to G. H.* is undoubtedly the author's most dramatic work in which she struggles with the more opaque side of life and language. An allegory of life and death, the novel reveals Lispector's unique way of stripping away layers of meaning in order to transcend the frontiers between things real and imagined, things visible and invisible. The thin divide between love and hatred, between happiness and sorrow, between heaven and hell, has rarely been drawn with such power and precision.

Lispector sensed the puzzlement and disquiet this novel might cause her critics and readers. Writing the book brought her "an awkward happiness; but happiness nevertheless.":

> Language is my human effort. It is my destiny to go searching and my destiny to return empty-handed. But I return with the unsayable. The unsayable only comes to me through the breakdown in language. Only when the con-

struction is missing do I obtain what the construction failed to achieve.[17]

This statement has been verified by critics and translators of her work who have often compared her prose to certain experiments in musical composition, where variations are created around a central theme. Perhaps more than any of her other novels, *The Passion According to G. H.* illustrates the unparalleled individuality of her style as she struggles to transpose life's experiences into words without losing any of their truth or immediacy.

As the mother of two little boys, it was perhaps inevitable that Lispector should finally turn to writing stories for children; stories featuring those pet animals she so dearly loved. Like children themselves, she found animals had the power to enchant and disconcert her: "I tremble all over when I come into contact with animals or even so much as look at them. I seem to have a certain fear and horror of that living creature which is not human yet has the same instincts, although in animals those instincts are freer and indomitable."[18]

In 1967 she published *O Mistério do Coelho Pensante* (The Mystery of the Pensive Rabbit), and in the following year *A Mulher Que Matou Os Peixes* (The Woman who Killed the Goldfish). In fact these narratives have as much to say to adults as to children. On the surface they relate the adventures of the chicks, rabbits, monkeys, and dogs who graced the author's household at one time or another. The tone of these narratives is lively and colloquial. Lispector knows how to engage the eye and ear of her young audience. At a deeper level, however, they probe the mysterious links between the human and animal order and even the morals these stories convey are surprisingly sophisticated and direct: frank statements about mankind's need to covet and possess, our power to cherish and destroy. Reading between the lines, we find subtle meanings about the hypocrisies and prejudices that blight the adult word once the innocence and spontaneity of childhood wanes. *A Vida Íntima de*

Laura (The Secret Life of Laura, 1974) and *Quase de Verdade* (An Almost True Story, 1978), the latter engagingly narrated by her dog Ulysses, complete this quartet. The author would read these stories aloud to the children and their friends, sessions she found much more rewarding than any literary gathering, and the interesting dialogues that ensued led her to reflect:

> Why is it that when I write for children I am understood? Yet when I write for adults I suddenly become difficult? Should I write for adults with words and feelings suitable for children? Can I not speak to adults as between equals? How frustrating, dear God, but scarcely worth bothering about.[19]

But it did bother Lispector that readers should find her difficult to read when her main objective was to communicate without barriers.

She certainly achieves that objective in *A Legiao Estrangeira* (The Foreign Legion, 1964), a miscellaneous anthology of stories and chronicles that allows us to see Lispector under various guises. The chronicles offer her greater freedom to register shifts of mood: whimsical and serious, mawkish and provocative, flirtatious and withdrawn. Above all, the chronicles show just how closely she remained in touch with the world around her. Character sketches, travel notes, random quotations, conversations with friends and her own children betray unsuspected reserves of humor and compassion. The self-portrait became even richer in detail when her weekly contributions to the *Jornal do Brasil*, Rio's leading newspaper, were collected after her death under the general title *A Descoberta do Mundo* (Discovering the World). First published as a weekly assignment between 1967 and 1973, these articles, reminiscences, and press interviews with intellectuals, artists, musicians, poets, politicians and their wives reveal a woman of many facets. Light-hearted and playful one minute, stinging and lethal the next. Her dialogues with taxi drivers and housemaids are particularly revealing. Their little eccentricities and unpredictable reactions intrigued her. A simple journey by taxi often turns into a voyage of discovery once the question-and-answer sessions get underway between driver and passenger. Aninha, Jandira, Maria Carlota and all the other maids whom she employed at one time or another amused and intimidated her with their knowing ways and drollery. Her conversations with the street-wise find Lispector at her funniest, encounters with philanderers, con men and bores at her most aggressive; her moments of self-doubt and despondency at her most vulnerable. The deep humanity, the warmth and understanding we glean from these chronicles match up to Lispector's assessment of her main strength as a writer: "People who refer to my intelligence are, in fact, confusing intelligence with what I would call a knowing sensibility. Now that is something I really do possess."[20]

A serious accident in 1967 almost cost the writer her life. She had fallen asleep with a lit cigarette in one hand and the bedclothes caught fire. Accustomed to sleeping with the door and window open, a current of air soon spread the flames. She was rescued just in time by her eldest son but suffered severe burns to her right hand and legs. There are frequent references to this terrifying experience throughout her chronicles. The accident coincided with a period of nervous stress and financial difficulties. Painful skin grafts had to be carried out and the long months of convalescence affected her deeply. Life seemed to take on a new urgency and, although weary and depressed, she seemed determined to survive by taking on more and more commitments in the form of translations (sometimes completed by others), stories (often revised versions of work already published), and articles (sometimes surprisingly terse) for newspapers that did not conform to any set rules. The success of her interviews varied according to her mood and sense of rapport with the person being interviewed. With artists as creative as herself she sounds completely relaxed. But when interviewing influential members of Brazilian high society a note of mischief and even mockery creeps in. Her years as a diplomat's wife had made her somewhat wary and disillusioned. She could look the part but refused to take it seriously, and her description of ladies attending a luncheon party in "Social Column" is wickedly satirical:

> . . . dumb waiters, flowers and all this elegance . . . but if they were all entitled to this ambiance, they still seemed apprehensive about committing some faux-pas . . . One must assume that every one of the guests had her own little moment of crisis during this formal gathering. Each of them must have sensed, however momentarily, this acute and imminent danger of their coiffure coming apart and throwing the luncheon into chaos . . . Discreet women who form a kind of sisterhood, who recognize each other at a glance, and in praising each other they are praising themselves.[21]

After a nervous start, Lispector had gradually transformed the nature and scope of the chronicle. When she wrote the women's page for the *Correio da Manha* (Morning Post) from 1959 until 1960 under the pseudonym of Helen Palmer, she confined herself to fashion, cosmetics, mother care, home economics, recipes, and household tips. She gathered facts with flair and enthusiasm and knew precisely what her readers expected. The courage to bemuse and bewilder and then to deliver what they did not expect only came later. Yet even in her earliest assignments she could be slyly ironic, whether quoting from Dumas the Younger: "A woman's heart may be made of the most fragile tissue but is also the easiest to repair" or suggesting that "love and romance are not the two most powerful things in our life because hatred and fear are more difficult to control."[22]

She enjoyed life's little vanities as much as any woman, dressed tastefully, and used makeup to enhance her striking good looks. She was forever encouraging readers and friends to make the best of themselves. But for Lispector, painting one's face and dressing up was a serious business. The girls and women in her narrative use masks and adornments to play out travesties, baring or concealing their identity at will. Even the numerous portraits and photographs that survive of Lispector herself capture her in different poses. Her lips and eyes are particularly expressive and create an unmistakable aura of mystery and allure. I only met Lispector once. It was in the early seventies, soon after the publication of my translation of *Family Ties* in the United States. I can still see those extraordinary eyes looking into infinity as we sat there in silence, watching and waiting until we could no longer ignore each other's presence. Disconcertingly beautiful, she was also extremely gentle and hospitable, despite the sense of weariness as she began to relax and converse. But what I recall most clearly of all is the way in which she articulated sparse phrases in a voice as musical as that of her written prose.

Her output during the last ten years of her life was uneven but steady. She was haunted by ever-increasing bouts of depression and a frustrating lack of motivation. Between 1969 and 1977, the year of her death, she wrote another four novels and three collections of stories: Some of the material had already appeared with different titles or in another form. Most of these later narratives continue to pursue paths of self-discovery, though one senses Lispector is trying to find new sources of inspiration and to move in some new direction. The one outstanding work of this last phase, *A Hora da Estrêla* (The Hour of the Star, 1977) shows quite clearly that, despite her worst fears, Lispector's creative powers had not deserted her. Short even by her standards, this penultimate novel is extraordinarily dense and rich.

The plot is sparse and deceptively straightforward. The orphaned Macabea from the slums of Alagoas struggles for survival in an overpopulated Rio. Barely literate, ugly, and undernourished, she is one of the world's born losers. She has nothing to offer and expects nothing in return. Her sole ambition in life is to look like Marilyn Monroe. Innocent to the point of eccentricity, Macabea is superfluous and vulnerable in an aggressive metropolis. Her sudden demise under the front wheels of a yellow Mercedes driven by

a handsome foreigner is as unreal and absurd as all the other disasters that befall this hopeless misfit. The story of Macabea operates at three interdependent levels. Symbolically, this antiheroine
embodies the Brazilian legacy of poverty and ignorance. At another level, Macabea's blighted existence obliges us tot take a close
look at the human condition: "Who has not asked himself at some
time or other: am I monster or is this what it means to be a person?"[23] And at a third level, Lispector exploits Macabea's harsh
experiences to reveal her own deep-rooted fear of the abyss and the
Hell of Human Freedom.[24] As in all her narratives, the facts are
sonorous, but what the reader must look out for is that murmur
amidst the facts.

The social evils stalking Macabea are treated mainly as asides,
but we are in no doubt about where the author's sympathies lie.
Lispector is all too aware of the heroine's physical and emotional
hunger and of the solitude imposed by a vicarious existence. Educated, well-traveled, and socially privileged, Lispector was not indifferent to the plight of millions of fellow Brazilians who get
nothing out of life other than life itself. To those who accused her
of being naïve or apolitical, she explained: "It would indeed be
strange if I were to remain indifferent to life in my own country. I
may not write about social problems but I live them intensely."[25]

As a child, the sight of human deprivation and injustice in the impoverished Northeast caused her to tremble with rage. She studied
law in the hope that she might one day help to reform the country's
appalling penal system. She marched in Rio on behalf of students
debarred from education because they were unable to pay; and her
mistrust of politicians and their abuse of power comes over forcefully in chronicles such as "The Leader's Dream" and "In Memory
of the Man Who Stood Down."[26] She needed no persuading that
acts of charity are an unacceptable substitute for human justice and
social equality, and rejected the idea that want might enhance one's
spirituality. In one of her most pungent chronicles, "Hateful Charity," two telling encounters with Rio's destitute expose the humil-

iation, embarrassment, and hostility engendered by poverty in a divided society. No simple tale about those who have and those who have not, *The Hour of the Star* also exposes contrasting attitudes among the poor themselves. Lispector draws a sharp distinction between material and spiritual poverty: Macabea, her swaggering boyfriend Olímpico, the resentful doctor and loquacious Mme Carlota all react in different ways to their squalid reality.

The book is also a meditation on life and death as Macabea moves toward an irresistible destiny. Death is seen as transfiguration, an apotheosis capable of finally transforming Macabea into the Hollywood idol of her dreams:

> No one would teach her how to die one day: yet one day
> she would surely die as if she had already learned by heart
> how to play the starring role. For at the hour of death you
> become a celebrated film star, it is a moment of glory for
> everyone when the choral music scales the top notes.[27]

It is difficult to say with any certainty whether Lispector knew that she herself would soon be confronting death. Those who were close to her during the last months of her life insist that she never spoke of dying as the end approached. Yet how tangible death becomes as Macabea confronts her ultimate destiny. The sense of anguished postponement at the end of the novel is almost unbearably moving:

> [Macabea] clung to a thread of consciousness and mentally
> repeated over and over again: I am, I am, I am. Precisely
> who she was, she was unable to say . . . As she lay there, she
> felt the warmth of supreme happiness, for she had been born
> for death's embrace.[28]

The last two interviews Lispector gave betray a note of physical and mental fatigue. The first of these interviews was in Rio's Museum of Image and Sound in late October 1976. She claimed to be more disorganized than ever but was writing sporadically with even greater haste. She had more friends and admirers than ever before, yet writing remained that solitary act, a burden, and she felt that freedom would only be hers when she finally laid down her pen. The second interview, given in Sao Paulo in January the following year, was a much more harrowing affair. She agreed to be interviewed on television in the company of her friend and companion Olga Borelli, and the stills confirm that Lispector was already very ill. Looking remote and uneasy, she confessed to a permanent feeling of exhaustion that left her frustrated and irritated. When the interviewer asked, "Surely you find rebirth with each new work?" she gave a wan smile and assured him, "For the moment I'm dead but let's see if I can come back to life . . . For the moment I'm dead . . . I'm talking from my grave."[29]

Death held no fear for Lispector. In the closing pages of *The Hour of the Star* she comforts the reader: "Don't grieve for the dead: they know what they're doing . . . Death is instantaneous and passes in a flash."[30] One senses that she was spiritually prepared for her own quiet exit: She constantly reminded those around her: "God doesn't kill anyone. People simply die."[31]

Unaware of the seriousness of her illness, she allowed the doctors to operate for what she believed to be acute peritonitis. In fact, she was dying of cancer. The operation was carried out in late October and she hovered for forty-five days between life and death. She finally died on 9 December, the eve of her fifty-eighth birthday, and at the request of her family was buried in the Jewish cemetery in Rio.

The years have passed and Lispector continues to talk to us from the grave, tranquil in the knowledge that she lived up to the words on her tombstone: To stretch out my hand to someone is all I expected of happiness.[32] Now that her private papers are in the public domain, a fuller picture is beginning to emerge of this remarkable human being. Her correspondence with friends and relatives tended to be fitful and erratic. Her missives are almost telegraphic in style, her longer letters reserved for her children and fellow writers. How revealing to find her in the role of confidante, dispensing comfort and words of comfort to troubled souls, the clearest testimony of her sincerity when she wrote: "Loving others is the only salvation known to me. No one will be lost if they give love to others and receive a little love in return from time to time."

Some read her fiction for its sheer individuality, others for the lessons she imparts about life. She is rewarding on both counts. Haunted by enigmas she felt she must somehow decipher, she sought to communicate her vision of a fragile world without lapsing into "counterfeit emotions and creative lies." The truth she would have us cherish is that sorrow and joy, weakness and strength, life and death are simply the two sides of the same coin. Here is a writer who gradually seduces her readers by confronting them with the ineffable mysteries which shape our lives. No easy task. Like most of her characters, she found that living one's story was somehow easier than trying to narrate it.

Today her contribution to contemporary writing is universally acknowledged but it is worth noting that she thought of herself as being first and foremost Brazilian. The year spent away from Brazil caused her deep anguish. Despite her Ukrainian ancestry, Lispector identified completely with Brazil, and most of all with the northeastern provinces. Memories of her childhood, especially in Recife, evoked the authentic Brazil, where traditions and folklore had been preserved. A slight speech defect made her sound like a foreigner, but she was adamant that she had forged her soul and innermost thoughts with the Portuguese language, "a difficult language" to her mind but one she was able to transform and even reinvent by means of conceptual refinements, subtle nuances and bold experiments with syntax and phrasing.

Something of an acquired taste in her own country, she is today probably more widely known and read outside Brazil. So how is one to explain the secret of her appeal? The answer lies in one of the most memorable of her riveting perceptions: "Extreme happiness is almost indistinguishable from unhappiness. Both are so dramatic. Both are life."[33] This is the vision she consistently projects.

Alejandra Pizarnik:
THE SELF & ITS IMPOSSIBLE LANDSCAPES

ALICIA BORINSKY

⌒ ENIGMATIC, FREQUENTLY SOMBER, Alejandra Pizarnik's work is one of the most original among contemporary Hispanic women poets. She was born in 1936 in Buenos Aires, Argentina, to a family of eastern European Jewish immigrants. Drawn to the humanities and the arts, she immersed herself in the intellectual world of a very cosmopolitan Buenos Aires. She was admitted to the University of Buenos Aires in 1954, where she first majored in philosophy, then switched to literature but did not complete her degree, choosing instead to undertake painting under the direction of the surrealist artist Juan Batlle Planas. The different directions in which she channeled her talents were not seen as separate in the lively artistic Buenos Aires context of the time. Batlle Planas was a painter with profound links to literature; the connections among the arts and written language were frequently stressed in exhibitions, lectures, and readings.

Parisian and Buenos Aires intellectual and artistic concerns have traditionally been closely related. Traveling the road to Paris from

Buenos Aires has held a great fascination for *porteños*. Alejandra Pizarnik made her pilgrimage to Paris in 1960 and lived and worked there for a few years. Those years turned out to be crucial to her development. An avid reader of French literature, she translated into Spanish works by Antonin Artaud, Aimé Cesaire, Henri Michaux, and Yves Bonnefoy. She became close friends with Italo Calvino and Julio Cortázar. Remembered as shy by some of her close friends, she was able, nevertheless, to become closely associated with what remained of the surrealist movement in Paris. She was an active collaborator in several literary and scholarly journals from Europe and Latin America, among them *Les Lettres Nouvelles, La Nouvelle Revue Française, Sur, Zona Franca, Mundo Nuevo,* and *Papeles de Son Armadans*. She published several books of poetry and poetic prose, which were received quite positively.[1] Octavio Paz, the Mexican poet and Nobel laureate, wrote a preface to her book *Arbol de Diana* in 1962, hailing her as an original and strong talent. She was also the recipient of a Guggenheim Fellowship. At a time when poetry was already becoming a marginal genre, Alejandra Pizarnik managed to be recognized as an important writer and to support herself with various forms of literary work while continuing her activity in drawing and painting. Her romantic life, mostly lesbian, although some of her French acquaintances recall involvements with men, is made explicit in some of her poems. In 1972, back in Buenos Aires, she took her own life.

WHERE IS THE SELF?

Who was this woman? How did she view herself in her writing? Earlier in the century, Macedonio Fernández, the Argentine writer Jorge Luis Borges designated as his master, had produced a powerful dismantling of the very idea of a self. Through the use of radical humor, Macedonio expected to convince his readers of the fact that their individual identities were a mere illusion, born out of a belief in dogmatic forms of realism.[2] With a spirit akin to the festive side of dadaism, he wanted to fight against the established truths of nineteenth-century literature. Readers, he thought, had been taken in by a literature in which plots based on sex and money forced them away from a metaphysical encounter with eternity. The first step for attaining eternity was for him an overcoming of the self, which he saw as a fake. If people stopped believing that there was any particular weight attached to their identities, they would be able to step out of the constraints of time. Following up on his teachings, Borges envisioned once a dialogue with Macedonio in which they decided to commit suicide. The dialogue ends with one of the speakers saying that he is not sure whether they took their lives. The road taken by Macedonio involved punning, manufacturing neologisms, writing manifesto-like pronouncements; the one chosen by Borges has given us parallel worlds, a skepticism about individual identities, an erasure of difference over time.

Alejandra Pizarnik was aware of the Macedonio-Borges register and articulated her vision in an idiom that questions, from the outset, the weight of the visible. Her language plays with what's palpable and obvious so that we may have access to another realm. In her book *Arbol de Diana* (Diana's tree),[3] we read the following lines:

> *she undresses in the paradise*
> *of her memory*
> *she ignores the cruel destiny*
> *of her visions*
> *she is afraid of not knowing how to name*
> *what doesn't exist*
> (36)

The poem states what would become Pizarnik's most explicit concern: the assurances rendered by memory in opposition to another domain that is, nevertheless, dependent on memory. It is the one space that encompasses her visions, said to have a cruel destiny, of which the *she* invoked in the poem is unaware. Fear closes this section of the book. It qualifies silence, the impossibility of seizing with words that elusive territory of visions, stemming from memory. Undressed in that paradise, the *she* is about to become a victim of her own willingness to name what doesn't exist, because a terrible destiny awaits her visions. The perception of memory as paradise is, then, a mistake. Vulnerable, undressed, she is suspended between two separate temporal poles: the past experienced—mistakenly—as paradise, and the future that will correct any initial optimism by granting a cruel destiny to her visions. Being a young girl is more than a recollection for Pizarnik. The girl is evoked throughout her poetry as a presence, with a materiality that renders the uncanniness of time:

> *now*
> *in this innocent hour*
> *I and the girl I was sit down*
> *on threshold of my gaze*
> (36)

The poet is not merely her own youth. Rather, beyond the control of the voice giving us the poem, she takes on different existences. Pizarnik's language is anchored in still another avant-garde writer, Vicente Huidobro, who founded a school he named *creacionismo* in open revolt against mimetic literature. Like Macedonio, Huidobro did not want art to be a servile copy of what was regarded as "life." *Altazor,* a long poem emphasizing his aesthetic stands, contains some lines in which he addresses poetry as "señora arpa" (lady harpist) and asks her to stop producing a series of images he inventories. Pizarnik echoes Huidobro's resistance to the commonplaces of poetry in *Diana's Tree* when she says: "no more sweet metamorphoses of the silken girl / now a sleepwalker in the cornice of fog" (37). The sleepwalker in the cornice of fog agrees with the alternatives offered by Huidobro's influential poem. It refers to something almost unimaginable outside the written page by releasing the energy of language rather than its capacity to mimic a camera recording nature.

Creacionista image, then, daughter of the avant-garde, this girl is also a memory of somebody who, because of her very nature, did not exist in the immediate history of the self as autobiography. She is a girl who locates the poet's self in art and literature, granting her an existence in which the familiar in the narrow sense has been displaced by a wider realm of shared words and visions. Pizarnik's poetry finds its definition in the uncertainties engendered by the ambiguities of this situation. In a manner not unlike the one found in Borges's ubiquitous play against univocal identity, such as in "Borges and I," *Diana's Tree* suggests that there are at least two in the individual poetic persona. But unlike Borges, here the doubleness is seen as a parasitic rivalry:

> *Fear of being two*
> *on the way to the mirror:*
> *someone asleep inside me*
> *is eating and drinking me up*
> (47)

"Asleep inside me": In spite of the fear of partition, an interiority is affirmed ("inside me . . . eating and drinking me up"). The cannibalistic other acquires names and faces in Pizarnik's poetry. They are the girl (la niña), Madame Lamort, muerte (death), sombra (shadow), la reina muerta (the dead queen). *Diana's Tree* states the difficulties produced by this conception of the self in a process of estrangement from its own hypothetical origin. The voice retelling the poem is presented as having already been kidnapped, taken away: "to explain with words of this world / that a boat departed from me carrying me away" (37). Where did that boat go? What are the terms in which it is represented? Visually, it brings into the texts surrealistic images in the tradition of Pizarnik's painting teacher, Batlle Planas, and the Pre-Raphaelites. The effort to create a self separate from the autobiographical is expressed frequently in Pizarnik's poetry in terms of despair, solitude, orphanage, and nostalgia for a girl (la niña), but in another, more powerful layer of her writing, she poses insistently the challenge as a triumph in a battle:

> *Strange to wean myself*
> *from the hour of my birth*
>
> *you have built your house*
> *you have feathered your birds*
> *you have knocked at the wind*
> *with your own bones*
>
> *you have finished by yourself*
> *what no one began*
> (37)

In Pizarnik's land, the one to which she gains access by departing from "the hour of her birth," words and images take over with the insistence of an obsession ("una idea fija," as she says in one poem). The effect is to suggest to the reader that the function of poetry is an exploration of this territory, one in which the consideration of the fixed idea is to be conducted by the production of images and wordplay rather than by philosophical inquiry. Unlike other poets, then, of the "idea fija," with a marked preference for the marriage between philosophy and poetry, Pizarnik offers us a peculiarly tangible representation of the new space:

> *Days in which a distant word takes me over. I*
> *go through those days somnambulant and*
> *transparent. The beautiful automaton sings to*
> *herself, charms herself, tells herself cases and*
> *causes: nest of taut threads where I dance*
> *myself and cry for myself in my numerous*

funerals. (She is her mirror set on fire, her wait
in cold blazes, her mystical element, her fornication
with names growing by themselves in
the pale night.)
(37–38)

We understand now the dangers awaiting the third person singular, the *she* referred to in the beginning. The destiny of her visions implicates her not as an observer but rather as that which, transformed, keeps her somnambulant and transparent. Visions, then, confuse her with her own mirror set on fire, a refusal of the independence of each term in the mimetic process ("names growing by themselves in the pale night") and sweep away any possibility of attaining univocal identity. As she abandons her biographical family and gives herself up to the energy of words and images, the new space betrays her. She is going to be the one transformed; she will not be able to play and remain untouched. On the contrary, in the game, her very identity will become a pawn. Played-out player (*jugador jugado*, in Spanish), as her friend Julio Cortázar used to say about himself, Pizarnik will not celebrate her inclusion in this space as a triumph of eloquence. It is, on the contrary, the result of violence and contradiction: "This repentant song, guard behind my poems: / this song contradicts and gags me" (41).

If the song contradicts her as it gags her, how are we to read it? How to understand its music? In spite of the persistent statements about the unreliability of the writing self because of its separation from another, original one and its subsequent scattering, Pizarnik produces a remarkably coherent register for her poetry. The adventures of the self in fragmentation weaned away from birth are articulated in the idiom of the visual and poetic avant-garde. But perhaps more intriguingly, her poetry frequently states its relationship to the turn-of-the-century Latin American poetic movement initiated by Rubén Darío, known in Spanish as *modernismo*.[4] As for them, poetry is named in Pizarnik as song *(mi canto)*, the space of exploration as the garden *(el jardín)*. Swans, princesses, and queens so inseparable from the *modernista* poetics reappear in her work rewritten into a different script. Darío was one of the great believers in the idea that poetry was a medium for the presentation of a privileged reality. His swans, exotic birds, plants, art objects, gardens are cast in poems sure of their own capacity to create music, to entice and seduce the reader. Beauty, poetry, and music are made to celebrate their union. In a poem entitled "On a poem by Rubén Darío," Pizarnik says:

> *Seated at the bottom of a lake.*
> *She has lost her shadow,*
> *not the desire to live, to lose*
> *She is alone with her images.*
> *Dressed in red, she doesn't look*
>
> *Who has arrived to this place*
> *where no one ever arrives?*
> *The lord of deaths in red.*
> *The man masked by his expressionless face.*
> *the one who arrived to find her*
> *takes her away without himself.*
>
> *Dressed in black, she looks*
> *She who never knew to die for love and because of that*
> *learned nothing*
> *She is sad because she is not there.*
> (90)

The landscape is uncannily Darío's. The princess of his well-known "Sonatina" is now at the bottom of a lake (lakes being ubiquitous in Darío's poetry); the uncertainty of the cause for her sadness in "Sonatina" is addressed here and given a clear-cut resolution (she is alone with her images). In this way, the princess of "Sonatina" has gone from being the object observed and described by poetry (as in Darío's treatment) to storing images within herself, and the man who has arrived, ostensibly a figure for the poet, is not her savior, as "Sonatina" implies in a paternalistic tone, but death itself. Fond of color, like the *modernistas,* Pizarnik invents a death by color. Red death. In "Sonatina," the one dressed in red is a buffoon doing pirouettes. Pizarnik sweeps way from the red its ornamental function and makes it literally cover the poem with the intimation of a death that engulfs both princess and savior.

Does Pizarnik offer this poem as a rewriting of Darío that would simultaneously define her own poetic persona as taking control of an imagery to cast in a different light? In other words, is the re-casting of "Sonatina" such that we may think of the ultimate role of the writing self in this kind of poetry as being one of criticism and dark parody? The elements are undoubtedly there for such a response. But there is more. Pizarnik's poem is dedicated to the French writer Marguerite Duras, an author whose visions fre-quently approximate those of Pizarnik. The exploration of the fe-male gaze in Duras and the eloquence of inaction are, as we turn to the dedication, not only a tribute to Duras but also a correction of Darío's poem. Darío's question in "Sonatina": "The princess is sad? What is it that ails her?" (¿La princesa está triste? ¿Qué ten-drá la princesa?) is answered in terms of Duras. The rewriting of Darío has not been done for propping up a writing self, but rather to further strip it of authority.

In abandoning her own biography and offering herself (as a writer) as the very subject of poems that undo the univocity of the first person singular, Pizarnik seems to gain access to an ahistori-cal, utopian space. But the dissemination of tasks performed by the self produces a different genealogy, articulates the terms by which she may be recognized as part of another chain. Rather than start-ing from zero, then, she enters a preexistent domain, a tradition. Within that tradition, her writing becomes part of the continuum of the visual imagery of the Pre-Raphaelites and Surrealism, as well as a joke on the literary heritage of the Darío school. The fantasy of giving birth to herself through the abandonment of the hour of her birth has been displaced by the emergence of another set of poems, one that helps us to understand what would have otherwise remained mere statements of dislocation. The ways in which Pizarnik suggests the undoing of her individual voice perform the opposite of what she states explicitly. Firmly grounded in an alternative genealogy, even her jokes against tradition confirm her credentials and grant meaning to her writing. The self that she so wanted to erase in its biographical form ends up inscribed in the larger family of the avant-garde, intensified by the dialogue with contemporaries such as Marguerite Duras.

OF TERROR, VIOLENCE, AND HUMOR

Pizarnik's friends speak of a woman with a great sense of humor, adept at jokes. There was a certain childishness about her; her lack of capacity for dealing with the practicalities of life invited others to help and become, at the same time, partners in a suspension of the requisites of common sense. Although most of her poetry engages a dark, albeit playful, vision of imaginary spaces, her prose is written with a different voice. Among her most remarkable texts is one she devoted to a reading of the story of the "Bloody Countess," Erzsébet de Bathory, as recounted in a fictionalized biography by Valentine Penrose that appeared in France in 1962 under the title *La Comtesse sanglante.*[5] Pizarnik was fascinated by the life of a woman said to have murdered more than a hundred young maidens whose blood she would drink. These events, which took place in the early seventeenth century, moved the French writer Valentine Penrose to describe in great detail what she saw as the aesthetic dimension of blood and pain. Very akin to a surrealistic sensibility for which the Marquis de Sade and Gilles de Rais exercised transgressive authority, the deeds of the Bloody Countess appear to give a glimpse of what female desire might entail. Pizarnik, obviously impressed by Penrose's treatment of the subject, wrote about the loneliness that the countess must have experienced after she was walled in as punishment for her crimes. In a closing reflection about her life and deeds, Pizarnik talks about the unspeakable horror of life.

The countess's cruelty toward other women, the violation of their bodies, the ultimate objectification implied by murder fascinated Pizarnik. Pain, both as it is being felt and inflicted, rather than the celebration of female bonding in generosity, is the motif of the nightmarish female world evoked by Penrose. Julio Cortázar, with whom she was in frequent contact during her stay in Paris, was also struck by this case and included the countess as one of the recurring characters in his novel 62. *A Model Kit,* a continuation of his earlier *Hopscotch,* a work with which Pizarnik was very closely associated. The domain of the countess exercised the mesmerizing power of extreme pain inflicted without compassion. The refusal to psychologize femininity is all-pervasive in Pizarnik's work. Her choice is the distancing of an apathetic amoral gaze in the case of the countess, and a recording of the dissemination of the self in her poetry.

Pizarnik also wrote a number of short prose pieces, occasional plays of the theater of the absurd, and narratives. In those texts she engages in punning and other forms of wordplay, including the redefinition of everyday language by disassembling clichés. A reader used to the complicities elicited by her poetry, the secretive and subtle tone of her lines, cannot but be startled by the ubiquitous obscenities of her humorous prose pieces. Pizarnik's humor is genital, almost in a childish way. She delights in making words slide onto unexpected allusions that represent graphically body parts and sexual positions. Her amused view of language is a celebration of equivocations that sweep every sentence onto an arena of fluids, orifices, contacts. The little girl wandering in an unnamed garden, the abandonment of the self, the games with death are left aside in these pieces. Instead, there is a relentlessly, obsessive parodical tone. Leonor Fini's representations of the female body as well as

Bellmer's broken dolls evoke in a serious tone the puzzlement at female desire that Pizarnik names, jokingly, in her prose. The success of her poetry has relegated the prose to a second place, but her artfulness in producing a baroque festival of heckling sexual humor puts her on a level with Severo Sarduy. An original voice within the living heritage of the avant-garde, Alejandra Pizarnik explored both sides of laughter through her writing and may have become lost in one of its darkest alternatives when she decided to end her own life.

Marosa Di Giorgio:
URUGUAY'S SACRED POET OF THE GARDEN

TERESA PORZECANSKI
TRANSLATED BY NANCY ABRAHAM HALL

⌐ A WINTER'S NIGHT, damp and cold, in a small, makeshift theater inside an old Spanish-style house that has been renovated to turn-of-the-century standards. The audience waits, silently, or with barely a murmur, for the show to begin. Middle-aged men who have come straight from work, scruffy and tired-looking humanities students, women wrapped in heavy otter-skin coats, young girls with long hair and surprised expressions, perhaps forty people in all. It is July in the city of Montevideo, Uruguay. In the neighborhood called Cordón, the streets slowly quiet down. It has been a cold and difficult day. People want to get home to a hot meal.

Suddenly, on the dimly lit stage, and seemingly without feet, as if it had flown there, a figure appears wrapped in a long, black garment, above which glows a mass of red hair, almost the color of carrots. It is a woman: her face is smooth, her eyes half-closed behind thick glasses. It is Marosa Di Giorgio Medici, born in 1932 in Salto, Uruguay, the city of Horacio Quiroga and Enrique Amorim. She has come to recite her poetry.

"I was bewitched by things that spring from the ground. How do they get out? The Bromelias that seemed to be made of bright rose-colored porcelain, like the dawn, like nothing. With a thick cluster of green filaments."[1] Her voice is serious, deep, and has what can be called a silky quality. But what captures the audience is a series of verbal images that begins to build into an uninterrupted torrent of words. Something that seems to have begun long ago and has perpetuated itself since time immemorial.

"Altars appeared, made of nothing but Bromelias, kitchens, beds; the country brides carried them in baskets. And the snails, stiff as rocks, as eggs, their white shells and their bulging, rose-colored eyes."[2] Excessive and surprisingly colorful descriptions begin to expand within the imagination, slowly giving birth to the special universe of her poetry, as if the world were always being created for the first time.

FAR-AWAY ITALY

A descendant of Italian peasants from the area around Florence, Marosa identified with an idealized Italy that had disappeared before she was even born, the place where her paternal grandparents, Domenico Di Giorgio and Mariana Grossi, as well as her maternal grandparents, Eugenio Medici and Rosa Arresigor, had lived and worked as farmers, cultivated small plots of land, and raised a few animals. As part of the massive immigration to America of thousands of poor Italian peasants and artisans at the turn of the nineteenth century, Marosa's maternal grandparents, like so many others, made the journey in hopes of a better future. Tearing up ancient roots, Eugenio Medici established a Uruguayan branch of the family in Salto: "The grandfather's business dealings were imaginative, changeable. He became a grower, acquired two small farms in eastern Salto, 'San Antonio,' where he integrated the miracle of the Italian country house with lady's-mantle and fabulous oranges."[3] In years to come, a connection to the eternal mysteries and ambiguities of nature would be one of the central themes of Marosa's poetry.

SILK AND MULBERRY LEAVES

With tremendous zeal, Eugenio Medici worked to recreate the orchards of Florence. But in addition to olive trees, he cultivated silk worms and the requisite mulberry trees. A businessman whose schemes often lacked substance, he was a dreamer as well as a grower. In the family orchards, the fields full of olive trees, and the nests where the silkworm cocoons took shape, a little girl would grow up, and her poetic imagination would transform the way in which the countryside had, until then, been portrayed in Uruguayan literature.

Eugenio's marriage to Rosa Arresigor produced a daughter, Clementina Medici, who would be Marosa Di Giorgio's mother, and a strong presence in the education of her two daughters. Within the bosom of the extended family, made up of grandparents, uncles, aunts, parents, sisters, and cousins, there was an unquestioned sense of the patriarchal family structure, which had spurred Italian and Spanish immigration to Uruguay, and which, in rural areas, lasted throughout the first half of the twentieth century.

Some time later, the adolescent Pedro Di Giorgio arrived in the port city of Salto. With his father, he had undertaken an incredible forty-day journey: Toscana, Geneva, Marseille, Buenos Aires, Salto. When he got off the boat, the first person he spoke to was Clementina Medici, who fate had placed that day on the docks and who years later would become his wife. The couple had two daughters, Nidia and Marosa, both raised on the land and within the traditions of a strongly held Catholic faith.

SALTO, AN UNUSUAL CITY

"Is it possible to write the literary history of a city whose population, in over one hundred fifty years, has never exceeded 80,000 people?" asks L. Garet in a book devoted to the topic.[4] Salto, a city that could be deemed small, has given Uruguayan literature a surprising number of writers, storytellers, and poets of significance. Moreover, the city's cultural life, which includes literary magazines, theater groups, and cultural centers, is especially dynamic and varied.

According to Garet, however, poetry is predominant in Salto's creative life: "On radio programs and in newspapers so many poems are featured that, to no one's surprise, a newspaper editorial once appeared with gaps of blank space after every fourth line. According to the typesetter, he had become confused after setting a full page of poetry."[5] Visitors to the city are also surprised by poetry: "When one arrives in Salto, one is given, along with the usual information, a sheet paper on which a poem is printed."[6]

A city of orange groves, intense sunshine, and parks celebrated by local poets, it rises on the banks of a river that abruptly falls. Impossible to abandon even after one has left, Salto "is a city in northern Uruguay. Marked by waterfalls. That's how it got its name . . . I am from there. That's where I'm headed."[7]

AN IMPOSSIBLE BIOGRAPHY

A biography of Marosa Di Giorgio is not possible, at least not the usual kind of biography, one containing "reliable" facts pertaining to a so-called real life. In the case of Marosa, all the anecdotes, her everyday experiences, have an unreal quality to them, and the facts seem disconnected, to point toward outer limits:

> When I was three years old, my mother, who was nevertheless a Merciful Woman (and more so over time), she and I hunted (My God!) a butterfly, who lived for a very long time pressed between the pages of a book. I don't know how it happened. I can't forget. She was very beautiful. Large. Light blue like the sky. That young lady, with filament-like extremities, and a dress made of pure soul! I hope she is with Mama in Heaven, and that I can be reunited with them.[8]

A HIERATIC TRIO

Within a pure and sustained Catholic faith, Marosa's First Communion, which took place at the *Templo del Carmen,* marks her passage from girlhood to adolescence: "Nidia and I wore white organdy, sky-blue shawls, and carried stalks of white lilies. The Immaculate Mary outfits. There were photographs, a small celebration, and I fainted."[9] Similarly, Marosa's high school years were characterized by a desire to define for herself a distinctive identity within the provincial life of the small city of Salto.

Marosa, her sister Nidia, and cousin Ilse formed a peculiar trio. They wore the obligatory pale school uniforms but used colorful makeup, put flowers in their hair, and wore earrings. Their appearance pointed to a need for fantasy that was probably not satisfied by the city's sleepy routine. Marosa recalls the effect of their appearance: "This upset the residents of gray, dull Salto. The world is divided into those who dream, and those who do not."[10]

LOSSES

Marosa's adolescence was also shaped by the deaths of close relatives, first her grandparents, then her father, and later, her grandmother, an exquisite cook and essential nurturer. "In the dark air, Grandmother, who always loved me, begins to shine, she combs my hair, she serves me coffee and squash preserves . . ."[11] All these losses are experienced in a magical way by a sensitive soul who turns pain and anguish into poetry, thus reviving the memory of the loved ones, and bringing them, dreamlike, into the present.

A degree in law, a youth spent in Salto, where, little by little, she cultivated an eccentric image and became the center of a circle of amateur poets and philosophers who frequented the downtown cafés, an occasional job as a society columnist for the local newspaper (Marosa usually wrote about the gowns worn by the bride, maid of honor, groom's sister, and other figures associated with a wedding), roles in plays, a desire to be a stage actress, poetry readings, and the impetus of literary magazines, all are elements that contributed to her poetry, a poetry of fantasy that departs from reality by boldly using multiple meanings of words.

THE BEGINNING

Precisely when her poetic vocation emerged is not known: "My literature began when I was born, or when I was four years old, as I walked through the mythical garden, and suddenly found myself in another dimension. Perhaps one morning I simply woke up that way."[12] The reliable facts, if there are any such things, are inserted into a "diffuse" biography that overlaps the work, and are transformed into various "voices": memories, reconstructions, revelations. "The extraordinary and fantastic nature of the 'facts' which appear in each composition (and even of the experiences recalled, or lived and expressed, by the first-person narrator) creates an atmosphere that transcends the unity of the text and provokes strong new semantic associations," writes R. Pallares.[13]

A strong and relevant presence in both Marosa's life and poetry is the extended family's country house, where her grandmothers and aunts lavishly maintained an enriched environment. The time spent at the house seems to be real, but it is also a period of initiation, and of loss of superhuman attributes: "Whenever the summer heat became too intense—I was still a child in those garden days—we would move our beds outside; then, everything would seem so strange. My relatives would fly a bit; but then they would go to sleep; I would stay awake and scrutinize the sky; among the stars the ancient ships would continue to do battle."[14]

Childhood, and especially a childhood spent in the gardens, is a source of hallucinations and dreams: everything that grows, lives, and breathes is manifested, as in ancient myths, through signs. Even the image of self is seen as a vision: "If I look at myself, I see a little girl absorbed in her work, as if she were looking in a mirror; a solitary, passionate, innocent, visionary little girl."[15] Poetry is introduced into the child's world by means of recognizable signs: "I experienced annunciations. A voice that I heard during adolescence in the corridor of the house. I heard it three times, it was as if someone were talking to me about poetry." Such annunciations continue into adulthood: "How do I see myself? Pierced by an arrow. From my long, red hair (which, of course, I wouldn't change, but which nevertheless, constitutes a sign), towards the poem, towards writing."[16]

In this way, a childhood without limits stops to consider the poetic experience, and to explore itself as it discovers the world, fear, or play:

> I remember a terrible childhood. Ilse, Nidia and I, frozen
> under the weak sun. Or entering and leaving the house,
> for years. The ghost-like trees, under which there were live
> stones; black ones, white ones, gray ones, striped ones, with
> curved backs. We would stroke them with our hands, or
> touch them with a stalk, until we began to shake; they would
> open a languid, weakening eye, which could see for only a
> second.[17]

THE PRESENT

In the early eighties, Marosa Di Giorgio moved to Montevideo with her elderly mother. At first, they both rented apartments in collective buildings or rooming houses. They lived on the social security income that the father had left to his wife and unmarried daughter. A few years later, when her mother was quite ill, Marosa moved to a modest apartment in the Cordón neighborhood of the city. Clementina Medici died in 1990, at the age of 85, following a long illness, during which her daughter cared for her. Since her mother's death, Marosa has lived alone. She does not hold a job, and she has not worked since she came to Montevideo. She remains single. She has not had children. She claims she has never had a partner, and no one knows of any lovers or boyfriends with whom she might have lived, or had even a brief relationship. A few years ago the Uruguayan government awarded her a small monthly pension on which she can draw for the rest of her life.

THE EXTRAORDINARY

For Marosa Di Giorgio, the natural world is also supernatural: "Everything is extraordinary. Impossible to believe. And yet, there it is. We are living it."[18] From the surrounding, everyday, familiar contexts come extreme, exaggerated, marvelous worlds. Surprising transformations emerge from what is insignificant, taken for granted, unnoticed. Intensely metaphorical language, and a syntax "characterized by representation and intense punctuation," gradually weave the extraordinary into a context of verisimilitude accessible to the reader.[19] It is not a matter of distant, abstract, and metaphysical poetry: the unreal is concretely there, almost made solid in the images, woven into a logic that is immediately understood by the reader:

> My grandmother was very good at hunting down insects and dressing them. She kept them alive, to the great delight and amazement of her customers and guests. In the evenings we would sit at the little tables in the garden, with little plates and saltshakers. We were surrounded by rose bushes, and motionless, snow-covered, unique roses.[20]

THE SAVAGE MIND

Working outside the tradition of nativism, and further still from *costumbrismo* and the idealized and epic masculine perspective that casts country dwellers as wild, silent, and rebellious creatures, Marosa Di Giorgio began, as early as 1954, to put forth a new poetic perception. She offered a strikingly original vision of the relationship between the small farmers of northern Uruguay and the flora and fauna of the region. One could perhaps speak of a cosmology of the garden, of an anthropomorphization of the natural world, of a transubstantiation of the allegorical dimensions of myth, of nature as something sacred, alive, animated:

> The animals spoke; my father's cows, horses, birds, sheep.
> Long, reasoned discourses, speeches; they talked to each
> other and to the humans, as they searched for fruit, mush-
> rooms, salt. I would walk through the woods and see the
> sun set in several places at once; four or five round suns,
> white as snow, made of long filaments.[21]

An anthropological approach to Marosa Di Giorgio's work could be based on the concept developed by C. Levi-Strauss in his classic study *The Savage Mind*. By "savage mind," Levi-Strauss does not mean the mind of savages, but rather the mind in a savage state, as opposed to the "cultivated, domesticated mind." The latter is subject to discipline, a certain order, so as to produce particular results. Both domesticated and savage minds coexist in contemporary society, to a greater or lesser degree, and in diverse combinations, although increasingly, the cultivated mind predominates over that in a savage state. However, there are still some residual spaces in which the mind exists in a savage state, as in the case of art. Art is still an element of the savage state of mind.

A symbolist impulse and scrupulous attention to the ordering of the concrete can make the savage mind both analytic and synthetical. In the case of Marosa Di Giorgio's intensely visual poetry, images are placed first in space rather than in time. There is no logical progression, therefore, from yesterday to tomorrow, but rather the intense presence of a reality independent of the present, underscored by the ordered repetition of seasons, cycles, natural phenomena, births and deaths that point to a dimension that has neither a beginning nor an end.

All her writing is characterized by careful observation of the natural and human environment in its most subtle details. The result is not an analytic description of the phenomena but a perceptive global synthesis, primordially sensitive and emotionally charged with meaning, that stirs immediate sensual empathy in the reader. The author handles the pure, perceptive data of consciousness just as they appear in the world around her, without "domesticating" them through a filter of rationality.

Plot is minimal because temporal dimensions constantly dissolve into spatial ones. Any facet or detail can unexpectedly become the protagonist and then disappear into the heterogeneous abundance of the captured totality. Poetry of images, not ideas, lyrical poetry for canvasses, directly visual renditions of a rare and original emotional landscape.

RECOGNITIONS

And there are themes that guide the reader toward certain recognition, such as the action of devouring in order to nourish and transform the self: "The clients arrived trying not to be seen. Some asked for bats, the most expensive item, or fireflies. Others wanted thick cream-colored butterflies, with a sprig of mint and a tiny little snail. And I remember when we served that large black butterfly, which seemed to be made of velvet, so reminiscent of a woman."[22] She speaks of devouring bodies, body parts, animals, plants, in order to merge the marvelous other-world with the self, a process that allows us to take on qualities we lack. That intimate and ultimate fusion with the world is curiously present, not only within the mythologies of diverse cultures from all over the planet but also in the cosmologies that explain the origin of human life, or the origin of death.

A second characteristic is the intense perception of the sacred, in its angelic as well as diabolic sense. More than its enunciation, she captures its presence: "God is here. God speaks. Sometimes at night, when I least expect it, his face, his forehead, immense and diminutive like a star, appears among my things. Scintillating and steady. He's been hanging around the house for years."[23] The modality of these priestly acts, which seek to transcend the profane world and establish direct communication with divine beings, is ancient. Far from religious poetry, however, Marosa Di Giorgio's work places what is sacred within a familiar, everyday context. In this way, it operates as a variant of the traditional reading of reality, without losing its connection to it.

FEMALE GESTATION

Another recurring theme is that of gestation, from whose matrix—at times a women, at times nature—emerges the "initial egg" or first cause. The image of the egg appears many times in Marosa Di Giorgio's poetry:

> I laid a white, pure, brilliant egg. It looked like an oval-
> shaped star. Years before I had laid a different one, sky-blue,
> and another, rose-colored. But this one was pure, white, bril-
> liant, it was the most beautiful. I put it in a cup, and shielded
> it with my hand so that it would not lose its shine. I cared
> for it discreetly, with a certain feigned indifference. Other
> women were jealous, insidious; they criticized me. Os-
> tensibly, they covered their shoulders and dropped their
> hemlines.[24]

This gestation implies permanent motherhood, the result of a fertile sexual act, brought on by the already noted fusion of the vegetable, animal, and human kingdoms. In her writing, the female is at once nature and animal, woman and insect, a variety of flowers and stars, an existential coupling whose roots remain mysterious: "I cannot say what hatched from the egg, because I do not know. But whatever it was, it still follows me: its filial and sweet shadow swoops down on me."[25]

The reiteration of vital circles, the nurturing of relatives and animals, the care given to the processes of growth and development, the mourning of the dead, the vigilance of the world, and a world that repeats itself in immanence are traditional themes linked to the female in the mythologies of many civilizations, including Greece. The vigilant figure of the mother is ever present, serving as a model of female filiation from one generation to another, forming a web of identity that connects women with one another: "Of all the girls, only our cousin Poupee had a fairy outfit . . . her mother made [it] for her; deep blue like the sky, and at times, pale and wide like the air . . . We watched her in terror, and with a bit of sadness; we retreated, our empty hands outstretched in her direction."[26]

A LYRIC POETRY OF THE GARDEN

No other writer, or literary school—nativist or folklorist—has bestowed on the countryside, the garden, the farm, the rural landscape of Uruguay, the lyricism of Marosa Di Giorgio's poetry. In her work, the Uruguayan landscape, certainly less abundant than the exuberant tropics and regions of Central America, is imbued with magic. Perhaps the magic is not as dramatic as that created by Quiroga, or as ironic as that of Felisberto Hernández, but in form as well as content, it clearly opposes the literature of the city.

Faced with the brutality of urban life, which divorces the individual from his or her feelings and forces people to live removed from nature, the rural world of Marosa Di Giorgio offers its subjects a symbolic, emotive, and immediately apparent unity between humans and the earth, an invitation to capture the sacred sense of nature. Faced with the city as a gray, apathetic, and, according to J. C. Onetti, a nihilistic and intensely chauvinistic place, the lyrical poetry of Marosa Di Giorgio's garden offers a respite, a possibility of life's exaltation, the regeneration of things, and a slow ascension into the realms of the meaning of existence.

Notes

SOFÍA OSPINA DE NAVARRO

1. The biographical data included here are based on a collection of newspaper articles that appeared around the time of Sofía Ospina's death in 1974. These articles, as well as a collection of books written by Sofía Ospina, were sent to Colombia by Clara Inés Navarro de Uribe to Bertha Olga Ospina, now living in the United States, who remembers her great aunt with deep affection and has been most generous in sharing memories as well as the printed materials that have made this chapter possible.

2. Citations to the books quoted here (translated by this writer) are annotated as follows: *Don* indicates *Don de gentes* (1969), *CC* indicates *Cuentos y crónicas* (1926), and *AC* indicates *La abuela cuenta* (1964).

VICTORIA OCAMPO

1. This is an expanded and updated version of an article, "Victoria Ocampo: 'A Thirst for the Ultimate,'" originally published in *Visvabharati Quarterly* (West Bengal, India) 44 (November 1978–April 1979): 113–29.

This journal was founded by Rabindranath Tagore, is located at Visvabharati University, and is available from Xerox University Microfilms.

2. On this subject, see my forthcoming book, *Rereading the Spanish American Essay: Translations of 19th and 20th Century Women's Essays* (Austin: University of Texas Press, 1995), in which various scholars elucidate the nature and significance of women's essays in Latin America.

3. A biographical study along with a selection of her essays translated into English: *Victoria Ocampo: Against the Wind and the Tide* (New York: George Braziller, 1979; Austin: University of Texas Press, 1990).

4. *Autobiografía II: El imperio insular* (Buenos Aires: Ediciones Revista Sur, 1980), 60. Ocampo's six-volume autobiography was published posthumously between 1979 and 1984. I had access to the manuscript copy at her home in San Isidro, where she would occasionally debate with me the merits of publishing or burning it; needless to say, I argued passionately for the former, although I was never entirely sure that these debates weren't just Victoria's way of testing reader response to what her memoirs contained and getting a handle on how they would be received by readers of a different generation and culture.

5. Letter dated 11 June 1907, written in Buenos Aires. From an unpublished collection of correspondence saved by Delfina Bunge and privately bound as a gift to Victoria. Portions of these letters are included in *Autobiografía II,* 77–139; quotes cited here are from the originals, written in French and translated by myself, as are all translations in this paper, except from Ocampo's book on T. E. Lawrence.

6. Victoria Ocampo, "Página sobre Dante," *Testimonios,* 7th ser. (Buenos Aires: Ediciones Sur, 1967), 28.

7. "Prefacio y confesión," *Sur* (Special issue devoted to Gandhi) (January–December 1975): 5.

8. "Desde Bengala," *Testimonios,* 10th ser. (Buenos Aires: Ediciones Sur, 1977), 115–16.

9. In her seventies, Ocampo turned down an offer from the Argentine government to be ambassador to India, claiming that the diplomatic life and tropical climate held no allure for her at that age.

10. This letter was dated July 23, 1908, and was written in Buenos Aires.

11. See *A Woman of Genius: The Intellectual Autobiography of Sor Juana Inés de la Cruz,* trans. with an introduction by Margaret Sayers Peden (Salisbury, Conn.: Lime Rock Press, 1982).

12. This letter has no specific date but is from early October 1908. It is noteworthy that some of the more intimately revealing letters (or parts there of) were not included in the *Autobiografía,* perhaps because they might have merited further explanation, which Ocampo chose not to provide at the time.

13. Ocampo, "Página sobre Dante," 28.

14. From the author's interview with Borges on August 14, 1962.

15. Victoria Ocampo, "La mujer, sus derechos y sus responsabilidades," *Testimonios,* 2d ser. (Buenos Aires: Ediciones Sur, 1941), 260–63.

16. Sylvia Molloy has suggested that Ocampo's reliance on a male-authored canon was evidence of her female dependency and "lack of writerly authority." Molloy, *At Face Value: Autobiographical Writing in Spanish America* (Cambridge: Cambridge University Press, 1991), 72–73. I have responded to this in a paper entitled "Reciprocal Reflections: Specular Discourse and the Self-Authorizing Venture," in *Reinterpreting the Spanish American Essay.*

17. Victoria Ocampo, "Malraux: Dos parejas de *La Condition Humaine,*" *Testimonios,* 10th ser., 201.

18. Victoria Ocampo, "Vísperas de guerra," *Testimonios,* 2d ser., 477.

19. Victoria Ocampo, "La mujer y la guerra en los Estados Unidos," *Testimonios,* 3d ser. (Buenos Aires: Editorial Sudamericana, 1946), 274.

20. Ibid., 275.

21. Quoted in Victoria Ocampo, "El caso de Drieu la Rochelle," in *Soledad sonora* (Buenos Aires: Editorial Sudamericana, 1950), 19.

22. Ibid., 25.

23. Victoria Ocampo, "Dar a los hombres conciencia de su propia grandeza," *Testimonios,* 10th ser., 124.

24. In 1974 Malraux received the Nehru Prize in New Delhi. In his speech of acceptance, reprinted in the special issue of *Sur* devoted to Gandhi, he expresses this admiration. See *Sur* (January–December 1975), 7–12.

25. Ocampo, "Malraux: Dos parejas," 205.

26. From conversations between the author and Victoria Ocampo in January 1977, two months after Malraux's death. At that time, Victoria decided to publish a special issue of *Sur* in memory of Malraux; it appeared later that year and included three of her own articles, also published in the tenth volume of her *Testimonios.*

27. Quoted in Victoria Ocampo, "El año de Gandhi," *Testimonios,* 8th ser. (Buenos Aires: Ediciones Sur, 1971), 19. During a brief visit to Argentina in 1947, where he was Victoria's guest, Camus refused to submit to Peronist censorship by speaking in public.

28. Ibid., 20–21.

29. Ibid., 22.

30. See *338171 T. E.: Lawrence of Arabia,* trans. David Garnett (New York: E. P. Dutton, 1963).

31. Ibid., 15 and 13.

32. Victoria Ocampo, "El hombre que murió (D. H. Lawrence,)" *Testimonios,* 1st ser. (Madrid: Revista de Occidente, 1935), 231.

33. Ocampo, *338171 T. E.,* 17–18.

34. Ibid., 76.

35. Ibid., 127–28.

36. Victoria Ocampo, "Felix culpa," *Testimonios,* 5th ser. (Buenos Aires: Ediciones Sur, 1957), 191.

37. Her last essay on the subject, "Am Sam Dram (El enigma de T. E. Lawrence)," was published in *La Nación* in August 1976 and can be found in *Testimonios,* 10th ser., 75–86.

38. Gandhi, *Gandhi on Non-Violence,* ed. and with an introduction by Thomas Merton (New York: New Directions, 1965), 24.

39. Ocampo, *Autobiografía II,* 177.

40. Victoria Ocampo, "A propósito de una cita suprimida y de un aforismo de los Upanishads," *Testimonios,* 5th ser., 12.

ALFONSINA STORNI

1. This chapter is an abbreviated version of the essay "The Journalism of Alfonsina Storni: A New Approach to Women's History in Argentina," in *Seminar on Feminism and Culture in Latin America. Women, Culture and Politics in Latin America* (Berkeley and Los Angeles: University of California Press, 1990), 105–29.

For assistance with research in Buenos Aires, I am grateful to the staff of the Biblioteca Nacional of Buenos Aires; to Washington and Teresita Pereyra, who generously allowed me to use their private library; to Lea Fletcher; and to Susana Zanetti. All translations from Spanish are my own.

2. Two of the best studies on her poetry include: Rachel Phillips, *Al-*

fonsina Storni: From Poetess to Poet (London: Tamesis, 1975) and Mark Smith-Soto, *El arte de Alfonsina Storni* (Bogotá: Ediciones Tercer Mundo, 1986).

3. For biographical information, see the chronology by Mabel Mármol in Conrado Nalé Roxlo, *Genio y figura de Alfonsina Storni* (Buenos Aires: Eudeba, 1964), 5–20. For more listings, see Marta Baralis, *Bibliografía argentina de artes y letras* (Buenos Aires: Fondo Nacional de las Artes, 1964).

4. For a historical overview of the period in Argentina, see David Rock, "Argentina from the First World War to the Revolution of 1930," in *Cambridge History of Latin America*, vol. 5, *1870–1930*, ed. Leslie Bethell (Cambridge: Cambridge University Press, 1986), 419–52. Another perspective focusing on women is found in Donna Guy, *Sex and Danger in Buenos Aires: Prostitution, Family, and Nation in Argentina* (Lincoln: University of Nebraska Press, 1991).

5. The most complete history of women in Latin America is Francesca Miller, *Latin American Women and the Search for Social Justice* (Hanover, N.H.: University Press of New England), 1991.

6. Quoted in Phillips, *Alfonsina Storni*, 126.

7. Alfonsina Storni, "Entre un par de maletas a medio abrir y la manecilla del reloj," *Revista Nacional* 1, no. 2 (February 1938): 216–17.

8. Ibid., 214.

9. Phillips, *Alfonsina Storni*, 6. See also 1–14.

10. Carlos Alberto Andreola, *Alfonsina Storni: Inédita* (Buenos Aires: n.p., 1974), 98.

11. Roxlo, *Genio y figura de Alfonsina Storni*, 10.

12. Carlos Alberto Andreola, *Alfonsina Storni: Vida, Talento, Soledad* (Buenos Aires: Plus Ultra, 1976), 299.

13. Lily Sosa de Newton, *Las argentinas de ayer a hoy* (Buenos Aires: Ediciones Zanetti, 1967), 216.

14. María del Carmen Feijóo, "Las feministas," in *La vida de nuestro pueblo* (Buenos Aires: Centro Editor de América Latina, 1982), 5–6. For more information on the women's movements in Argentina and the Southern Cone, see: Miller, *Latin American Women;* María del Carmen Feijóo, "Las luchas feministas," *Todo Es Historia* 128 (January 1978): 6–23; Asunción Lavrin, *The Ideology of Feminism in the Southern Cone, 1900–1940*, Latin American Program Working Papers 169 (Washington,

D.C.: Wilson Center, Smithsonian Institution, 1986); and Cynthia Little, "Education, Philanthropy, and Feminism: Components of Argentine Womanhood, 1860–1926," in *Latin American Women: Historical Perspectives,* ed. Asunción Lavrin (Westport, Conn.: Greenwood Press, 1978), 235–53.

15. As both Asunción Lavrin and Cynthia Little point out in their previously cited studies, the Socialist Party was outspoken in its defense of women's rights, supporting suffrage, the right to absolute divorce, paternity investigations, and legal equality of both legitimate and illegitimate children. See Lavrin, *Ideology of Feminism,* 8, and Little, "Education, Philanthropy, and Feminism," 243.

16. For biographical data on Alicia Moreau de Justo, see Mirta Henault, *Alicia Moreau de Justo* (Buenos Aires: Centro Editor de América Latina, 1983) and Sosa de Newton, *Las argentinas,* 142–43, 148, 191.

17. In her review for *Nuestra Causa* of Storni's *Languidez,* Adela García Salaberry (teacher, journalist, and secretary of the Unión Feminista Nacional) defended Storni's work, calling her "uno de los más originales genios líricos de América" and "nuestra más genial poeta" (*Nuestra Causa* 2, no. 22 [April 1921]: 230). In the same year, the magazine records an "Homenaje a Alfonsina Storni" presented by the Unión Feminista Nacional, on the occasion of her poetry prize in the municipal competition. Mirta Henault states that Storni was also a contributor to *Nuestra Causa* (77). I have not, however, been able to examine those issues of the magazine.

18. Alfonsina Storni, "Un tema viejo," *La Nota* 4, no. 194 (25 April 1919): 501.

19. Sosa de Newton, *Las argentinas,* 148–49.

20. *La Nota* 4, no. 202 (27 June 1919): 682.

21. *Nuestra Revista* 4, no. 34 (April 1923): 45–47. The same article was originally published in *La Nación,* 14 November 1920, p. 9.

22. *La Nota* 5, no. 210 (22 August 1919): 878.

23. *La Revista del Mundo* (Buenos Aires), August 1919, p. 12–19.

24. *La Nota* 5, no. 22 (14 November 1919): 1173.

25. *La Nota* 4, no. 194 (25 April 1919): 500.

GABRIELA MISTRAL

1. "The commentators (I don't know how many books and articles have been written about G. M. chewing over this image that so satisfies manly

pride) impose on us the simplified silhouette of a woman going to pieces alongside a tomb in a single, terrible love. Surely these commentators have dreamed of such a love for themselves and have wanted such a woman—resembling a force of Nature—who is destroyed in a fatal knot of love and death in which they themselves are origin and object" (Introduction, x).

2. "A song is a wound of love opens things to us. You, coarse man, are aroused by a woman's belly, the heap of woman's flesh. We go forth aroused, we receive the lance-stroke of all the beauty of the world, because the starry night was to us a love as acute as carnal love."

VIOLETA PARRA

1. This section of the chapter is drawn in part from Inés Dölz-Blackburn, "Valorización y perfil de Violeta Parra a través, de la prensa chilena, 1967–90: una evaluación cronológica y crítica." This monograph is composed of an extensive introductory critical essay and annotated dated newspaper articles on Parra (1967–90) written mostly in Chile. I have added additional commentaries, a product of my many years of reflection on Parra's scholarship and work.

2. Among the many critics and scholars of Parra's literary works come to mind a few university professors in the United States: Marjorie Agosín (Wellesley College, Massachusetts), Fernando Alegría (Emeritus, Stanford University, California), Inés Dölz-Blackburn (University of Colorado, Colorado Springs, Colorado), Armando Epple (University of Oregon, Oregon), Naomi Lindstrom (University of Southern California, California), and Klaus Müller-Berg (University of Chicago, Illinois). In Chile, we must mention: Alfonso Alcalde, Jorge Edwards, Juan Andrés Piña, and Ignacio Valente. In Germany, the critic and professor Manfred Englebert (University of Gotina) is an important voice in Parra's evaluation.

A new approach to her biography was attempted by Carmen Oviedo in the best seller *Mentira todo lo cierto. Tras la huella de Violeta Parra* (1990). This book was published after many years of research and is based mainly on testimonies.

3. The lyrics of the love songs can be consulted in the anthologies of Violeta Parra, edited by Alfonso Alcalde, Juan Andrés Piña, and Javier Martínez Reverte. The political songs appear in the Martínez Reverte's anthology (65–99). For the critical study of these songs, refer to: Agosín

and Dölz-Blackburn, *Santa de pura greda,* and Dölz-Blackburn, "Violeta Parra y la expresión de la conciencia social" (Folklore Americano, 1994).

4. This section is drawn in large part from Agosín and Dölz-Blackburn, "Biography" and "Décimas en su concepto ideológico feminista," in *Santa de pura greda,* 13–21 and 98–118. Additional commentaries are based on Gina Cánepa, "La canción de lucha en Violeta Parra"; Dölz-Blackburn, "La mujer marginal" (*Letras Femeninas,* forthcoming); and Adriana Castillo, "Las *Décimas.*"

5. This section is based on the letters of Violeta Parra published by Isabel Parra in *El libro mayor.* Some of the commentaries are taken from Dölz-Blackburn, "La mujer marginal." Refer also to Agosín and Dölz-Blackburn, "Las Décimas" in *Santa de pura greda;* and Dölz-Blackburn and Agosín, *Violeta Parra o la expresión inefable* (1992).

6. The translation is mine.

CECILIA ANSALDO

1. I think that it is relevant to point out that in Spanish America we distinguish the school/high school teacher as the "maestra/maestro" who must attend the "Escuela Normal" to acquire her/his diploma.

2. See Jean Franco, "Going Public: Reinhabiting the Private," in *On Edge,* ed. George Yúdice et al. (Minneapolis: Minnesota University Press, 1992), 65–83. César A. Chalela, "Women of Valor: An Interview with the Mothers of Plaza de Mayo," in *Surviving Beyond Fear,* ed. Marjorie Agosín (New York: White Pine Press, 1993).

3. Today there are some eighty women organizations in Ecuador.

MARTA TRABA

1. *El problema de la existencia del artista latinoamericano* (Bogotá: Revista Plástica, 1956).

2. Traba, Marta, *Problemas del arte en Latinoamérica* (México: Revista Siempre, 1964).

RIGOBERTA MENCHÚ

1. Kay B. Warren, "Transforming Memories and Histories: The Meanings of Ethnic Resurgence for Mayan Indians," in *Americas: New Inter-*

pretive Essays, ed. Alfred Stephan (New York: Oxford University Press, 1992), 197–201; and Kay B. Warren, ed. *The Violence Within: Cultural and Political Opposition in Divided Nations* (Boulder, Colo.: Westview Press, 1993).

2. Rigoberta Menchú, *I, Rigoberta Menchú: An Indian Woman in Guatemala,* ed. Elisabeth Burgos-Debray (London: Verso Press, 1984), 245.

3. Others include Domitila Barrios de Chungara with Moema Viezzer, *Let Me Speak! Testimony of Domitila, A Woman of the Bolivian Mines* (New York: Monthly Review Press, 1978); and Elvia Alvarado, *Don't Be Afraid Gringo: A Honduran Woman Speaks from the Heart,* trans. and ed. Medea Benjamin (New York: Harper and Row, 1987).

4. Dinesh D'Souza, *Illiberal Education: The Politics of Race and Sex on Campus* (New York: Free Press, 1991), 72.

5. Rigoberta Menchú, *Me Llamo Rigoberta Menchú y así me nació la conciencia* (Mexico: Siglo XXI, 1985).

6. Menchú, *I, Rigoberta,* 244.

7. Ibid., 246.

8. Ibid., 189.

9. Warren, "Transforming Memories," 190–93.

10. Rigoberta Menchú y Comité de Unidad Campesina, *Trenzando el futuro: luchas campesinas en la historia reciente de Guatemala* (Donostia, Spain: Tercera Prensa, 1992), n.p. Translation mine.

11. "Guatemalan Indian Accepts a Nobel," *New York Times International,* 11 December 1992.

JULIA DE BURGOS

1. The biographical information comes from: Yvette Jiménez de Báez, *Julia de Burgos: Vida y poesía* (San Juan: Editorial Coquí, 1966); and Edgar Martínez Masdeu, *Cronología de Julia de Burgos,* in *3 Cuadernos del Congreso Internacional Julia de Burgos 1992* (San Juan: Ateneo Puertorriqueño, 1992).

2. Julia de Burgos, *Desde la Escuela del Aire: Julia de Burgos. Textos de radio teatro escritos por Julia de Burgos.* In *6 Cuadernos del Congreso Internacional Julia de Burgos 1992* (San Juan: Ateneo Puertorriqueño, 1992).

3. See Jiménez de Báez, *Julia de Burgos,* 22 n. 5.

4. See ibid., 44.

5. *Pueblos hispanos* was founded in 1943. It was published from February 13, 1943, to October 7, 1944. The director was Juan Antonio Corretjer; Consuelo Lee Tapia de Lamb was the administrator; Clemente Soto Vélez was the editor in chief. A total of eighty-seven issues were published.

6. Letter to her sister Consuelo from Cuba. Quoted by Juan Antonio Rodríguez Pagán in *Julia De Burgos . . . periodista en Nueva York. 1 Cuadernos del Congreso Internacional Julia de Burgos 1992* (San Juan: Ateneo Puertorriqueño, 1992).

7. See Jiménez de Báez, *Julia de Burgos*, 67.

8. See Pagán, *Julia De Burgos . . . periodista en Nueva York*, 77–78.

9. José Emilio González, "Algo más sobre la vida y la poesía de Julia de Burgos," in *Julia o la intimidad de los instantes. 5 Cuadernos del Congreso Internacional Julia de Burgos 1992* (San Juan: Ateneo Puertorriqueño, 1992), 13.

10. Julia de Burgos, "A Julia de Burgos," in *Poema en veinte surcos* (Río Piedras: Ediciones Huracán, 1982 edition), 9. Subsequent reference will be to this edition and will appear in the text.

11. Luz María Umpierre, "Metapoetic Code in Julia de Burgos' *El mar y tú*: Towards a Revision," in *In Retrospect: Essays on Latin American Literature*, ed. Elizabeth S. Rogers and Timothy J. Rogers (York, S.C.: Spanish Literature Publishing, 1987), 85–94.

12. Julia de Burgos, *Canción de la verdad sencilla* (Río Piedras: Ediciones Huracán, 1982), 7. Subsequent reference will be to this edition and will appear in the text.

13. Ivette López Jiménez, "Julia de Burgos: los textos comunicantes," *Sin Nombre* 10, no. 1 (April–June 1979): 54.

14. In an unpublished article, Heather Rosario Sievert has pointed out the correspondence that exist in the aesthetics of Julia de Burgos and the symbolist poets.

15. Eliana Rivero, "Julia de Burgos y su visión poética del ser," *Sin Nombre* 11, no. 3 (1980): 51–57.

16. Julia de Burgos, "Poema de la íntima agonía," in *El mar y tú* (Río Piedras: Ediciones Huracán, 1986 edition), 45. Subsequent reference will be to this edition and will appear in the text.

17. María Solá, ed., *Julia de Burgos: Yo misma fui mi ruta* (Río Piedras: Ediciones Huracán, 1986 edition). See her introduction, 7–48.

18. Solá, ed., *Julia de Burgos*, 158.

ELENA PONIATOWSKA

1. Portions of this chapter have appeared in Kay Garcia's *Broken Bars: New Perspectives from Mexican Women Writers Spanish America* (Albuquerque: University of New Mexico Press, 1994).

DELMIRA AGUSTINI

1. Clara Silva, *Genio y figura de Delmira Agustini* (Buenos Aires: Ceibo, 1968), 154.

2. Sylvia Molloy, "Dos lecturas del cisne: Rubén Darío y Delmira Agustini," in *La sartén por el mango,* ed. Patricia Elena González and Eliana Ortega (Río Piedras: Ediciones Huracán, 1985), 60.

3. José P. Barrán and Benjamín Nahum, *El Uruguay del novecientos* (Montevideo: Ediciones de la Banda Oriental, 1979), 16.

4. Ibid., 681–69.

5. Silva, *Genio y figura de Delmira Agustini,* 106.

6. Silva, *Genio y figura de Delmira Agustini,* 27.

7. Delmira Agustini, *Obras poéticas* (Montevideo: Talleres Gráficos de Institutos Penales, 1940), 55–57.

8. Silva, *Genio y figura de Delmira Agustini,* 102.

9. Ibid., 64.

10. Arturo Sergio Visca, *Correspondencia íntima de Delmira Agustini y tres versiones "De lo inefable"* (Montevideo: Ediciones Biblioteca Nacional Uruguay, 1978), 37.

11. Ibid., 16.

12. Ibid., 63.

13. Ibid., 64–65.

14. Emir Rodríguez Monegal, *Sexo y poesía en el 900* (Montevideo: Editorial Alfa, 1969), 44.

15. Agustini, *Obras poéticas,* 143.

16. Silva, *Genio y figura de Delmira Agustini,* 46.

CLARICE LISPECTOR

1. Interview in Clarice Lispector, *A Paixao Segundo G. H.,* ed. Benedito Nunes (Florianopolis: Universidad Federal de Santa Catarina, Coleçao Arquivos, 1964) 296.

2. Clarice Lispector, *Near to the Wild Heart,* translated by Giovanni Pontiero (New York: New Directions, 1990) 81.

3. Ibid., 138.

4. Ibid., 157.

5. Clarice Lispector, "The Making of a Novel," in *Discovering the World* (Manchester, U.K.: Carcanet, 1992) 372.

6. Clarice Lispector, *Family Ties,* translated by Giovanni Pontiero (Austin: University of Texas Press, 1987) 23.

7. Lispector, *Family Ties,* 43–44.

8. Clarice Lispector, "Some Useless Explanation," in *Discovering the World,* 313.

9. Clarice Lispector, "Preciousness," in *Family Ties,* 79.

10. Clarice Lispector, "Mystery in Sao Cristóvao," in *Family Ties,* 112.

11. Ibid.

12. Clarice Lispector, "The Chicken," in *Family Ties,* 30.

13. Clarice Lispector, "The Crime of the Maths Teacher," in *Family Ties,* 119.

14. Clarice Lispector, "Animals," in *Discovering the World,* 439.

15. Olga Borelli, *Clarice Lispector, Esboço para um possive reitrato* (Rio de Janeiro: Nova Frontiera) 218.

16. Clarice Lispector, *The Apple in the Dark,* translated by Gregory Rabassa (New York: Knopf, 1967) 321.

17. Benedito Nunes, preface to *A Paixao Segundo G. H.,* xxviii.

18. Lispector, "Animals," 436.

19. Clarice Lispector, "Hermetic," in *Discovering the World,* 107.

20. Clarice Lispector, "A Knowing Sensibility," in *Discovering the World,* 198.

21. Clarice Lispector, "Social Column," in *Discovering the World,* 249–52.

22. Columns written for the *Correio do Manha* (Morning Post), Clarice Lispector Archives (CL. 01), Ruy Barbosa Foundation, Rio de Janeiro.

23. Clarice Lispector, *Hour of the Star* (Manchester, U.K.: Carcanet, 1986) 15.

24. Ibid., 36.

25. From author's conversation with Giovanni Pontiero.

26. "In Memory of the Man Who Stood Down," on the resignation of

President Jânio Quadros, who stepped down on 25 August 1961, less than seven months after taking office.

27. Lispector, *Hour of the Star,* 28.

28. Ibid., 83.

29. Interview with Julio Lerner published in *Shalom* (Sao Paulo), August 1992, 69.

30. Lispector, *Hour of the Star,* 85.

31. Interview with Olga Borelli in Sao Paulo, August 1992.

32. Borelli, *Clarice Lispector,* 34.

33. Borelli, *Clarice Lispector,* 19.

ALEJANDRA PIZARNIK

1. See by Alejandra Pizarnik: *La tierra más ajena* (Buenos Aires: Botella al Mar, 1955), *La última inocencia* (Buenos Aires: Ediciones Poesía, 1956), *Las aventuras perdidas* (Buenos Aires: Altamar, 1958), *Arbol de Diana* (Buenos Aires: Sur, 1962), *Extracción de la piedra de la locura* (Buenos Aires: Sudamericana, 1968), *Nombres y figuras* (Barcelona: La Esquina, 1969), *La condesa sangrienta* (Buenos Aires: Acuarius, 1971), *El infierno musical* (Buenos Aires: Siglo XXI, 1971), and *Los pequeños cantos* (Caracas: Arbol de Fuego, 1971). Collections of texts: *El deseo de la palabra* (Barcelona: Ocnos, 1975), *Poemas* (Buenos Aires: Centro Editor de América Latina, 1982), *Textos de Sombra y últimos poemas* (Buenos Aires: Sudamericana, 1982), and *Obras Completas* (Buenos Aires: Corregidor, 1990; rev. ed., 1994).

2. For a study of the critique of the self and the connections between Macedonio Fernández and Borges, see Alicia Borinsky, *Theoretical Fables* (Philadelphia: the University of Pennsylvania Press, 1993).

3. Unless otherwise indicated, the quotations and page numbers correspond to: Frank Graziano, *Alejandra Pizarnik. A Profile* (Boulder, Colo.: Logbridge-Rhodes, 1987). Translations by Maria Rosa Fort, Frank Graziano, and Suzanne Jill Levine.

4. Not to be confused with the American use of the term *modernism.*

5. See Valentine Penrose, *La Comtesse sanglante* (Paris: Gallimad, 1962).

MAROSA DI GIORGIO

1. Marosa Di Giorgio, *La liebre de marzo* (Montevideo: Calicanto, 1981), 87.

2. Ibid.

3. MDG interviewed by Wilfredo Penco, *El País Cultural* (Montevideo), 20 April 1990.

4. Leonardo Garet, *Literatura del Salto* (Salto: Intendencia Municipal de Salto, 1990), 9–11.

5. Ibid., 404–5.

6. Ibid., 405.

7. MDG interviewed by Teresa Porzecanski, August 1993.

8. Ibid.

9. Penco, *El País Cultural.*

10. Ibid.

11. Ibid.

12. MDG interviewed by Wilfredo Penco, *Correo de los Viernes* (Montevideo), 20 November 1981.

13. Ricardo Pallares, "Marosa Di Giorgio: Liebre en marzo como en febrero," in *Tres mundos de la lírica uruguaya actual* (Montevideo: Ediciones de la Banda Oriental, 1992), 45.

14. Penco, *El País Cultural.*

15. MDG interviewed by J. Malaia, *La Semana de El Día,* 14 November 1981.

16. MDG interviewed by R. Mascaro, *El País Cultural,* (Montevideo), no. 159.

17. MDG interviewed by Teresa Porzecanski, August 1993.

18. Marosa Di Giorgio, *Los papeles salvajes,* vol. 2 (Montevideo: Arca Editorial, 1991), 140.

19. Pallares, "Marosa Di Giorgio," 46.

20. Ibid., 44; and Di Giorgio, *Liebre de marzo,* 19.

21. Garet, *Literatura del Salto,* 369.

22. Ibid.

23. Di Giorgio, *Papeles salvajes* 1:173.

24. Di Giorgio, *Liebre de marzo,* 39.

25. Ibid., 39–40.

26. Di Giorgio, *Papeles salvajes* 2:229.

Bibliography

SOFÍA OSPINA DE NAVARRO
WORKS BY DE NAVARRO

La abuela cuenta. Medellín: Ediciones La Tertulia, Editorial Granamérica, 1964; Medellín: Imprenta Departamental de Antioquia, 1975.

La buena mesa: sencillo y práctico libro de cocina. 1942. Reprint, Medellín: Promotora de Ediciones y Comunicaciones Ltda., 1982.

La cartilla del hogar. 4th ed. Medellín: Editorial Granamérica, 1972.

Crónicas. Medellín: Susaeta, 1983.

Cuentos y crónicas. Prologue by Tomás Carrasquilla. Medellín: Tipografía Industrial, 1926.

Don de gentes: Comprimidos de cultural social. Medellín: Granamérica, 1958; Medellín: Editorial Colima, 1969.

Menos redes. Prologue by Alfonso Castro. Medellín: Editorial Granamérica, 1970.

Plays (Circulated in Manuscript)

Ascendiendo: Comedia en un acto y dos cuadras
La familia Morales: Comedia en tres actos

El favor de San Antonio
Una junta benéfica: Comedia en dos actos y en prosa
Un luto pasajero: Comedia en un acto
Milagro

WORKS ABOUT DE NAVARRO

Agudelo, Bernardo. "Cuatro mujeres en la historia de Antioquia." *Boletín histórico* 6 (February 1978): 93–100.

Angulo, Enriqueta. "'Resta feminidad a las mujeres la excesiva erudición' dice la Clara Matron Doña Sofía Ospina de Navarro." *Raza* (Medellín) 31 (April 1949): 6–7.

Anonymous. "Antioquia está de luto por la muerte de doña Sofía Ospina de Navarro." *El Colombiano,* 14 June 1974, pp. 1 and 8.

———. "La buena mesa de Doña Sofía." *El Tiempo,* 18 June 1974: 1B.

———. "Con Doña Sofía Ospina de Navarro: su carácter, sus pareceres, educación femenina, el sufragio de la mujer, su libro, problema social." *El Heraldo de Antioquia* (Medellín) 111 (16 October 1927): 1.

———. "Cuentistas colombianas." In *Varias cuentistas colombianas.* Bogotá: Editorial Minerva, 1936.

———. "Homenaje póstumo a Doña Sofía." *El Colombiano,* 15 June 1974.

Blair Gutiérrez, Bernardo. "Sofía Ospina de Navarro." *Gentes* (Medellín) 87 (May-June 1974): 9–11.

Cano, Ana María. "Reportajes contra la pared: entrevista con Sofía Ospina de Navarro." *El Mundo* (1962): 13–15.

Castro, Alfonso. "Sofía Ospina de Navarro." *Lectura Breve* (Medellín) 1, no. 4 (18 April 1983): 47–57.

Gutiérrez, Emilia. "La mujer antioqueña." *Panoramas* (Pereira-Caldas). Reprinted in Diana Rubens, ed. *Mujeres colombianas.* Quito: Editorial de El Comercio, 1940.

Gutiérrez Vélez, Raúl. "Sofía Ospina de Navarro." In *Grandes forjadores.* Medellín: Impresión Edinalco, n. d.

Hernández Suárez, Alvaro. "Sofía Ospina de Navarro." In *Antioquia: pueblos y figuras.* 2d ed. Medellín: Grupo Impresor, 1991.

Jaramillo, María Mercedes, Angela Inés Robledo, and Flor María Rodrígues-Arenas. "Ospina de Navarro, Sofía." In *¿Y las mujeres? En-*

sayos sobre literatura colombiana. Medellín: Editorial Universidad de Antioquia, 1991.

Londono Martínez, Alfonso. "Quién es quién: Doña Sofía Ospina de Navarro." *Raza* (Medellín) 2, no. 8 (1947): 66 and 74.

Mariester. "La abuela cuenta: una conversación con Doña Sofía Ospina." *El Colombiano* (Medellín) 951 (23 June 1974): 1–3.

Melo, Silvia Stella. "Navarro Sofía Ospina de: Cuentista—Acción Social." In *Valores femeninos de Colombia.* Bogotá: Editorial Carvajal, 1966.

Montana, Inés de. "Doña Sofía Ospina de Navarro." *El Espectador* (Bogotá), 19 September 1970, sec. 3.

Naranjo Balcázar, Rafael. "La vida y la obra de doña Sofía Ospina de Navarro." *Universidad de Antioquia* (Medellín) 178 (July–September 1970): 507–20.

Otero Muñoz, Gustavo. "Las escritoras colombianas." In *Resumen de historia de la literatura colombiana.* 3d ed. Bogotá: Editorial El Escolar, 1940.

Pérez Medina, Julián. "Mujeres de Antioquia. Sofía Ospina de Navarro." *Repertorio histórico de la Academia Antioqueña de Historia* (Medellín) 33, no. 233F (1980): 121–27.

———. "Sofía Ospina de Navarro." In *Mi raza.* Medellín: Copiyepes, 1986.

Romero de Nohra, Flor, and Gloria Pachón Castro. "Sofía Ospina de Navarro." In *Mujeres de Colombia.* Bogotá: Editorial Andes, 1961.

Sánchez López, Luis María. "Sofía Ospina de Navarro." In *Diccionario de escritores colombianos.* 2d ed. Bogotá: Plaza y Janes, 1982.

Velásquez Toro, Magdala. "Condición jurídica y social de la mujer." In *Nueva historia de Colombia: educación y ciencia, luchas de la mujer, vida diaria,* vol. 4. Bogotá: Planeta Colombiana Editorial, 1989.

GABRIELA MISTRAL
POETRY, PROSE, AND ANTHOLOGIES BY MISTRAL

Antología. Santiago: Zig-Zag, 1940.

Desolación. New York: Instituto de las Españas, 1922; Santiago: Zig-Zag, 1926.

Lagar. Editorial del Pacífico, Santiago, 1954.

Lecturas para mujeres. México: Secretaría de Educación, 1923; México: Porrúa, 1973.

Poesías Completas. Madrid: Aguilar, 1958.

Tala. Buenos Aires: Sur, 1938.

Ternura. Madrid: Saturnino Callejas, 1924; Buenos Aires: Espasa-Calpe, 1945.

POSTHUMOUSLY EDITED COLLECTIONS OF POETRY AND PROSE-POETRY

Lagar II. Dirección de Bibliotecas, Archivos y Museos. Santiago: Biblioteca Nacional, 1992.

Motivos de San Francisco. Edited by César Díaz-Muñoz Cormatches. Santiago: Pacífico, 1965.

Poema de Chile. Edited by Doris Dana. Santiago: Pomaire, 1967.

Reino: Poesía dispersa e inédita, en verso y prosa. Edited by Gastón von dem Bussche. Valparaíso: Universidad Católica, 1983.

VOLUMES OF CORRESPONDENCE

Hiriart, Rosario, ed. *Cartas a Lydia Cabrera: Correspondencia inédita de Gabriela Mistral y Teresa de la Parra.* Madrid: Torremozas, 1988.

Fernández Larraín, Sergio, ed. *Cartas de Amor de Gabriela Mistral.* Santiago: Andrés Bello, 1978.

Vargas Saavedra, Luis, ed. *Epistolario de Gabriela Mistral y Eduardo Barrios.* Santiago: Centro de Estudios de Literatura Chilena, Pontificia Universidad Católica de Chile, 1988.

Silva Castro, Raúl, ed. *Gabriela Mistral Epistolario, Cartas a Eugenio Labarca 1915–1916.* Santiago: Anales Universidad de Chile, 1958.

Arce, Magda, ed., with the collaboration of Eugenio García Carrillo. *Gabriela Mistral y Joaquín García Monge: Una correspondencia inédita.* Santiago: Andrés Bello, 1989.

Vargas Saavedra, Luis, ed. *Tan de Usted: Epistolario de Gabriela Mistral con Alfonso Reyes.* Santiago: Hachette and Universidad Católica de Chile. 1991.

VOLUMES OF SELECTED PROSE

Calderón, Alfonso, ed. *Croquis Mexicanos.* Santiago: Nascimento, 1979.

Céspedes, Mario, ed. *Recados para América: textos de Gabriela Mistral.* Santiago: Epesa, 1978.

———. *Materias: prosa inédita.* Santiago: Universitaria, 1978.

Dirección de Bibliotecas, Archivos y Museos. *Gabriela Mistral en La Voz de Elqui.* Vicuña: Museo Gabriela Mistral de Vicuña, 1992.

Esteban Scarpa, Roque, ed. *Elogio de las Cosas de la Tierra.* Santiago: Andrés Bello, 1979.

———. *Gabriela anda por el mundo.* Santiago: Andrés Bello, 1978.

———. *Gabriela piensa en . . .* Santiago: Andrés Bello, 1978.

———. *Grandeza de los oficios.* Santiago: Andrés Bello, 1979.

———. *Magisterio y niño.* Santiago: Andrés Bello, 1979.

Vargas Saavedra, Luis, ed. *Prosa Religiosa de Gabriela Mistral.* Santiago: Andrés Bello, 1978.

MAJOR CRITICAL/BIOGRAPHICAL SOURCES

Alegría, Ciro. *Gabriela Mistral Íntima.* 1968. Reprint, Cali, Colombia: Oveja Negra, 1980.

Alegría, Fernando. *Genio y figura de Gabriela Mistral.* Buenos Aires: Universitaria, 1966.

Bahamonde, Mario. *Gabriela Mistral en Antofagasta: Años de forja y valentía.* Santiago: Nascimiento, 1980.

Collectivo Isis Internacional. *Una palabra cómplice: encuentro con Gabriela Mistral.* Santiago: Casa de la Mujer La Morada, Isis Internacional, 1990.

Concha, Jaime. *Gabriela Mistral.* Madrid: Júcar, 1986.

Díaz Arrieta, Hernán. *Gabriela Mistral: Premio Nobel 1945.* Santiago: Nascimento, 1946.

Fariña, Soledad. *Lecturas de Mujeres.* Santiago: Taller Literatura la Morada, 1989.

Figueroa, Virgilio. *La Divina Gabriela.* Santiago: Imprenta El Esfuerzo, 1933.

Gazarian-Gautier, Marie-Lise. *Gabriela Mistral: The Teacher from the Valley of Elqui.* Chicago: Franciscan World Herald Press, 1975.

Guzmán, Jorge. *Diferencias Latinoamericanas (Mistral, Carpentier, García Márquez, Puig).* Santiago: Departamento de Estudios Humanísticos, Universidad de Chile, 1984.

Ladrón de Guevara, Matilde. *Gabriela Mistral: Rebelde magnífica.* 1957. Reprint, Santiago: Araucaria, 1984.

Samatán, Marta Elena. *Gabriela Mistral: Campesina del Valle de Elqui.* Buenos Aires: Instituto Amigos del Libro Argentino, 1969.

Scarpa, Roque Esteban. *La desterrada en su patria*. 2 vols. Santiago: Nascimento, 1980.

———. *Una mujer nada de tonta*. Santiago: Nascimento, 1976.

Silva Castro, Raúl. *Producción de Gabriela Mistral de 1912 a 1918*. Santiago: Anales Universidad de Chile, 1957.

Taylor, Martin C. *Sensibilidad religiosa de Gabriela Mistral*. Translated by Pilar García Noreña. Madrid: Gredos, 1975.

Teitelboim, Volodia. *Gabriela Mistral pública y secreta*. Santiago: BAT, 1992.

Vargas Saavedra, Luis. *El otro suicidio de Gabriela Mistral*. Santiago: Universidad Católica de Chile, 1985.

Villegas, Juan. *Estudios sobre poesía chilena*. Santiago: Nascimento, 1980.

Von dem Bussche, Gastón. *Visión de una poesía*. Santiago: Anales de la Universidad de Chile, 1957.

VIOLETA PARRA
WORKS

Parra, Violeta. *Cantos folklóricos chilenos*. Musical transcription by Gastón Soublette and photographs by Sergio Larraín and Sergio Bravo. Santiago: Nascimento, 1979.

———. *Décimas de Violeta Parra: Autobiografía en versos*. With an introduction by Pablo Neruda, Nicanor Parra, and Pablo de Rokha. Barcelona: Pomaire, 1976.

———. *Poésie populaire des Andes*. Translated by Fanchita Gonzáles-Batte. Paris: François Mampero, 1965.

Alcalde, Alfonso, ed. *Toda Violeta Parra. Antología presentada por Alfonso Alcalde*. Buenos Aires: Ediciones de la Flor, 1974.

Las últimas composiones de Violeta Parra. Santiago: Odeón Chilena, S.A., 1974. RCA 1347007, 1983.

Piña, Juan Andrés, ed. *Violeta Parra 21 son los dolores*. Santiago: Ediciones Aconcagua, 1978.

Martínez Reverte, Javier, ed. *Violeta Parra-Violeta del pueblo*. Madrid: Visor, 1983.

BIOGRAPHY

Agosín, Marjorie. "Violeta Parra." In *Spanish American Women Writers. A Bio-Bibliographical Source Book*, edited by Diane E. Marting,

427–35. Westport, Conn.: Greenwood Press, 1990.

Agosín, Marjorie, and Inés Dölz-Blackburn. "Biografía." In *Violeta Parra: Santa de pura greda. Un estudio de su obra poética.* Santiago: Planeta, Biblioteca Sur, 1988.

Alegría, Fernando. "Violeta Parra," In *Retratos contemporáneos.* New York: Harcourt, Brace and Jovanovich, 1979.

Huasi, Julio. "Violeta de América." *Casa de las Américas* (Havana) 65–66 (March-June 1971): 91–104.

Letelier, Alfonso. "In Memoriam. Violeta Parra." *Revista Musical Chilena* (Santiago) (April-June 1967): 109–11.

Manns, Patricio. *Violeta Parra.* Madrid: Ediciones Júcar, 1977.

———. *Violeta Parra. La guitarra indócil.* Concepción, Chile: Ediciones Literatura Americana Reunida, 1986.

Oviedo, Carmen. *Mentira todo lo cierto. Tras la huella de Violeta Parra.* Santiago: Editorial Universitaria, 1990.

Parra, Isabel. *El Libro Mayor de Violeta Parra.* Madrid: Ediciones Michay, 1985.

Radio Chilena. Santiago. "Recordando a Violeta Parra." 5 February 1989.

Radio Cooperativa Vitalicia. "Homenaje a V. Parra." 4 October 1986.

Rodríguez, Osvaldo. *Cantores que reflexionan. Notas para una historia personal de la Nueva Canción Chilena.* Madrid: Ediciones Literatura Americana Reunida, 1983.

Subercaseaux, Bernardo, and Jaime Londoño. *Gracias a la vida.* Santiago: Editorial Granizo-Céneca, 1982.

CRITICAL BOOKS

Agosín, Marjorie, and Inés Dölz-Blackburn. *Violeta Parra: Santa de pura greda. Un estudio de su obra poética.* Santiago: Planeta, Biblioteca Sur, 1988.

Dölz-Blackburn, Inés, and Marjorie Agosín. *Violeta Parra o la expresión inefable. Un estudio de su poesía, prosa y pintura.* Santiago: Planeta, 1992.

CRITICAL ARTICLES: A SELECTION

Agosín, Marjorie. "Bibliografía de Violeta Parra." *Revista Interamericana de Bibliografía* (Washington, D.C.) 32 (1982): 179–90.

———. "Reseña de *Cantos folklóricos chilenos* de Violeta Parra." *Literatura chilena: creación y crítica* 16 (January–March 1981): 34.

———. "Violeta Parra." In *Spanish American Women Writers. A Bio-Bibliographical Source Book,* edited by Diane E. Marting, 427–35. Westport, Conn.: Greenwood Press, 1990.

Arguedas, José María et al. "Análisis de un genio popular hacen artistas escritores." *Revista de Educación* (Santiago) 13 (December 1968): 67–76.

Barros, Raquel, and Manuel Danneman. "Violeta Parra, hermana mayor de los cantores populares." *Revista Musical Chinena* 12, no. 60 (June–August 1958): 71–77.

Bello, Enrique. "Homenaje a Violeta Parra." *Boletín de la Universidad de Chile* (Santiago) 74 (May 1967): 60–61.

Cánepa Hurtado, Gina. "La canción de lucha en Violeta Parra y su ubicación en el complejo cultural chileno entre los años 1960 a 1973." *Revista de Crítica Literaria Latinoamericana* (Lima, Peru) 9, no. 17 (1983): 147–70.

———. "La canción y poesía de Violeta Parra." Unpublished manuscript provided by Marjorie Agosín.

Castillo, Adriana. "Décimas de Violeta Parra o la superación de la conciencia de lo individual." *Ventanal* 2 (1981): 1–14.

Dölz-Blackburn, Inés. "El amor logrado o el alma en calma en la poesía de Violeta Parra." *Confluencia* 5, no. 2 (1990): 39–45. Excerpt from Dölz-Blackburn and Agosín, *Violeta Parra o la expresión inefable.*

———. "Introducción a la poesía amorosa de Violeta Parra: recolección, reelaboración, y creación." *Literatura Chilena. Creación y Crítica* 47–50 (1989): 159–69. Also in *Folklore Americano* 48 (1989): 11–20.

———. "La prensa y Violeta Parra 1967–90." *Revista Interamericana de Bibliografía* (Washington, D.C.) 41, no. 3 (1991): 409–536.

———. "Violeta Parra, heredera de la tradición de los cantores anónimos." *Letras Femeninas* 14, nos. 1–2 (1988): 80–89. Also in Agosín and Dölz-Blackburn, *Violeta Parra: Santa de pura greda,* 141–50.

———. "Violeta Parra. La mujer marginal y la mujer liberada en su poesía." *Letras Femeninas.* Forthcoming.

———. "Violeta Parra y la expresión de la conciencia social." Monograph. *Folklore Americano.* Forthcoming.

Englebert, Manfred. "Violeta Parra Lieder aus Chile." In *Zwiesprachige Anthologie*. Frankfurt: [**publisher?**] 1979.

Epple, Juan. "Discografía, Bibliografía y Filmografía de Violeta Parra." In *El libro mayor de Violeta Parra*, edited by Isabel Parra. Madrid: Ediciones Michay, 1985.

———. "Notas sobre la cueca larga de Violeta Parra." *Cuadernos Americanos* (Mexico) 124, no. 5 (May–June): 232–48.

———. "Preguntas, por Violeta Parra a Angel Parra." *Cahiers du Monde Hispanique et Luso-Bresilien* 48. University de Toulouse-Le Mirail: Service des Publications, 1987. Also in *Mundo* 1, no. 3 (Summer 1987): 65–71.

———. "Reseña de *El libro mayor de Violeta Parra*." *Literatura Chilena. Creación y Crítica* 32–34 (July-December 1985): 66.

———. "Violeta Parra y la cultura popular chilena." *Literatura Chilena en el Exilio* 1, no. 2 (April 1977): 4–11.

González Bernejo, Ernesto. "Entrevista a Isabel Parra." *Crisis* 28 (August 1975): np.

González Vergara, Ruth. "Violeta Parra: Testimonio de un patrimonio mayor." *Araucaria* (1985): 193–99.

Lindstrom, Naomi. "Construcción y deconstrucción individual en un texto de Violeta Parra." *Literatura Chilena. Creación y Crítica* (Los Angeles) 9 (Summer-Fall 1985): 33–34, 56–60.

Martí Fuentes, Adolfo. "La poesía popular de Violeta Parra." *Casa de las Américas* (Havana) 69 (November-December 1979): 203–6.

Moreno, Albrecht. "Violeta Parra y la Nueva Canción Chilena." In *Studies in Latin American Popular Culture*, vol. 5. Morris, Minn.: University of Minnesota, 1986.

Müller-Bergh, Klaus. "Fulgor y muerte de Violeta Parra." *Revista Interamericana de Bibliografía* (Washington, D.C.) 28 (January–March 1978): 47–55.

Orrego Salas, Juan. "La Nueva Canción Chilena: Tradición, espíritu y contenido de su música." *Literatura Chilena en el Exilio* 4, no. 2 (1980): 2–7.

Subercaseaux, Bernardo, and Jaime Londoño. "Notes on Violeta Parra: From Folklore to Chilean Lore." In *Papers in Romance*, vol. 2. Seattle: University of Washington, 1978.

CECILIA ANSALDO

Ansaldo, Cecilia. "Interview by Patricia Varas," 24 July 1993.

Carreño, Antonio. *La dialéctica de la identidad en la poesía contemporánea.* Madrid: Editorial Gredos, 1982.

Chalela, César A. "Women of Valor: An Interview with the Mothers of Plaza de Mayo." In *Surviving Beyond Fear,* edited by Marjorie Agosín. New York: White Pine Press, 1993.

Franco, Jean. "Going Public: Reinhabiting the Private." In *On Edge. The Crisis of Contemporary Latin American Culture,* edited by George Yúdice and Jean Franco. Minneapolis: Minnesota University Press, 1992.

———. *Plotting Women. Gender and Representation in Mexico.* New York: Columbia University Press, 1989.

Heilbrun, Carolyn G. *Writing a Woman's Life.* New York: Ballantine Books, 1988.

Martillo Monserrate, Jorge. "Guayaquil de mis desvaríos." *El Universo,* 31 March 1992.

CARMEN NARANJO
WORKS BY NARANJO

América. San José: Educa (Editorial Universitaria Centroamericana), 1972.

Camino al mediodía. San José: Editorial Costa Rica, 1968.

Canción de la ternura. San José: Ediciones Elite de Lilia Ramos, 1964.

El caso 117 . . . Educa (Editorial Universitaria Centroamericana), 1965.

Cinco temas en busca de un pensador. San José: Ministerio de Cultura, Juventud y Deportes, 1977.

Cultura: La acción cultural en Latinoamérica. Estudio sobre la planificación cultural. San José: Departamento de Publicaciones del Instituto Centroamericano de Administración Pública, 1978.

Diario de una multitud. San José: Editorial Universitaria Centroamericana, 1974.

Estancias y días. With Graciela Moreno. San José: Editorial Costa Rica, 1985.

Hacia tu isla. San José: N.p., 1966.

Homenaje a Don Nadie. San José: Editorial Costa Rica, 1981.

Hoy es un largo día. San José: Editorial Costa Rica, 1974.

Memorias de un hombre palabra. San José: Editorial Costa Rica, 1968.

Mi guerrilla. San José: Editorial Universitaria Centroamericana, 1984.

Misa a oscuras. San José: Editorial Costa Rica, 1967.

Nunca hubo alguna vez. San José: Editorial Universidad Estatal a Distancia, 1984.

Ondina. San José: Editorial Universitaria Centroamericana, 1985; Havana: Casa de las Américas, 1988.

Los perros no ladraron. San José: Editorial Costa Rica, 1966.

Por las páginas de la Biblia y otros caminos de Israel. San José: N.p., 1976.

Responso por el niño Juan Manuel. San José: Editorial Conciencia Nueva, 1971.

Sobrepunto. San José: Editorial Universitaria Centroamericana, 1985.

"La voz." In *Obras breves del teatro costarricense,* vol. 1. San José: Editorial Costa Rica, 1977.

TRANSLATIONS

"The Flowery Trick," "The Journey of Journeys," and "Inventory of a Recluse." In Yolando Oreamuno, ed. *Five Women Writers of Costa Rica.* Beaumont, Tex.: Asociación de Literatura Femenina Hispánica, 1976.

"Listen." *Mundus Artium* 7, no. 1 (1975): 87.

There was never . . . Pittsburgh, Penn.: Latin American Literary Review, 1989.

ELENA PONIATOWSKA
BOOKS BY PONIATOWSKA

¡Ay vida!, no me mereces. Mexico City: Joaquín Mortiz, 1985.

Dear Diego: Affectionately, Quiela. Translated by Katherine Silver. New York: Pantheon Books, 1986.

De noche vienes. Mexico City: Ediciones Era, 1991.

Domingo 7. Mexico City: Ediciones Océano, 1982.

Fuerte es el silencio. Mexico City: Ediciones Era, 1980.

La "Flor de Lis." Mexico City: Ediciones Era, 1988.

Gaby Brimmer. Mexico City: Editorial Grijalbo, 1979.

Hasta no verte, Jesús mío. Mexico City: Ediciones Era, 1969.

Lilus Kikus. Los Presentes series. Mexico City: Ediciones Era, 1985.

Massacre in Mexico. Translated by Helen R. Lane. New York: Viking Press, 1971.

Mujeres de Juchitán. Mexico City: Editorial Toledo, 1988.

Nada, nadie: Las voces del temblor. Mexico City: Ediciones Era, 1988.

La noche de Tlatelolco. Mexico City: Ediciones Era, 1971.

Palabras cruzadas. Mexico City: Ediciones Era, 1961.

Querido Diego, te abraza Quiela. Mexico City: Ediciones Era, 1990.

Tinísima. Mexico City: Ediciones Era, 1992.

Todo empezó en domingo. Mexico City: Fondo de Cultura Económica, 1963.

El último guajolote. Mexico City: Cultura/SEP, 1983.

Works About/Including Poniatowska

Agosín, Marjorie. "The Message: Elena Poniatowska." In *Landscapes of a New Land: Fiction by Latin American Women.* Buffalo: White Pine Press, 1989.

Dever, Susan. "Elena Poniatowska: La crítica de una mujer." In *Mujer y literatura mexicana y chicana, culturas en contacto,* edited by Aralia López González. Mexico City: Coloquio Fronterizo, 1988.

Dimitriou, Agnes L. "Entrevista con Elena Poniatowska." *Letras Femeninas* 16, no. 1–2 (Spring-Fall 1990): 125–33.

Flori, Monica. "El mundo femenino de Marta Lynch y Elena Poniatowska." *Letras Femeninas* 9, no. 2 (1983): 23–30.

Foster, David William. "Latin American Documentary Narrative." *Publications of the Modern Language Association of America* 99, no. 1 (January 1984): 41–55.

Fox-Lockert, Lucia. "Elena Poniatowska: *Hasta no verte, Jesús mío* (1969)." In *Women Novelists of Spain and Spanish America.* Metuchen, N.J.: Scarecrow Press, 1979.

González, Patricia, and Eleana Ortega. "Testimonios de una escritora: Elena Poniatowska en micrófono." In *La sartén por el mango, encuentro de escritoras latinoamericanas.* San Juan, Puerto Rico: Ediciones Huracán, 1985.

Jorgensen, Beth E. "La intertextualidad en *La noche de Tlatelolco* de Elena Poniatowska." *Hispanic Journal* 10, no. 2 (Spring 1989): 81–93.

Miller, Beth Kurti. "Elena Poniatowska." In *Mujeres en la literatura,* 2d ed. Toluca: Universidad Autónoma del Estado de México, 1982.

Ocampo, Aurora M. *Cuentistas Mexicanas Siglo XX.* Mexico City: Universidad Nacional Autónoma de México, 1976.

Poniatowska, Elena. "And Here's to You, Jesusa." Translated by Gregory Kolovakos and Ronald Christ. In *Lives on the Line: The Testimony of Contemporary Latin American Authors,* edited by Doris Meyer. Berkeley and Los Angeles: University of California Press, 1988.

Sefchovich, Sara. "Elena." *Nexos* 13, no. 151 (July 1990): 10–11.

Steele, Cynthia. *Beyond the Pyramid: Politics, Gender, and The Mexican Novel, 1968–1988.* Austin: University of Texas Press, 1992.

———. "Entrevista: Elena Poniatowska." *Hispamerica* 18 (August-December 1989): 89–105.

Tatum, Charles M. "Elena Poniatowska's *Hasta no verte, Jesús mío.*" In *Latin American Women Writers: Yesterday and Today.* Pittsburgh: Latin American Literary Review, 1977.

DELMIRA AGUSTINI

Agustini, Delmira. *Obras poéticas.* Montevideo: M. García, 1940.

Alvar, Manuel. *La poesía de Delmira Agustini.* Sevilla: Publicaciones de la Escuela de Estudios Hispanoamericanos, 1958.

Barrán, José P., and Benjamín Nahum. *El Uruguay del novecientos.* Montevideo, 1979.

Cabrera, Sarandy. "Las poetisas del 900." In *La literatura uruguaya del 900.* Montevideo, 1950.

Koch, Dolores. "Delmira, Alfonsina, Juana y Gabriela." *Revista Iberoamericana* 132–33 (July–December 1985): 722–29.

Medina Vidal, Jorge et al. *Delmira Agustini: seis ensayos críticos.* Montevideo, 1982.

Molloy, Sylvia. "Dos lecturas del cisne: Rubén Darío y Delmira Agustini." In *La sartén por el mango,* edited by Patricia Elena González and Eliana Ortega. Río Piedras, Ediciones Huracán, 1985.

Riestra, Sylvia, and Alvaro Díaz Berenguer. *Delmira y su mundo.* Montevideo, 1982.

Rodríguez Monegal, Emir. *Sexo y poesía en el 900.* Montevideo, 1969.

Silva, Clara. *Genio y figura de Delmira Agustini.* Buenos Aires: Ceibo, 1968.

Visca, Arturo Sergio. *Correspondencia íntima de Delmira Agustini y tres versiones "De lo enefable."* Montevideo, 1978.

Zum Felde, Alberto. *Proceso intelectual del Uruguay.* Montevideo, 1967.

MAROSA DI GIORGIO

Los papeles salvajes, vols. 1 and 2. Montevideo: Araca Editorial, 1991. These volumes contain the complete works of Marosa Di Giorgio: *Poemas* (1954), *Humo* (1955), *Druida* (1959), *Historial de las violetas* (1965), *Magnolia* (1965), *La guerra de los huertos* (1971), *Está en llamas el jardín natal* (1971), *Gladiolos de luz de luna* (1974), *Clavel y tenebrario* (1979), *La liebre de marzo* (1981), *Mesa de esmeralda* (1985), *La falena* (1987), *Membrillo de Lusana* (1991), and *Misales* (1993).